The protection of human rights of irregular migrants

Elisa Fornalé

The protection of human rights of irregular migrants

The case of Morocco

Peter Lang
Bern • Berlin • Bruxelles • Frankfurt am Main • New York • Oxford • Wien

Bibliographic information published by die Deutsche Nationalbibliothek

Die Deutsche Nationalbibliothek lists this publication in the Deutsche Nationalbibliografie; detailed bibliographic data is available on the Internet at ‹http://dnb.d-nb.de›.

British Library Cataloguing-in-Publication Data: A catalogue record for this book is available from The British Library, Great Britain

Library of Congress Cataloging-in-Publication Data

Fornalé, Elisa.
The protection of human rights of irregular migrants : the case of Morocco / Elisa Fornalé.
pages cm
Revision of the author's thesis (doctoral)--University of Palermo, 2011.
Includes bibliographical references and index.
ISBN 978-3-0343-1273-8
1. Illegal aliens–Morocco. 2. Foreign workers–Legal status, laws, etc.–Morocco. I. Title.
KSW3025.F67 2012
342.6408'3–dc23

Cover illustration: from iStockphoto.com © by mustafahacalaki
Cover design: Didier Studer, Peter Lang AG

ISBN 978-3-0343-1273-8 pb. ISBN 978-3-0351-0512-4 eBook

Hochfeldstrasse 32, CH-3012 Bern, Switzerland
info@peterlang.com, www.peterlang.com

Printed in Switzerland

Acknowledgements

I express my most sincere gratitude to Curtis Doebbler (co-supervisor of my PhD thesis) for his strong support and inspiring encouragement.

Special thanks are also due to Giovanni Distefano (University of Neuchâtel), Amarelle Cesla (University of Neuchâtel) and Marion Panizzon (World Trade Institute, University of Bern) for the intellectual stimulation they gave me during this project. I have also greatly benefited from discussions with Piyasiri Wickramasekara and Tina Freyburg during the development of the dissertation.

I am grateful to all the members of the Doctoral Programme on "Human Rights: Evolution, Protection and Limits" at the University of Palermo for long conversations and the confidence they placed in my work. I mention in particular my co-supervisor Professor Fulvio Vassallo Paleologo, Isabel Trujillo, Francesco Viola, and Aldo Schiavello.

I gratefully acknowledge the grants I received from the Italian Ministry of Foreign Affairs, the *Fondation pour des bourses d'études italo-suisses*, the Swiss Academy of Humanities and Social Sciences, and the Equality Office (University of Neuchâtel) that made it possible for me to conduct research for this doctoral project at the University of Neuchâtel, to present and to publish the results of my work.

I would like to thank all the staff at Peter Lang (in particular Martina Räber) for their patience and kind help during the publication process. Thanks also to Evan de Riel and Ilaria Bracchetti for their excellent work in proofreading and editing the text.

I must thank my family, Oriana, Antonio, and Emanuele, for all their support and love. Finally, I extend my heartfelt gratitude to Francesco for *everything*.

Contents

Foreword

by Dr. Curtis F.J. Doebbler

> We can see that migration is both a cause and a consequence of political and economic change. International migration, like trade, is a fundamental feature of the post-war liberal order.
> James F. Hollifield, *Trade, Migration and Economic Development the Risks and Rewards of Openness* 38 (2007).

> The drama of the refugees and the undocumented migrants can only be effectively dealt with amidst a spirit of true human solidarity....
> Judge A.A. Cançado Trindade, *Juridical Condition and Rights of Undocumented Migrants*, Concurring Opinion in the Advisory Opinion OC-18, Ser. A No. 18 (17 September 2003).

Irregular migration is one of the most pressing problems confronting the global community today. It is also one of the most misunderstood problems confronting States. Nevertheless, government policies are often developed without a clear understanding of the law and especially the restrains on government's discretion that are provided by international law protecting the fundamental rights of all human beings. Dr. Fornalé takes on the challenge of identifying not only the problems of definition of irregular migrants, but also reminds us of the restraints on governments' discretion that are provided by international law.

Dr. Elisa Fornalé has produced a significant contribution to our understanding of irregular migration at a crucial time when economic crisis, climate change and many other pressures are contributing to this phenomenon. Her book is based on significant research that explores how migration has been dealt with by States in the past and delineates the limits of States discretion that are provides by international law. It provides vital advice for policymakers and experts in migration as well as thought provoking perspective on the plight of irregular migrants and the responsibilities of governments for migrants.

The book contributes to the development of international law related to irregular migrants. This is a topic of significant and timely importance in several parts of the world, including in Europe and specifically as concerns Mediterranean Europe's relationship with North Africa. Dr. Fornalé's insightful discussion of Morocco's treatment of irregular migrants sheds light on the relationship that Europe has established with this North African State.

The contemporary relevance of the topic is illustrated by the author's extensive use of contemporary sources. Irregular migration is a topic that is frequently in the news and will be discussed at the highest diplomatic levels within the United Nations in the coming years. For example, a UN High Level Dialogue on Migration is currently scheduled for 2013.

After describing the plight of irregular migrants and what we mean when we use this term, Dr. Fornalé identifies many of the most relevant sources of law and legal practice relating to migrants rights. The book considers hundreds of books, academic articles, UN documents, and more than a hundred and fifty international and domestic cases.

The author's ultimate argument is that we need to complement the existing framework of legal protections for irregular migrants. It is a convincing argument made in a manner that contributes to our understanding and development of international law and how to use it to deal with migration.

* * *

The book starts with the challenging task of grappling with the definition of irregular migrants. It provides a good overview of the complex problem of terminology, particularly its socio-legal consequences. At the heart of the problem is the difference between illegal and irregular migrants. Dr. Fonalé's discussion of this difference is logical and well thought out. She concludes that States often define irregular migrants in a manner that is used for an excuse for increasing restrictive measures against the migrants.

Having described the inescapable problem of definition, Dr. Fornalé goes on to provide an overview of the international law applicable to the human rights of migrants. She describes the most important sources of international human rights law, examining them critically and with reference to cases in which these rights have been applied. While not an exhaustive discussion of the law, Dr. Fornalé chooses the examples she uses judiciously and in a manner that provides a lucid description of the applicable law. Perhaps most valuably, always reminding the reader that this law is intended to be interpreted and applied to provide the highest degree of protection possible to the fundamental human rights of all human beings irrespective of their status.

In her description of the international law protecting irregular migrants, Dr. Fornalé also appropriately indicates where there are gaps in this law. This critical consideration of the law is good food for thought for anyone involved in the reform of existing laws or the creation of new laws to deal with irregular or other types of migration. The identification of the applicable law and where it needs improving is also a valuable contribution to the research relating to the protection of migrants. This provides both governments with guidance in setting migration policy and migrants' advocates assistance for defending the rights of migrants.

Finally, the discussion of the treatment of irregular migrants in Morocco provides a useful example of how the international human rights law could contribute to protecting migrants. Dr. Fornalé who spent significant time in Morocco researching the plight of irregular migrants provides a well-informed insight into both the problems irregular migrants face in Morocco and how inroads to dealing with these problems might be made using international human rights law.

Dr. Fornalé has taken on a topic for which there is currently inadequate literature and has provided the reader a very interesting exploration of the most fundamental rules of international law that must guide government's action concerning irregular migrants.

Abbreviations

AFVIC	*Association des familles des victimes de l'immigration clandestine* (Association of families of victimes of illegal migration)
AJIL	American Journal of International Law
BO	*Bulletin Officiel* (Official Journal)
CAT	Committee against Torture)
CCDH	*Conseil Consultatif des droits de l'homme* (Consultatif Committee of Human Rights)
CEDAW	Committee on the Elimination of Discrimination Against Women
CERD	Committee on the Elimination of Racial Discrimination
CESCR	Committee on Economic, Social, and Cultural Rights
CHR	Commission on Human Rights
CMW	Committee on the Protection of the Rights of All Migrant Workers and Members of Their Families
CRC	Committee on the Rights of the Child
EU	European Union
GADEM	*Groupe antiraciste d'accompagnement et de défense des étrangers et migrants* (Antiracist Group for the support and defence of migrants and foreigners)
GCIM	Global Commission on International Migration
GMG	Global Migration Group
HCR	High Commissioner for Refugees
HRC	Human Rights Committee
ICCPR	International Covenant of Civil and Political Rights
ICECR	International Covenant of Economic and Cultural Rights
ICJ	International Court of Justice
ICMC	International Catholic Migration Commission

ICRMW	International Convention on the Rights of Migrants Workers and Members of Their Families)
ILC	International Labour Conference
ILO	International Labour Organization
IOM	International Organization for Migration
JO	Journal Official
MSF	*Médecins Sans Frontières* (Doctors without borders)
NGO	Non Gouvernamental Organization
OHCHR	Office of the High Commissioner for Human Rights
REMALD	*Revue marocaine de l'administration publique et du developpement*
SR	Special Rapporteur
SRHRM	Special Rapporteur on the Protection of Human Rights of Migrants
TPI	*Tribunal de Première Instance* (Tribunal of First Instance)
UMA	Union of Maghreb Arab
UN	United Nations
UNHCR	United Nations High Commissioner for Refugees
WGAD	Working Group on Arbitrary Detention

Introduction

Ci siamo accorti dell'esistenza di un diritto ad avere diritti (e ciò significa vivere in una struttura in cui si e' giudicati per le proprie azioni e opinioni) solo quando sono comparsi milioni di individui che lo avevano perso e non potevano riacquistarlo a causa della nuova organizzazione globale del mondo.

H. Arendt[1]

Recently, the phenomenon of so-called "irregular" migration has become an issue of international concern, highlighting several critical issues pertinent to the intersection of protecting migrants in these circumstances and implementing international human rights law. All around the world this phenomenon, which is finding its definition in the irregularity of its being, increasingly attracts media attention through the dissemination of information, denunciation of abuses, and violations of migrants' rights.

Just to illustrate my argument I cite the case of Burundi, where numerous incidents (around 800) of arbitrary expulsion and detention of foreigners from different countries raised concerns.[2] Collective expulsion and deportation has taken place in Angola and Congo.[3] The issue of irregular migrant workers is also growing in Thailand, where civil society is seeking increased respect for these migrants' basic human rights against employers' abusive practices.[4] Violent attacks

1 HANNAH ARENDT, LE ORIGINI DEL TOTALITARISMO 410-411 (Giulio Einaudi Editore, 2009).

2 SRHRM, *Report submitted by the Special Rapporteur on the human rights of migrants, Jorge A. Bustamante, Addendum, Communications sent to Governments and replies received*, at 4, U.N. Doc. A/HRC/14/30/Add.1 (May 25, 2010).

3 *Id.* at 10 and 16.

4 Human Rights Watch, *From the Tiger to the Crocodile–Abuse of migrant workers in Thailand*, February 2010.

against foreign nationals have occurred in South Africa[5] and in Kuwait.[6] Xenophobic attitudes and related intolerance are also targeting irregular migrants in the Dominican Republic and in Mexico.[7]

Irregular migration is now a relevant topic on the agenda of the international community.[8] In this regard, there has been a lack of recognition on the part of international organizations that irregular migration and human rights protection are a concern for everyone.[9] Irregular migration was considered only as a matter of a domestic nature or an internal matter of states. However, this attitude has been changing recently, as it has moved gradually from being treated as a domestic matter to a full-fledged human rights issue. By 2005, the Global Migration Group (chaired in 2011 by the United Nations High Commissioner for Human Rights, Navanethem Pillay), was openly acknowledging that[10]

5 Refugee Studies Centre, *Forced Migration Review No. 34,* 62 (Issue No. 34, February 2010).

6 *See* SRHRM, *supra* note 2, at 36.

7 *Id.* at 37.

8 DAUVERGNE CATHERINE, JURISPRUDENCE FOR AN INTERCONNECTED GLOBE, Ashgate Press, Burlington (2003).

9 Navanethem Pillay stated: "Through its leadership of the GMG in the coming months, OHCHR seeks to promote and mainstream a human rights approach to migration within the United Nations system, highlight key migration and human rights themes at the international level", Press Release, OHCHR, Joint hands to protect the human rights of all migrants (Sep. 8, 2010) <www.ohchr.org/ EN/NewsEvents/Pages/GMG.aspx> (last visited Jun. 20, 2012).

10 The Global Migration Group (GMG) brings together several international agencies that cooperate in the field of migration (for instance ILO, IOM, World Bank, WIPO, UNDP, UNESCO, and UNHCR, United Nations Children's Fund). The GMG was established in 2006 recognizing that "that international migration is an important, complex and multi-dimensional issue, and that, properly managed, in full respect for the human rights and international legal principles at issue, migration benefits individuals and societies, and can make an important contribution to the early achievement of the internationally agreed development goals and objectives, including the Millennium Development Goals", *see* GMG, Terms of Reference, *available at* <www.globalmigrationgroup.org/uploads/what-is-gmg/Final%20GMG%20Terms%20 of%20Reference_prioritized.pdf> (last visited Jun. 20, 2012).

> Too often, States have addressed irregular migration solely through the lens of sovereignty, border security or law enforcement, sometimes driven by hostile domestic constituency. Although States have legitimate interests in securing their borders and exercising immigration controls, such concerns cannot, and indeed, as a matter of international law do not, trump the obligations of the State to respect the internationally guaranteed rights of all persons, to protect those rights against abuses, and to fulfill the rights necessary for them to enjoy a life of dignity and security.[11]

This explicitly highlights the role that national policies and legal measures play in ensuring that all migrants–whether regular or irregular–enjoy basic human rights.

This is particularly relevant if we consider actual border-crossings in the Euro Mediterranean region.[12] At the United Nations, particular attention has been paid to this issue, especially through the mandate and work of the former UN Special Rapporteur on the Human Rights of Migrants, prof. Jorge Bustamante. Bustamante observed that the general trend is an increase in the abuse of irregular migrants through the migration process (in the countries or territories of origin, transit, and destination).[13] In fact the irregular migratory flows into and out of each country are complex and, in some instances, the issue of political asylum tends to become linked with irregular movement. In response to these complex patterns of human mobility, maintaining a clear distinction between refugee protec-

11 Press Release, OHCHR, Statement on Protecting the Human Rights of Irregular Migrants (Sep. 30, 2010).

12 NINNA NYBERG SORENSEN (ED.), MEDITERRANEAN TRANSIT MIGRATION (Danish Institute for International Studies, 2006).

13 SRHRM, *Promotion and protection of all Human Rights, civil, political, economic, social and cultural rights including the right to development, Report of the Special Rapporteur on the human rights of migrants, Jorge Bustamante*, U.N. Doc. A/BRC/7/12 (Feb. 25, 2008). On this vein, the prof. François Crépeau, the new SRHRM launched in March 2012 a one-year "Regional Thematic Study: Management of the External EU borders and its impact on the human rights of Migrants". This study will assess the current challenges in protecting the rights of migrants, particularly in irregular situation, focusing on the Euro Mediterranean Region.

tion imperatives and migration control strategies becomes a challenge.[14]

This book will highlight some of the human rights violations perpetrated against irregular migrants in transit countries, beginning with the examination of the pattern and dynamics of transit migration towards Morocco and the European countries, because the dynamics of unauthorized migration have received extensive media coverage but little academic attention. In particular the research will focus on the national legal practice of Morocco in the context of identifying the exact scope of states' obligations relevant to irregular migration with regard to migrants' protection. I will argue that the responsibility of third countries in the field of asylum and migration to take measures to prevent such violations must be assessed against the broader framework of state obligations derived from the interaction of different legal orders, both universal and regional in scope.

Today a growing number of people across international borders by choosing routes that fall outside of the so-called legal channels. These irregular movements may occur by land, by sea, or by air, and in most cases qualify as South–North or South–South movements, although there is growing evidence that they cannot be traced from developing countries.[15] The "push factors" which compel thousands of people to migrate are often mixed and complex, many individuals who take irregular paths hardly fit into any of the categories into which legal or political construction tries to crystallize them.[16] Sometimes several reasons impel individuals to leave their countries and cross national borders, or a set of interrelated factors may contribute to increase the incentives and imperatives that drive these individual to

14 Ibrahim Awad, Keynote Speech at the Meeting of Experts and Policymakers on Irregular Migration into and through Southern and Eastern Mediterranean Countries, European University Institute, January 2009, *available at* <www.euie.eu> (last visited Oct. 25, 2010).

15 GMG, *International Migration and Human Rights*, Global Migration Group, Geneva, 2008, at 43.

16 FRANK DUVELL (ED.), ILLEGAL IMMIGRATION IN EUROPE, BEYOND CONTROL 289–310 (Palgrave, 2005).

move, sometimes within their region and sometimes between continents.[17]

This situation applies not only to the case of violations of admission rules, but also if sudden changes occur to the national regulations addressing the status of foreigners: it could happen that migrants themselves are not aware that they are violating domestic laws.[18] For instance, immigration policy reforms may contribute to the increase of so-called irregular migration by expanding the definition of "irregular migrants" to include tolerated migrants.[19]

Public debates and political agendas treat this topic as a legal or security issue, paying scant heed to the needs of migrants for protection and increasing their vulnerability to different forms of abuse and violations.[20]

Irregular migrants are a heterogeneous group: they may have specific needs and, in some cases, they are entitled to access to the protection afforded by the international human rights framework. Firstly, more and more individuals cross borders and are in need of protection because of the critical political situation or national conflicts in their countries of origin that make impossible for them to go back.[21] Secondly, it is relevant to note that migration is a dynamic

17 Alexander Betts, *Towards a Mediterranean Solution? Implications for the Region of Origin,* 18 INTERNATIONAL JOURNAL OF REFUGEE LAW 652, 656 (2006); ILO, *International Labour Migration: a rights-based approach*, ILO, Geneva, 2010, at 31.

18 CATHERINE DAUVERGNE, MAKING PEOPLE ILLEGAL: WHAT GLOBALISATION MEANS FOR MIGRATION AND LAW 19 (Cambridge University Press, 2008).

19 See for instance in Jordan 2007, the legal status of more than 200,000 Egyptian migrant workers suddenly changes as a result of legal reform which undermined the migrants' capacity to legally stay in the country. Mohamed Olwan, *Irregular Migration in Jordan–A Policy of No Policy* (CARIM Analytic and Synthetic Notes 2008/60, 2008).

20 ELSPETH GUILD, SECURITY AND MIGRATION IN THE 21ST CENTURY 1–3 (Polity Press, 2009).

21 Frank Düvell, *The Pathways in and out of Irregular Migration in the EU: A Comparative Analysis, Special Issue*, 13 EUROPEAN JOURNAL OF MIGRATION LAW 275, 288 (2011).

process and in some cases the protection needs raised by the individuals are direct consequences of that dynamic nature.

Beyond the individual reasons that push a person to leave his or her country of origin, migrants may be facing situations of abuse and rights violations during the migratory process.[22] There are several groups of people who illustrate this: 1) stranded migrants may be exposed to the worst forms of violation or abuse linked with the uncertainty of their stay, such as being deprived of any legal opportunity to leave the country, making them trapped; 2) victims of trafficking, who are forced to move and are subjected to physical abuses and exploitation; 3) smuggled migrants and people suffering other kinds of abuse during their travel, who may be in need of psychological assistance;[23] 4) individuals subject to removal orders may be exposed to violence or inhuman treatments if sent back to their countries of origin or to their transit countries.[24]

22 GMG, *Background Paper, Rooting migration policies in human rights: ensuring the rights of all migrants and improving human development outcomes*, Global Migration Group, May 2010.

23 ICMC raised the need to develop international and national mechanisms to provide satisfactory conditions of medical assistance, nutrition, and hygiene to individuals affected. ICMC, *Improving responses to boat people and other migrants injured or traumatized crossing borders*, Geneva, April 2008.

24 *See* Betts, *supra* note 17, at 656. Exemplary is the case of Congolese migrants expelled from Angola to Congo. Between 2003 and 2009, around 3000 Congolese were expelled. Their conditions of deportation were unacceptable, they were subjected to sexual violence, including rape, and deprived of any kind of assistance and protection. OCHA, *Congolese expelled from Angola*, DR Congo Situation Report No. 1, 21 July 2008. As confirmed by the report submitted by SRHRM, *see* SRHRM, *supra* note 2, at 10.

a. Objectives

The present analysis aims to explore the significant legal and institutional gaps and their implications for affording adequate human rights protection. The existing nexus between human rights and migration is not a new one, and most of the doctrine affirms the application of human rights standards to migrants.[25] Nevertheless, the legal situation of international migrants in relation to their enjoyment of human rights is complex and overlapping layers of norm creation and norm application characterize it. [26] These layers include national, transnational, and international regulations and forums, as well as binding and non-binding regulations.

This analysis takes its starting point from this apparent consensus to assess this nexus between human rights and irregular migration in transit countries, taking Morocco as its case study.

The interest on irregular migrations in Morocco is closely linked to its position as a destination and transit country, which an increasing number of migrants reach and find themselves for several reasons (as it will be described later) *stranded.* In Morocco, as in other Maghreb countries, most migrants come from Sub-Saharan Africa.[27] The reasons for these irregular movements are varying and diverse: economic migrants, who do not have the right to enter or to stay and are employed in irregular conditions; rejected asylum-seekers also become irregular if they remain in the country of asylum; and the so-called transit migrants. The latter group tends to be linked with the first, due to the failure of most transit migrants to cross the Mediter-

25 Stephanie Grant, *The recognition of migrants' rights within the UN human rights system: the first 60 years*, *in* ARE HUMAN RIGHTS FOR MIGRANTS? CRITICAL REFLECTIONS ON THE STATUS OF IRREGULAR MIGRANTS IN EUROPE AND THE UNITED STATES 25–47 (Marie-Benedicte Dembour & Tobias Kelly eds., Routledge, 2011).

26 GHOSH BIMAL, ELUSIVE PROTECTION, UNCERTAIN LAND: MIGRANTS' ACCESS TO HUMAN RIGHTS, IOM, Geneva (2003).

27 *See* NYBERG SORENSEN, *supra* note 12, at 129.

ranean, remaining in North Africa under very precarious living conditions and denied access to the labour market.[28]

This analysis highlights some of the human rights violations perpetrated against irregular migrants, dealing with the examination of the patterns and dynamics of transit migration. In particular this book focuses on the national legal practice of Morocco in the context of identifying the exact scope of states' obligation towards irregular migration with respect to the approach to migrants' protection. I argue that the responsibility of third countries in the field of migration to take measures to prevent violations is to be assessed against the broader framework of states' obligations derived from the interaction of different legal orders, of both universal and of national scope. In order to assess how the norms of international law are applicable to migrants in irregular situations and to accentuate the normative gaps derived from the scattering of norms among various legal regimes, the book outlines general trends of worldwide human rights standards, including international agreements, regional instruments, and European Union migration policies.

b. Methodological considerations

The nature and intensity of movements between countries and regional context is influenced by national and administrative border procedures, which persist, with different levels of permeability.[29] At the national level, each state develops laws that govern domestic migration policies and protect the rights of migrants. Yet, state authority is increasingly limited by international legal norms. In many situations there is a gap between the rights which migrants, both

28 Franck Düvell, *Crossing the Fringes of Europe: Transit Migration in the EU's Neighbourhood* (COMPAS WP-06-33, University of Oxford, 2008).

29 SASKIA SASSEN, PERDIENDO EL CONTROL? LA SOBERANIA EN LA ERA DE LA GLOBALIZACION (Editions Bellaterra, 2001).

regular and irregular, enjoy under international law, and the difficulties they experience in the countries where they live, work, and travel across. This gap between the principles agreed by governments and the reality of individuals' lives underscores the vulnerability of migrants in term of human rights protection.[30] It is undisputed that migration law is regulated by a diversified body of rules, specifically at a substantive level (international human rights law, international refugee law).

This investigation will provide an overview of the key points emerging from the various levels (international and national) and types (migration, human rights, refugees) of regulation that characterize the extreme variety of the actual panorama and debate. This analysis will provide a better understanding of the failings and flaws of such approaches.

The international migration regime is undergoing a process of fragmentation, which reflects the recognized development of international law.

In the context of migration, many elements have a key role in this fragmentation: the strong presence of the sovereign authority paradigm to regulate and protect migrant rights, and the ambiguity o complex and different regimes (at the international, regional, and bilateral levels) with the emergence of different modes of governance, involving new actors, such as international organizations.[31]

It is undisputed that migration law is regulated by a diverse body of rules, specifically at a substantive level (hard and soft law provisions, primary and secondary rules).

The work of several authors, as Betts,[32] Aleinikoff,[33] examine how soft law mechanisms and instruments have a "persuasive au-

30 JORGE A. BUSTAMANTE, MIGRACION INTERNATIONAL Y DERECHOS HUMANOS (Universidad Nacional Autonoma de Mexico, 2002).

31 Marion Panizzon, *Migration and Trade: Prospects for Bilateralism in the face of skill-selective Mobility Laws*, 11(2) MELBOURNE JOURNAL OF INTERNATIONAL LAW 96, 96–140 (2011).

32 ALEXANDER BETTS (ED.), GLOBAL MIGRATION GOVERNANCE (Oxford University Press, 2011).

thority", even if they do not have a binding nature, to place human rights instruments in the migration context and to define how they apply to this specific group.

It is relevant in this context to highlight how the adoption of soft law instruments contributes to develop international law. As described by Prof. Kalin and Dr. Schrepfer,

> soft law can be understood as instruments and norms that create more than merely political or moral obligations and less than legal obligations, i.e. they 'share a certain proximity to law and have a certain legal relevance, but at the same time they are not legally binding *per se* as a matter of law.'[34]

Soft law allows non-state actors to experiment with new approaches and to advance the creation of new international standards to govern international relations. These regulations are more flexible and may play a significant role in improving the protection of irregular migrants; in this context specific instruments will be analysed as resolutions, general comments, recommendations, and opinions adopted by the United Nations bodies. In addition soft law instruments elaborated by the United Nations High Commissioner for Refugees and International Labour Organization, will be take under consideration to define the advantages and disadvantages of a hard *versus* soft law approach.

---

33 Alexander Aleinikoff, *International Legal Norms on Migration: Substance without Architecture*, *in* INTERNATIONAL MIGRATION LAW, DEVELOPING PARADIGMS AND KEY CHALLENGE 467–479 (Ryszard Cholewinski, Richard Perrouchoud & Euan MacDonald eds., Asser Press, 2007).

34 Walter Kalin & Ninna Schrepfer, *Protecting People Crossing Borders in the Context of Climate Change Normative Gaps and Possible Approaches* 73 (UNHCR, Legal and Protection Policy Research Series, 2012).

c. The book's structure

The book is divided in two sections to investigate several critical issues related to the intersectionality between the protection of human rights and irregular migration, adopting a theoretical perspective in the first part and an empirical perspective in the second, through an in-depth analysis of a selected case study: migratory movement to and through Morocco.

The first section, *International Legal Frameworks and Migration*, looks at the evolution of the normative framework for protecting migrants' rights, with a deep insight on international human rights standards. Moving from the overall theoretical framework, the analysis will address also specific legal regimes (e.g. asylum law or labour migration law) that are relevant for specific categories. The aim of the analysis is to strengthen the interplay between the normative and the practical level and to better understand how the responses formulated meet the challenges of irregular migration. To this end, the role played by institutional mechanisms, such as the United Nations Committee, will be described.

Chapter 1 deals with the absence of universally accepted legal terminology regarding the phenomenon of irregular migration. The use of definitions depends on national provisions and this lack of a uniform and coherent framework risks jeopardizing the implementation of existing legal safeguards.

Chapters 2 and 3 give a comprehensive overview of international and regional instruments that are the key elements of the normative framework, even if fragmented, to be invoked for the human rights protection of irregular migrants.

Chapter 4 attempts to move the analysis on the implementation of those standards, exploring how the current evolution and development of international human rights law inform state practices and jurisprudence in the field of migration.

Section 2, *Irregularity of Migration Issues in Morocco*, brings the discussion from the international to the national level, offering an overview of the different legal and political responses formulated by the government of Morocco in migration policy and seeking to identify the challenges and the practical problems that Morocco is facing in transposing international legal standards to the national level.

Chapter 5 gives a description of main features of the migration phenomenon, adopting an historical perspective. In particular, the chapter pays specific attention to the influence played by European Union regulations and how the European harmonization of return policy impacts transit countries, including Morocco.

Chapter 6 examines the development of the legal framework for migration, taking main constitutional provisions into account. Peculiar to Morocco is the recent adoption of the main legal instrument in the field of migration law, which consolidated and innovated the antiquated and fragmented national normative framework.

Finally, Chapter 7, drawing on fieldwork conducted in Beni Mellal and Rabat, highlights some of the human rights violations and abuses against irregular migrants, to enable the reader to connect the realities of irregular migration with the current status of norms.

1. Irregular migrants and migration law: some issues of definitions

1.1. "Irregular" versus "illegal" migrants: towards terminological coherence

The need to adopt definitions is crucial for advancing the common understanding of the migration process, but at the same time it may have a profound impact on the public perceptions of migrants. The absence of generally agreed upon definitions and terms in this context is partly a symptom of the difficulties in conceptualizing the nature of the inquiry.[35]

In fact, if, on one side, the on-going debate on this issue is more oriented to attribute and identify a specific status entitlement to all kinds of protection and rights, then on the other side, this approach reveals its limitations through the development of generic categories into which the migrants are placed, and it reflects a state-centred approach instead of considering characteristics inherent to migrants.[36]

Preliminarily, from a legal perspective the term foreigner is used to refer to persons who are not citizens of their country of residence, but this definition, as highlighted by Prof. Marie-Claire Foblets, is at risk of being "*faussement simple, la réalité déborde largement la formule*".[37] In fact, the legal status of foreigners, as it will be described later, is at the

35 Ségolène Barbou de Place, *Les étrangers "saisis" par le droits: enjeux de l'édification des catégoires juridiques de migrants*, Dossier: Usages et paradoxes des catégorisations en migration, 128 (22) MIGRATIONS SOCIETE 35 (2010).

36 *See* DAUVERGNE, *supra* note 8, at 16.

37 (Deceptively simple, in reality it goes far beyond this definition–Translation provided by the author), Marie-Claire Foblets, *Diversité et catégories de personnes*, *in* L'ÉTRANGER FACE AU DROIT 128 (Jean-Yves Carlier ed., Bruylant 2010).

mercy of different assessments, depending on a variety of factors, such as their individual plans, their intentions to stay, and their professional and personal backgrounds.[38] From this perspective, each attempt to define foreigner by reference to uncertain indicators risks remaining vague and inconsistent.[39] At the same time, the definition adopted by different instruments and regimes at international, regional, and national levels makes it extremely complex to outline the legal boundaries of this status.[40]

This analysis, which is aware of the fact that among different categories of foreigners, migrants in irregular situation have emerged as a fundamental challenge for states to comply with their human rights obligations, cannot be excluded from dealing with the implications of the way in which individuals are conceptualized.

Increasingly the use–or better the abuse–of different terms such as "illegal" or "clandestine migrant" has recurred in recent years, and the definition of "illegal migration" is a result of political decisions made by states.[41] Some scholars have argued that with respect to state adoption of laws, it is only in the moment when the state itself elaborates and adopts the rules governing entry and exit that the situation is perceived as illegal.[42] The existence or presence of one foreigner in their own territory violates so many norms that consequently the concept of illegal migration is configured. Other similarly believe that the category of "illegal migration" is an artificial construct without fixed meaning[43] and the negative connotations that follow from the

38 Stephen Castles, *The Factors that Make and Unmake Migration Policies,* 38(3) INTERNATIONAL MIGRATION REVIEW 852 (2004).

39 *See* Barbou de Place, *supra* note 35, at 40.

40 BOGUSZ BARBARA, CHOLEWINSKI RYSZARD, CYGAN ADAM & SZYSZCZACK ERIKA (EDS.), IRREGULAR MIGRATION AND HUMAN RIGHTS: THEORETICAL, EUROPEAN AND INTERNATIONAL PERSPECTIVES 3 (Martinus Nijhoff Publishers, The Hague, 2004).

41 For an historical overview of the concept of "illegal immigration", *see* DUVELL, *supra* note 16, at 298–297.

42 *See* DAUVERGNE, *supra* note 8, at 200–201.

43 Bensaad Ali describes a direct link between the development of securitarian migration policies and the creation of artificial categories in *"statuts distincts":*

use of such terminology may affect the individuals claiming protection.[44]

Most international organizations have addressed this concern, invoking the need to adopt "fairly neutral" language when addressing these issues, as noted by the Commissioner for Human Rights, Thomas Hammarberg:

> The choice of language is very important to the image which the authorities project to their population and the world. [...] Illegal immigration as a concept has the effect of rendering suspicious in the eyes of the population (including public officials) the movement of persons across international borders. The suspicious is linked to criminal law–the measure of legality as opposed to illegality.[45]

Similarly, the Special Rapporteur on Human Rights of Migrants (SRHRM) raised specific concerns on the current tendency on the

---

transit, immigration de travail, installation derrière laquelle pointe surtout le besoin de cerner et identifier un mouvement spécifique de transit vers l'Europe. L'irrégularité sur le plan formel est également générée par la nouvelle perception sécuritaire des circulations migratoires. La notion "sans papiers", apparue récemment, traduit le passage d'une circulation traditionnelle avec tolérance a un durcissement sécuritaire et n'a pas la signification qu'on lui prête ailleurs. (Different statuses: transit, economic migration, stay, beyond these the need is raised to identify and to label the transit movements to Europe. From a formal perspective, irregularity is conceived from the new "securitization" perception of migratory flows. The concept of "undocumented", recently adopted, translate the shift from a traditional tolerated movement to the securitization approach and it does not have the same meaning everywhere–Translation provided by the author), Ali Bensaad, *L'irrégularité de l'immigration en Mauritanie: une appréhension nouvelle, conséquence d'enjeux migratoires externes* 8 (CARIM, 2008/76, 2008).

44 Vincent Chetail (ed.), Mondialisation, Migration et Droits de l'Homme: Le droit international en question 13–133 (Bruylant, Vol. No. I, 2007).

45 Council of Europe Commissioner for Human Rights, *Criminalization of Migration in Europe: Human Rights Implications* 8 (CommDH/Issue Paper commissioned and published by Thomas Hammarberg, Council of Europe, 2009).

part of host governments for the criminalization of irregular migration.[46]

The main criticism of "illegal" is that only an act can be illegal, and to refer to foreigners that way could generate negative effects with regard to their protection.[47]

In dealing with irregular migrants, the use of inaccurate language may facilitate ambiguous situations in which migrants are identified as "not" being "legal" persons by destination countries in relation to the respect and protection of their basic rights.

The basic consideration in this context is that even if the migrant entered or stayed in a country in violation of national migration law, this situation does not deprive an individual of his or her basic human rights.

In fact, the "illegal" migrant as a category has the immediate and unavoidable effect the denial of his or her existence, despite the recognition of international human rights standards, and this can have much more serious effects of non-compliance to the application of these universal standards.[48]

Groenendijk, stated that the use of this label disqualify human beings "most of undocumented persons have some places in the world where they live lawfully".[49]

For these reasons, this attempted categorization, which results in excluding some individuals from "the right to have rights", is incompatible with the basic principles of the international human rights protection framework, as art. 6 of the Universal Declaration of Human rights which states that "Every human being has a right to recognition before the law".

An alternative solution is to refer to his or her status and use the term "migrant" for the individual. So it is preferable to use other

46 *See* SRHRM, *supra* note 13, at 5.

47 Agnieszka Kubal, *Conceptualizing semi-legality in migration research* (IMI Working Paper No. 58, 2012).

48 *See* BOGUSZ, CHOLEWINSKI, CYGAN & SZYSZCZACK, *supra* note 40, at 462.

49 *Id.* at 10.

terms such as "a migrant in an irregular situation" or "in irregular status".[50]

This analysis uses "migrant in irregular situation" to capture the various situations of people staying without the necessary residence permit.

As stated by Prof. Fargues,[51] within this concept, several individuals are concerned: individuals who try or succeed at crossing international borders without the necessary documents; migrants who no longer have the right to stay; individuals who are engaged in remunerated activity without conforming to national law; students working without authorization; legal migrant workers who have lost their jobs during the contract period; and migrants born from irregular parents who become irregular without crossing any borders.[52]

At the same time it is relevant to note that in many situations the boundaries between irregular migratory flows and the waves of forced migration of refugees and asylum seekers appear blurred, as will be described in the context of sub-Saharan migration to European countries. In light of this, it is often extremely difficult to apply formal definitions in practice, and in most cases the easy solution is to put each situation under the broader umbrella of irregular migration, with serious consequences for the protection needs of individuals.

Also of particular relevance, as stressed by Prof. Guild, is that also the use of this term could give rise to criticism because "irregularity" has no legal definition–leading to a normative vacuum–and the legal content of this concept, irregularity, is not defined, and its precise meaning is entirely based on national legal frameworks without a clear, shared understanding.[53]

50 Dita Vogel, Anna Triandafyllidou & Franck Duvell, *Introduction*, 49(5) INTERNATIONAL MIGRATION 48, 50 (2011).

51 Philippe Fargues, *Irregularity as normality among immigrants South and East of the Mediterranean* 6 (CARIM No. 02, 2009).

52 Frank Duvell, *Illegal immigration in Europe: patterns, causes and consequences* 3 (COMPAS, 2006).

53 Elspeth Guild, *Who is an irregular migrant?, in* IRREGULAR MIGRATION AND HUMAN RIGHTS: THEORETICAL, EUROPEAN AND INTERNATIONAL

In any case, it is urgent to encourage the adoption of terminology that constitutes a more neutral solution, given that these individuals are unable to regularize their status, and thus their presence in the countries where they are found is denied.

In addition, it is difficult to develop general categories able to be used on every continent, as it requires making an artificial abstraction from the socio-cultural context in which the migration flows take place. Prof. Awad argued that

> with regard to 'irregular migration' and the implied policies to address it, the concept does not seem very appropriate when applied between countries showing space continuity and sharing history, cultures, languages, markets, ethnic groups and ancient, established, traditions of human movement.[54]

For instance, it is interesting to make explicit reference to current terms used in Morocco, *Hrig, Hareg, Harrag* (respectively, "irregular migration", "clandestine", and "smuggler") which contain the Arabic root h–r–g, meaning "burn".

As illustrated in detail by the International Organization for Migration (IOM), these terms recall "symbolically" the military campaign conducted by Tarik Ibn Zyadm, well-known for completing the Arab Muslim conquest of Spain. Once he arrived in Spain, Tarik made the order to burn all the ships so that no one could escape before the Christian soldiers. After this, it seems that the strait that separated Morocco and Spain was called Gibraltar, distorsion of Jabel Tariq, and "according to the the Moroccan Arabic dialect "*hrag lourac*" means to burn all documents, recalling the one who lacks documents".[55]

PERSPECTIVES 3 (Barbara Bogusz, Ryszard Cholewinski, Adam Cygan & Erika Szyszczack eds., Martinus Nijhoff Publishers, 2004).

54 *See* Awad, *supra* note 14, at 11.

55 IOM, *Traite transnationale des personnes. Etat de lieux et analyse des réponses au Maroc*, Rabat, (August 2009), at 19 (Translation provided by the author).

1.1.1. At the international level

At the international level migration semantics have evolved. In fact, if either were used without distinction terms as "illegal" or "irregular", at the present there is a growing effort to refer in all official documents to migrants as "undocumented" or "irregular situation".[56] This change reflects the concern referring not to individual as such, but to his or her specific situation. The General Assembly of United Nations in its Resolution 3449 (XXX) of 1975 (Measures to ensure human rights and dignity of all migrant workers), urged all

> United Nations organs and specialized agencies concerned to utilize in all official documents the term 'non-documented' or irregular migrant workers, to define those workers that illegally and/or surreptitiously enter another country to obtain work.[57]

In particular it is appropriate to distinguish between "documented" and "undocumented migrants", and the expressions often used as alternatives, "authorized" and "unauthorized migrants". The latter set has to be preferred because it is frequent that many migrants, legally authorized to be in the countries or not, have some kind of documents, even if these documents are not readily available. Recently, a specific attention to the terminology adopted was invoked by several international actors, as the Committee on Migrant Workers:

> The Committee is generally concerned about the association of irregular migration with criminality and the use of the term "illegal migrants" rather than migrants in a "non-documented" or an "irregular situation", which is the terminology used in the Convention. In this regard, the Committee is concerned that a considerable number of migrant workers in the State party are non-documented and that their irregular migration status is considered a criminal offence punishable by imprisonment and/or fines under Law No. 08-11 of 25

56 Catherine Dauvergne, *Challenges to sovereignty: migration laws for the 21 century* 2 (UNHCR, Evaluation and Policy Analysis Research, Working Paper No. 92, July 2003).

57 G.A., *Measures to ensure the human rights and dignity of all migrant workers*, G.A. Res. 3449 (XXX) (Dec. 9, 1975).

June 2008. 19. The Committee is concerned that migrant workers in an irregular situation in the State party do not effectively enjoy a range of the rights guaranteed to all migrant workers under the Convention, including rights relating to conditions of work and terms of employment (art. 25), the right to join trade unions and associations (art. 26), the right to social security (art. 27) and the right to medical care (art. 28).[58]

Also at regional level, several bodies advocate for the notion of irregular migration and for a rejection of the "illegal" concept in the case of migration. Also this terminology has been adopted by several regional organizations whose official policy is to avoid the negative term "illegal".[59]

1.1.2. The European dimension

At the European level, the recent adoption of the Returns Directive presented an opportunity to address this issue of definitions, to identify coherent and clear terminology.[60] According to Prof. Guild, the diffusion of divergent practices and legal perceptions at the national level could affect the uniform application, or even the uniform interpretation, of Return Directive provisions so long as there is no "defi-

58 CMW, *Concluding observations of the Committee on the Protection of the Rights of All Migrant Workers and Members of Their Families, Algeria*, ¶18–19, U.N. Doc. CMW/C/DZA/CO/1 (May 19, 2010).

59 *See* e.g. that the Council of Europe resolution adopted in 2006 "prefers to use the term 'irregular migrants'", Council of Europe, Parliamentary Assembly, *Human rights of irregular migrants,* Resolution No. 1509, 2006, point 7. Also the Association of South East Asian Nations (ASEAN) uses this terminology: "migrant workers who, through no fault of their own, have subsequently become undocumented." ASEAN, *Declaration on the Protection and Promotion of the Rights of Migrant Workers*, 13 January 2007.

60 Sergio Carrera & Massimo Merlino, *Undocumented Immigrants and Rights in the EU* 11 (CEPS, December 2009).

nition independent of the vagaries of national law, which can determine EU status of regularity and irregularity."[61]

Neither in this occasion were discussions able to innovate and modify the terminology adopted, and Article 3 of the Directive defines "illegal stay" as "the presence on the territory of a Member State of a third-country national who does not fulfil, or no longer fulfils the conditions of entry as set out in Article 5 of the Schengen Borders Code or other conditions for entry, stay or residence in that Member State."[62]

The European institutions, with rare exceptions,[63] and most of the member states do not have particular interest in this debate and they use the term "illegal migrants" or other terms synonymously.[64]

61 Espeth Guild, *Written Evidence, Q 384, in* House of Lords, *Illegal migrants: proposal for a common EU returns policy, Report with Evidence,* 32nd Report of Session 2005-06, 120, 2006; Ryszard Cholewinski, *The criminalization of migration in EU law and policy, in* WHOSE FREEDOM, SECURITY AND JUSTICE? EU IMMIGRATION AND ASYLUM LAW AND POLICY 301–336 (Annaliese Baldaccini, Elspeth Guild & Helen Toner eds., Hart, 2007).

62 *See* Vogel, Triandafyllidou & Duvell, *supra* note 50, at 50. Directive 2008/115/EC of the European Parliament and of the Council of 16 December 2008 on common standards and procedures in Member States for returning illegally staying third-country nationals, OJ L 348/98, 24 Dec. 2008 (hereinafter "the Return Directive").

63 *See* the Opinion adopted by the European Economic and Social Committee and the definition of "Undocumented persons" at art. 4.8.1: "The EESC does not see an undocumented person as a person without rights: consequently, the EU and the Member States should protect their fundamental rights. The expression 'illegal immigration', when referring to migrants, requires some clarification. Although it is not legal to enter a country without the proper documents and authorisations, people who do so are not criminals. The link made in much of the media and in political speeches between irregular immigration and crime does not reflect reality, and stirs up fear-driven and xenophobic attitudes among the population of the host country. The Committee considers that certain Member States need to provide better protection of the fundamental rights of undocumented immigrants, and that the EU should consider them as one of the most vulnerable groups, preventing their labour exploitation and by ensuring their access to health services, other social services and education for minors", Opinion of the European and Social Com-

1.2. Irregular migration to and through Southern Europe: transit migration

Among the categories mentioned above to which irregular migrants belong, I would like to focus particularly on transit migration. Even though there is no generally accepted definition of this phenomenon, a growing number of people find themselves in a situation called "transit".[65] It has become so common that in addition to countries of origin and destination, an intermediate category has emerged: transit countries.[66] In particular, in the last several years this phenomenon of transit migrants has attracted attention from international organizations (e.g. IOM, UNHCHR) and academics, and also at the normative level, some countries, such as Algeria,[67] are adopting specific regulatory reforms to explicitly refer to this category, putting in this classification everybody who crosses the border and making an arbitrary distinction among foreigners who enter and stay in the receiving countries. This distinction is very dangerous because it implies a situation where migrants are not entitled to any protection because

---

mittee on Respect for fundamental rights in European immigration policies and legislation, SOC/335-CESE 1710/2009 (Nov. 4, 2009).

64 Also in the case-law developed by the European Court of Justice we find the use of terms as "illegal migrant". "By this question, the referring court asks whether Article 12 EC precludes national rules which exclude nationals of member States of the European Union from receipt of social assistance benefits which are granted to illegal immigrants". *Vatsouras,* 4 June 2000, C-22/08 ¶48. European Court of Justice, *Said Shamilovish Kadzoev*, on the interpretation of Article 15 of the "Return Directive" (2008/115) and the length of detention.

65 *See* NYBERG SORENSEN, *supra* note 12; *See* Düvell, *supra* note 21, at 3; Philippe Poutignat, *Transit, etc.*, 13 CAHIERS DE L'URMIS (2011).

66 Michael Collyer, *L'immigration clandestine en Méditerranée en 2006*, ANNUAIRE DE LA MEDITERRANEE 288, 288 (2007); Michael Collyer & Hein de Haas, *Developing dynamic categorisation of «transit» migration*, POPULATION, SPACE AND PLACE (forthcoming 2012).

67 Youssef Courbage, *Changements et perspectives de la population dans le sud de la Méditerranée,* ANNUAIRE DE LA MEDITERRANEE 40, 41 (2007).

their final destination is Europe, allowing the transit countries to try and avoid any duty to protect them.

As rightly observed by Courbage, the concept of "transit migration" has been initially adopted by EU member states to involve neighbouring countries and to share the responsibilities of migration management, as the EU itself was identified as the concrete destination of a massive influx of migrants.[68] Unfortunately, this concept is overly vague, and the absence of a shared legal understanding of its meaning creates perverse effects.[69] Most of the Maghreb countries use the EU's concept to state that they agree that it is appropriate to deny the Maghreb countries' own nature as immigration countries, and promote a juridical distortion between the categories of foreigners who find themselves in countries of the Maghreb; a part of the migrants seem to escape from the application of laws that govern resident aliens.[70]

As argued by some scholars, in particular by Prof. Fargues's analysis, it is possible to identify three forms of irregular migration, namely economic migrants (who move in search of employment), asylum seekers, and transit migrants, who can find themselves without lawful immigration status in a country in which they are physically present.[71]

In this context, economic migrants have been motivated to leave their countries of origin by the extremely poor living conditions and lack of financial resources, and in most cases they are from sub-Saharan or Asian countries.[72] However, from a practical perspective, they share the same condition of irregularity with others, even if they left their countries for different reasons. Being in irregular situation may have certain implications, as they enjoy limited access to legal

68 *See* Courbage, *supra* note 67, at 41.

69 Michael Collyer, Frank Duvell & Hein de Haas, *Critical Approaches to Transit Migration*, POPULATION, SPACE AND PLACE (forthcoming 2012).

70 PAPADOPOULOU-KOURKOULA ASPASIA, TRANSIT MIGRATION, THE MISSING LINK BETWEEN EMIGRATION AND SETTLEMENT (Palgrave, 2008).

71 *See* Fargues, *supra* note 51, at 14.

72 *See* NYBERG SORENSEN, *supra* note 12, at 5.

protection and basic rights such as health care and freedom from inhuman treatment, they are precluded from accessing diplomatic protection, they are unable to leave the country where they are, and they are forced to hide from the police during the day.

I would use the following definition of "transit country", adopted by the Committee on Migrant Workers: "any State through which the person concerned passes on any journey to the State of employment or from the State of employment to the State of origin or the State of habitual residence"[73] and "transit migrants" are persons who were initially trying to reach another destination–typically Europe, North America, or the Gulf States–but found themselves stuck at the gate of their intended destination due to the adoption of restrictive policies for entry and stay of aliens and increasing border control. This phenomenon deserves increasing attention to the new challenges for states in terms of human rights protection.[74] As stated by the Global Commission on Migration "migrants who move for economic reasons may become destitute and vulnerable to human rights abuses while they are in transit, and require protection and assistance, even if they do not have a valid claim to refugee status".[75]

In addition, it is possible to observe the increasing reference to "stranded migrants" to identify migrants who find themselves in the situation described above.[76] Even if this definition, formulated at the international level for the first time in 1982,[77] is more of an operational definition than a legal one, it has the merit of informing the

73 CMW, *Working Paper*, U.N. Doc. CMW/C/2/L.1 (Mar. 25, 2005).

74 GCIM, *Migration in an Interconnected World: New directions for actions", Report of the Global Commission on International Migration*, October 2005, at 40.

75 *Id.* at 40.

76 Stephanie Grant, *The Legal Protection of Stranded Migrants*, IN INTERNATIONAL MIGRATION LAW: DEVELOPING PARADIGMS AND KEY CHALLENGES 29–48 (Ryszard Cholewinski, Richard Perruchoud & Euan Macdonald eds., TMC Asser Press, 2007).

77 Rebecca Dowd, *Trapped in transit: the plight and human rights of stranded migrants* 1 (UNHCR, Research Paper No. 156, 2008).

debate over categorization in attempting to develop a clear understanding of the meaning of this status.[78]

1.2.1. *Mixed migratory flows*

As mentioned above, migratory movements today are of a mixed nature, including migrants moving for economic reasons, refugees and asylum seekers, victims of trafficking, and vulnerable people in an irregular situation.[79]

It is possible to identify how the two phenomena of irregular migrants and asylum seekers, particularly in the case of transit migration, are intermingled–their experiences overlap, and they begin the same journeys through the same routes. In particular, as stated by Aspasia Papadopoulou

> on the one hand, persons in need of international protection increasingly take the irregular migration path in order to reach European territory; they enter the first asylum country illegally and may also remain in the country undocumented, hoping to for asylum in another European country at a later stage. Rejected asylum seekers also become irregular when they remain in the country of asylum after the rejection of their claim. On the other hand, persons that seek to migrate to Europe but are not in need of protection tend to enter the asylum system, hoping to use this as an alternative means of immigration.[80]

78 Amnesty International highlights that "Many migrants are stranded in countries of transit or destination: they have been denied the right to enter and remain legally, but are unable to return to their countries of origin. Some migrants cannot return to their countries of origin due to continuing insecurity, because there is no legal means to get there, or because it is impossible in practice for them to return". Amnesty Int'l, *Spain and Morocco: failure to protect the rights of migrants–Ceuta and Melilla–One year on*, Amnesty International Publications, 2006.

79 *See* PAPADOPOULOU-KOURKOULA, *supra* note 70, at 91.

80 Aspasia Papadopoulou, *Exploring the asylum-migration nexus: case study of transit migrants in Europe*, 23 GLOBAL MIGRATION PERSPECTIVE 1 (2005).

In light of this, there is clearly an urgent need for further attention to the identification of migrants and refugees to provide them with appropriate protection. Therefore, it would be more useful to address the legal protection of refugees together with the situation of irregular migrants. It is imperative that "protection measures" and "migration management" should form part of a coherent framework.[81]

This has been highlighted by the definition of "mixed migration flows" provided by the United Nations High Commissioner for Refugees (UNHCR), which focus on the different protection needs of different groups and to avoid jeopardizing the protection afforded to recognized refugees. Moreover the collective dimension of migration makes this distinction difficult, in particular because of the difficulty of identifying the different categories of people concerned and the standards of protection to be granted to these persons.[82]

Given the far-reaching complexity of this phenomenon, states are more inclined to report refugees and asylum seekers in irregular migratory flows, using them as justification for increasing restrictive control measures. As a consequence, the UNCHR highlighted the need to take this distinction into account and the 10 Point Action Plan on Refugee Protection and Mixed Migration[83] was adopted during the Euro–African Convention on Migration and Development that took place in Rabat in 2006.

81 *See* ICMC, *supra* note 23.

82 Alexander Betts, *Towards a "Soft Law" Framework for the Protection of Vulnerable Irregular Migrants,* 22 INTERNATIONAL JOURNAL OF REFUGEE LAW 209, 209 (2010).

83 "The Plan is meant to guide States and other stakeholders in developing sound protection strategies within a context of mixed migration and focuses on: 1. cooperation among key partners; 2. data collection and analysis; 3. protection-sensitive entry systems; 4. reception arrangements; 5. mechanisms for profiling and referral; 6. differentiated processes and procedures; 7. solutions for refugees; 8. addressing secondary movements; 9. return arrangements for non-refugees and alternative migration options; 10. information strategy". UNHCR, *Refugee Protection and Mixed Migration: A 10–Point Plan of Action*, January 2007, *available at* <www.unhcr.org/refworld/docid/45b0c09b2.html> (last visited Jun. 20, 2012).

The elaboration of this Action Plan highlights the protection needs of refugees in the framework of mixed-migratory flows. The UNHCR is taking important steps to implement the provisions of this Action Plan in North Africa, towards the direct mobilization of these countries, reluctant to endorse a burden-sharing approach and more oriented to address these issues though the prism of national security.[84] Even though there is a consensus on the relevance of this Action Plan, invoking the development of a comprehensive and coherent approach in the field of migratory policies on the issues at stake, it suffers from implementation challenges, which are due to a deep lack of institutional and normative structures at the national level.[85]

84 Johannes Van Der Klaauw, *Refugee rights in times of mixed migration: evolving status and protection needs*, 28 REFUGEE SURVEY QUARTERLY 59, 79 (2009).

85 Nicole Guimezanes, *La lutte contre l'immigration clandestine dans l'Union Européenne et les Etats membres,* 326 REGARD SUR L'ACTUALITÉ 86, 88 (2006).

Section I
International legal frameworks and migration

2. Intersection between the establishment of human rights and the protection of irregular migrants

2.1. Introduction

Within the traditional categories of migration, migrants in irregular status represent the group that raises the most significant challenge in terms of legal protection. Preliminarily, it could be argued that the attention devoted to their situation is a positive step taken to incrementally recognize their protection needs and that this approach, as will be shown later, allows the inclusion of migrants in the protection of human rights regimes.[86] At the same time, their existence testifies to the failure of an entire body of law, namely migration law, incapable of dealing with the challenges emerging around the world.[87]

2.1.1. The "vulnerability" of migrants in irregular situation

The global debate on international migration has been precipitated by the need to formulate and adopt adequate and specific responses to ensure the protection of specific vulnerable groups,[88] exposed to

86 *See* DAUVERGNE, *supra* note 18, at 20–21.

87 *See* Foblets, *supra* note 37, at 141; Gregor Noll, *Why Human Rights Fail to protect Undocumented Migrants*, 12 EUROPEAN JOURNAL OF MIGRATION AND LAW 241, 244 (2010).

88 In particular through the work of Bustamante on immigration we have an articulated definition of vulnerability: "Vulnerability is understood here as a

potential abuses given the critical socio-economic and cultural living conditions outside their countries of origin.[89]
As stated by the United Nations

> the situation of vulnerability in which migrants frequently find themselves, owing, inter alia, to their absence from their states of origin and to the difficulties they encounter because of differences of language, custom and culture, as well as the economic and social difficulties and obstacles for the return to

---

social condition of powerlessness ascribed to individuals with certain characteristics that are perceived to deviate from those ascribed to the prevailing definitions of a national. Vulnerability is a social condition associated with outcomes of impunity for those who violate the human rights of those migrants labeled as deviants (Becker 1968). One of the most important elements of this definition is that vulnerability is not an inherent characteristic of individuals who emigrate from their countries of origin. More precisely, vulnerability is not inherent to racial characteristics, or to a country or an ethnic origin, or to the conditions of underdevelopment of the country or the region of origin. Vulnerability is not a condition brought by an immigrant to a country of destination, regardless of the legality of his or her entry or stay in a given country. In this sense, the causes of vulnerability should not be confused with the causes of immigration. In general terms, international migrations, whether for job purposes or family reunification, are indeed provoked by the interplay of factors located in both the country of origin and the country of destination. It could be said then, that international migrations are, in general, the result of a combination of endogenous and exogenous causes. In contrast, the vulnerability of a migrant as a subject of human rights is an endogenous condition, both at the country of origin and at the country of destination, each independent from the other." Jorge B. Bustamante, *Immigrants vulnerability as subjects of human rights*, 36 INTERNATIONAL MIGRATION REVIEW 333 (2002).

89 This is discussed by a range of authors. *See* e.g. Vincent Chetail & Gilles Giacca, *Who Cares? The Right to Health of Migrants* (2009), in REALIZING THE RIGHT TO HEALTH 225–226 (Mary Robinson & Andrew Clapham eds., Swiss Human Rights Book, Vol. 3, 2009). Commission on Human Rights (CHR), Fifty-fourth Session, *Report of the Intergovernmental Working Group of Experts on the human rights of Migrants "Measures to improve the situation and ensure the human rights and dignity of all migrant workers"*, U.N. Doc. E/CN.4/1998/76 (Mar. 10, 1998).

their states of origin of migrants who are non-documented or in an irregular situation.[90]

In light of this, the three UN Special Rapporteur on the human rights of migrants[91] have affirmed that the human vulnerability of migrants is dictated not only by common factors mostly emphasized in the current cultural discourses against foreigners (such as racism, xenophobia, and prejudice), but in a certain way this state of vulnerability depends on the "distribution of power within the State".[92] This approach recognizes that this situation is closely related to the power migrants have (according to its etymological meaning), as "lack of empowerment", that "derives from the existence of a power structure which shows that in any given national society, some have more power than others".[93]

Navanethem Pillay has recently recognized that the condition of vulnerability faced by irregular migrants affects their (in)ability "to seek protection and relief from the authorities of countries of origin, transit or destination".[94] The perception or *de jure* division of migrants into categories cannot permit the "widespread–and mistaken–view that migrants are somehow not entitled to the full protection of human rights law, often because of the belief that only citizens are

90 G.A., *Protection of migrants*, G.A. Res. 54/166, ¶5, U.N. Doc. A/RES/54/166 (Feb. 24, 2000).

91 Gabriela Pizarro (1999–2005), Jorge A. Bustamante (2005–2011), and F. Crépeau (2011–present). CHR, *Human rights of Migrants*, U.N. Doc. E/CN/RES/2005/47 (Apr. 20, 2005) and HRC, *Human rights of Migrants: Mandate of the Special Rapporteur on the human rights of migrants*, U.N. Doc. A/HRC/RES/8/10 (Jun. 18, 2008).

92 SRHRM, *Report of the Special Rapporteur on the human rights of migrants,* U.N. Doc. E/CN.4/2000/82 (Jan. 6, 2000). *See* Chetail & Giacca, *supra* note 89.

93 CHR, *Working paper of Jorge A. Bustamante, Chairman/Rapporteur of the Working Group of intergovernmental experts on the human rights of migrants*, U.N. Doc. E/CN.4/AC.46/1998/5 (Oct. 8, 1998). *See* Chetail & Giacca, *supra* note 89.

94 Press Release, OHCHR, Statement on Protecting the Human Rights of Irregular Migrants (Sep. 30, 2010).

entitled to these rights."[95] The global economic crisis and security concerns are additional matters that could have serious implications for the rights of irregular migrants, potential victims of abuses and violations.[96]

As Prof. Chetail and Dr. Giacca have shown, even the individual condition is very different: there are common barriers that undermine the possibility for providing a comprehensive legal framework with the primary objective of advocating for better protection and avoiding abuses.[97] In this regard, a specific focus of this analysis is devoted to identifying more clearly the legal and practical constraints that can affect the implementation of the existing international legal framework.[98] The analysis also takes into consideration that states

95 François De Varennes, *Strangers in Foreign Lands–Diversity, Vulnerability and the Rights of Migrants* 9 (UNESCO–MOST Working Paper No. 9, 2003).

96 *See* Chetail & Giacca, *supra* note 89, at 226–227.

97 This point is well argued by Abdelmalek Sayad, who has considered in detail the relationship between human rights violations and the situation of vulnerability of irregular migrants "*l'immigré est dissocié de tout ordre nationaliste [...]; cette dissociation a fait de lui un homme abstrait [...], un espèce d'homme qui serait hors de toutes les déterminations ou appartenances [...], l'homme idéal en somme, celui-là que postule paradoxalement l'expression 'les Droits de l'Homme'*("The migrant is dissociated from every nationalist order [...] this dissociation has created an abstract individual [...], a kind of individual outside any sense of belonging [...], in short the ideal man, whose paradoxical situation represents 'the rights of man'–Translation provided by the author). Sayad Abdelmalek, *Etat, Nation et Immigration: l'ordre national a l'épreuve de l'immigration*, 27–28 MEDITERRANEAN PEOPLE 187, 188–190 (1984).

98 As will be described later, the binding nature of human rights is not sufficient to guarantee their effectiveness, in fact the debate needs to take this direction, giving an appropriate relevance to the implementation of international standards: "*Dopotutto, i diritti dell'uomo erano stati definiti inalienabili perche' si presumeva che fossero indipendenti dai governi ; ma ora si scopri' ce, appena gli individui perdevano la protezione del loro governo ed erano costretti a contato sul minimo di diritti ch dovevano aver acquistato con la nascita, non trovavano nessuna autorita' disposta garantirlo*". *See* ARENDT, *supra* note 1, at 404.

may react by formulating restrictive migration policies to face national security concerns.[99]

The purpose of this section is to outline the general human rights framework, to give a better account of the impact of specialized international instruments and how they are translated into "effective protection regimes" to strengthen the ability of irregular migrants to make claims of human rights violations.[100]

In particular, David Weissbrodt, during his mandate as Special Rapporteur of the Sub-commission on the Promotion and Protection of Human Rights, has nurtured the debate on this issue by explicitly stating that non-citizens,[101] from a broad perspective, should be guaranteed, with few exceptions, the same protections as citizens.[102] In fact, the rights of non-citizens are an issue of concern because they are in many cases deprived of basic human rights, and this reality has been exacerbated by their status as non-nationals. This situation well illustrates the significant gap between the rhetorical and the pragmatic approaches in the implementation of international legal norms relating to migration.[103]

99 Stephanie Grant, *International Migration and Human Rights,* Report prepared for the GCIM, Geneva (2005), at 21. The author highlights as "a powerful obstacle to all rights is ignorance and many migrants know little about what their rights are, or how to claim them".

100 *See* Grant, *supra* note 25, at 26.

101 Answering the question "Who is a non-citizen?" Weissbrodt gives the following explanation: "They include migrants, that is individuals who are engaged in a remunerated activity in a state of which they are not a national. Non-citizens also include refugees, asylum seekers, and immigrants who have entered a new country for reasons of family reunification. They are also non-immigrants, that is, individuals who enter the country without the intent to remain on a permanent basis", David Weissbrodt, *The Protection of non-citizens in International Human Rights Law, in* DEVELOPING PARADIGMS AND KEY CHALLENGE 221 (Ryszard Cholewinski, Richard Perrouchoud & Euan MacDonald eds., Asser Press, 2007).

102 David Weissbrodt, *Final Report of the Special Rapporteur, The rights of non-citizens*, U.N. Doc. EC/CN.4/Sub. 2/2003/23 (May 26, 2003).

103 *See* GCIM, *supra* note 74, at 58: "There is an urgent need to fill the gap that currently exists between the principles found in the legal and normative

This section begins with an illustrative description of the most significant international instruments in this context, focusing on key instruments that are increasing the attention of the international community on these issues. Against the normative framework, the last part looks at some fundamental rights that migrants enjoy regardless of their status and highlights some positive achievements in the empirical dimension.

2.2. International law and irregular migration

International law has been influenced by the entry of human rights and their normative development into the international arena, in particular in relation to migrants' protection.[104] As described by Prof. Chetail, the "intrusion" of human rights upon the international legal order and the related normative expansions have had relevant impact on international law in general, challenging the "theory of two spheres". This theory was based on the distinction between on the one side domestic law to regulate relationships between the state and individuals, and on the other side the external sphere for the relationship between states, regulated by international law. The treatment of foreigners was part of this distinction: "*le droit International y avait sa place pour la simple raison que la position juridique de l'étranger s'assimilait à*

---

framework affecting international migrations and the way in which legislation, policies and practices are interpreted and implemented at national level."

104 This is a strong theme of Chetail's analysis, Vincent Chetail, *Migration, Droits de l'homme et souveraineté, in* MONDIALISATION, MIGRATION ET DROITS DE L'HOMME: LE DROIT INTERNATIONAL EN QUESTION 13 (Vincent Chetail ed., Bruylant, Vol. I, 2007); RICHARD PLENDER, INTERNATIONAL MIGRATION LAW (Martinus Nijoff Publishers, Dordrechtt, 1988); SYLVIE SAROLEA, DROITS DE L'HOMME ET MIGRATIONS: DE LA PROTECTION DU MIGRANT AUX DROITS DE LA PERSONNE MIGRANTE (Bruylant, Bruxelles, 2006); CARMEN TIBURCIO, THE HUMAN RIGHTS OF ALIENS UNDER INTERNATIONAL AND COMPARATIVE LAW (Martin Nijoff Publishers, The Hague, 2001).

une relation Etat à Etat".[105] After this change, international law entered into a new era to be understood no more as a tool for regulating an inter-state community, but a law for international communities as such. In light of this, international law becomes a prominent instrument, as stated by Prof. Abi-Saab "*le droit International est condamné à devenir de plus en plus le droit interne de l'humanité*".[106]

As argued by Prof. Chetail, even if international law is constantly changing and it is extremely difficult to foresee future evolutions, the peculiarity of international human rights treaties is that they have an objective nature that permits overcoming the logical reasoning that governs traditional treaties in the state–state relationship. "The synallagmatic logic is less present, and these treaties may give birth to rights and duties for a third subject: the individual".[107] Their objective nature aims to protect rights and liberties for foreigners and citizens alike.[108] In principle, migrants, regardless of legal *status*, enjoy the

105 Michel Virally observes in this respect how "*l'introduction de la protection de droits de l'homme dans l'ordre juridique international n'entraine pas simplement une modification du contenu du droit international, c'est la définition même de ce droit qui est remise en cause.*" (The introduction of human rights in the international legal order has modified not only international law, but the very definition of law itself is affected-Translation provided by the author). *See* Chetail, *supra* note 104, at 49–50.

106 George Abi-Saab, *Humanité et communauté internationale dans la dialectique du droit international*, *in* MELANGES EN HONNEUR DU PROFESSEUR RENE-JEAN DUPUY 11 (Pedone, 1991). *See* Chetail, *supra* note 104, at 50.

107 "In such a convention the contracting States do not have any interests of their own; they merely have, one and au, a common interest, namely, the accomplishment of those high purposes which are the *raison d'être* of the convention. Consequently, in a convention of this type one cannot speak of individual advantages or disadvantages to States, or of the maintenance of a perfect contractual balance between rights and duties. The high ideals which inspired the Convention provide, by virtue of the common will of the parties, the foundation and measure of all its provisions", in International Court of Justice (ICJ), *Advisory Opinion of 28 May 1951*, *Reservations to the Convention on the Prevention and Punishment of the Crime of Genocide*, Advisory Opinion, 1951 I.C.J. 15 (May 28), I.C.J. Reports, 23. *See* Chetail, *supra* note 104, at 51.

108 "There is nothing in the legislative history of these prescriptions to suggest any intent to exclude aliens from protection", in Myres McDougal, Harold Lasswell & Chen Lung-Chu, *The Protection of Aliens From Discrimination and*

protection conceptualized by norms of international law, being that these provisions are adopted as obligations *erga omnes*,[109] obligations that may give raise to international obligations for states in case of violations.[110]

The application of international human rights instruments to aliens has been mandated by the General Assembly in several instances, as the Universal Declaration establishes that there are human rights of all individuals, not only citizens of the state where they live,[111] and as in several resolutions adopted by the General Assembly for the protection of migrants, e.g.: "*Tous les Etats doivent protéger pleinement les droits de l'homme fondamentaux universellement reconnus des migrants, en particulier des femmes et des enfants, quelle que soit leur situation légale*".[112]

World Public Order: Responsibility of States Conjoined with Human Rights, 3 AJIL 432, 432 (1976).

109 "When a State admits into its territory foreign investments or foreign nationals, whether natural or juristic persons, it is bound to extend to them the protection of the law and assumes obligations concerning the treatment to be afforded them. These obligations, however, are neither absolute nor unqualified. In particular, an essential distinction should be drawn between the obligations of a State towards the international community as a whole, and those arising vis-à-vis another Stat in the field of diplomatic protection. By their very nature the former are the concern of all States. In view of the importance of the rights involved, all States can be held to have a legal interest in their protection; they are obligations *erga omnes*", in ICJ, *Barcelona Traction Light and Power Company (Belgium v. Spain),* of 5 February 1970, I.C.J. Reports 1970, ¶33.

110 SOCIÉTÉ FRANÇAISE POUR LE DROIT INTERNATIONAL, RESPONSABILITÉ DES ÉTATS, COLLOQUE DU MANS, Pedone, Paris (1999).

111 "Recognizing that the protection of human rights and fundamental freedoms provided for in international instruments should also be ensured for individuals who are not nationals of the country in which they live", G.A., *Declaration on the Human Rights of Individuals who are not Nationals of the Country in which They Live*, U.N. Doc. A/RES/47/144 (Dec. 13, 1985).

112 Resolutions of the General Assembly on the protection of migrants: G.A., *Protection of migrants*, U.N. Doc. A/RES/55/92 (Feb. 26, 2001); G.A. *Protection of migrants*, U.N. Doc. A/RES/56/170 (Feb. 28, 2002), G.A., *Protection of migrants*, U.N. Doc. A/RES/57/218 (Feb. 23, 2003); G.A., *Protection of migrants*, U.N. Doc. A/RES/58/190 (Mar. 22, 2004); G.A., *Protection of migrants*, U.N.

In fact, the doctrine asserts that migrants have human rights and need to be protected by the norms that have been created in a more general framework.[113] As stated by prof. Lillich

> What the International community is witnessing today is a major change–the significant of which cannot be overstated–in the way in which the rights of aliens are protected: from the classic system of diplomatic protection by alien's state of nationality, invoking the traditional International law governing the treatment of aliens, to the direct protection of the individual alien's rights through this use of national and international procedures to enforce a set of reformulated international norms.[114]

The usage of different terms as "Everyone has the right to [...]", "All persons [...]", and also in the negative formulation "No one shall be [...]" are significant signs of a global approach.[115]

Also the Charter of the United Nations could be a relevant starting point in the analysis[116] "the primary source of many of the most fundamental norms of contemporary International law",[117] to strengthen the "collective duty" to protect all individuals. In particular, Articles 55 and 56 make explicit reference to the obligation to protect human rights. This provision obliges the United Nations to promote the "universal respect for, and observance of, human rights and fundamental freedoms for *all* without distinction as to race, sex, language or religion."[118]

Doc.A/RES/59/194 (Mar. 18, 2005); G.A., *Protection of migrants*, U.N. Doc. A/RES/60/169 (Mar. 7, 2006); G.A., *Protection of migrants*, U.N. Doc.A/RES/61/165 (Feb. 27, 2007) e G.A., *Protection of migrants*, U.N. Doc. A/RES/62/156 (Mar. 7, 2008).

113 *See* BOGUSZ, RYSZARD, ADAM & SZYSZCZACK, *supra* note 40, at 9.

114 RICHARD B. LILLICH, THE HUMAN RIGHTS OF ALIENS IN CONTEMPORARY INTERNATIONAL LAW 3 (Manchester University Press, Manchester, 1984). *See* Chetail, *supra* note 104, at 51.

115 RYSZARD CHOLEWINSKI, MIGRANT WORKERS IN INTERNATIONAL HUMAN RIGHTS LAW 47 (Clarendon Press Oxford, Oxford, 1997).

116 Charter of the United Nations, adopted on 26 June 1975 and came into force on 24 October 1945.

117 *See* LILLICH, *supra* note 114, at 41.

118 Art. 55 subsection (c). (Emphasis added by the author).

A clear distinction needs to be made between the legal analysis of the existing legal framework and the translation of these standards into an effective protection regime; the linkages between these two dimensions will be addressed to identify their lights and shadows.

The first part describes the main legal provisions underpinning the issues of migrant protection contained in the Universal Declaration on Human Rights (1948),[119] in the International Covenant on Civil and Political Rights (ICCPR),[120] and in the International Covenant on Economic, Social, and Cultural Rights (ICESCR).[121] Even if the UDHR does not have legal force, it is widely recognized as the first and fundamental step in the articulation of the idea of universal human rights, and today most of its principles are considered part of customary law.[122] The adoption of the two International Covenants is also part of this process and gave legal effects to the rights included in the UDHR.

It is important to recall that the Universal Declaration of Human Rights makes explicit the principle that human rights apply to every individual, regardless of immigration status. At the same time, the ICCPR formulates several rights without making any distinctions in their implementation, and the ICESCR explicitly requires states to adopt measures to increase the available resources for granting protection to all individuals. Exceptions are admissible only if they attempt to realize a legitimate aim[123] and they are proportional to reach

119 Universal Declaration of Human Rights, U.N. GA Resolution A (III), adopted on 10 December 1948.

120 International Covenant on Civil and Political Rights adopted on 16 December 1966 by the General Assembly and came into force on 23 March 1976, 999 *UNTS* 14668.

121 International Covenant on Economic, Social and Cultural Rights, adopted on 16 December 1966 by the General Assembly, and came into force on 23 March 1976, 993 *UNTS* 3.

122 *See* Chetail, *supra* note 104, at 59.

123 Joan Fitzpatrick, *The human rights of migrants, in* MIGRATION AND INTERNATIONAL LEGAL NORMS 169 (Alexander T. Aleinikoff & Vincent Chetail eds., Asser Press, 2003).

this aim.[124] Attention is needed to contemplate, in opposition to international standards, the rights included in specific instruments to understand their role for migrant workers.[125] Specific attention will be applied to some categories of migrants, such as migrant workers, and the international standards to regulate their status to understand how they are implemented.[126]

2.2.1. *The principle of non-discrimination*

The general principle of equal rights for all is widely recognized by major human rights treaties, including being set forth in Article 2 of the Universal Declaration on Human Rights.

124 The Committee on the Elimination of Racial Discrimination (CERD) stated in its *General Recommendation No. 14 on the definition of racial discrimination (Forty-Second Session, 1993)*, ¶2, U.N. Doc. A/48/18 (Mar. 22, 1993), that: "The Committee observes that differentiation of treatment will not constitute discrimination if the criteria for such discrimination, judged against the objectives and purposes of the Convention, are legitimate or fall within the scope of article 1, paragraph 4, of the Convention. In considering the criteria that may have been employed, the Committee will acknowledge that particular actions may have varied purposes. In seeking to determine whether an action has an effect contrary to the Convention, it will look to see whether that action has an unjustifiable disparate impact upon a group distinguished by race, colour, descent, or national or ethnic origin". In addition the Human Rights Committee noted in this context made an exception "if the criteria for such differentiation are reasonable and objective and if the aim is to achieve a purpose which is legitimate under the Covenant". HRC, *General Comment No. 18, Non-discrimination (Thirty-Seventh Session, 1989), Compilation of General Comments and General Recommendations*, 146, U.N. Doc. HRI/GEN/1/Rev.6 (2003).

125 According to international law different treatment is allowed, and in some cases belonging to a certain category may be considered a legitimate criteria for discrimination. Jean François Flauss, *Entre souveraineté nationale et droits de l'homme*, *in* L'ETRANGER FACE AU DROIT 68 (Jean-Yves Carlier ed., Bruylant, 2010).

126 *See* CHOLEWINSKI, *supra* note 115, at 47.

Everyone is entitled to all the rights and freedoms set forth in this Declaration, without distinction of any kind, such as race, colour, sex, language, religion, political or other opinion, national or social origin, property, birth or other status. Furthermore, no distinction shall be made on the basis of political, jurisdictional or international status of the country or territory to which a person belongs, whether it is independent, trust, non-self-governing or under any other limitation of sovereignty.

Retracing the *travaux préparatoires* the member states explicitly changed the original phrasing of this article from "without distinction as to race [...]" to "without distinction of any kind, such as race [...]" to highlight that the proscription excludes *any* kind of discrimination and the list cannot be considered exhaustive.[127] In this regard, the Special Rapporteur, Diana Elles, raised the issue that the criteria mentioned in Article 2 have a "descriptive function", to allow them to have the criterion of nationality,[128] among others. [129]

Even in its general wording, specific provisions of the Declaration have been interpreted to exclude a distinction between citizens and non-citizens:

- Everyone has the right to freedom of movement and residence within the borders of each state (Article 13);
- Everyone has the right to leave any country, including his own, and to return to his country (Article 21).

Nevertheless, the ICCPR seems to adopt a more clear formulation. The Human Rights Committee, in its General Observation adopted

127 EIDE ASBJØRN, ALFREDSSON GUDMUNDUR, GORAN MELANDER, LARS ADAM REHOF & ROSAS ALLAN, THE UNIVERSAL DECLARATION OF HUMAN RIGHTS: A COMMENTARY 62 (Scandinavian University Press, 1992).

128 This is discussed by Prof. Jean-Yves Carlier, who explained how nationality could not be regarded as an objective or natural criteria, the way for instance race or age can. The alien is created by the legal system; this legal order makes the individual out of law and at the same time creates the opportunities for with a special status as refugee or statelessness. Jean-Yves Carlier, *Avant Propos*, *in* L'ETRANGER FACE AU DROIT 19 (Jean-Yves Carlier ed., Bruylant, 2010).

129 Sub-Commission on Prevention of Discrimination and Protection of Minorities, *International Provisions the Human Rights of Non-Citizens, Study prepared by the Baroness Elles*, U.N. Doc. E/CN.4/Sub.2/392/Rev.1 (1980).

in 1989, recognized that Art. 26 provided autonomous rights, prohibiting discrimination in law or in fact in any field of regulated and protected by public authorities.[130] In the International Covenant there are two different provisions: one horizontal provision, set out in Article 2 paragraph 1 that affirms the principle of non-discrimination, and Article 26, which contains a general provision against any form of discrimination.[131]

As highlighted by the doctrine, the criteria of nationality is not mentioned in this instrument and the interpretation holds that the words "such as" and "or other status" may encompass also the criteria of nationality.[132]

Based on the *travaux préparatoires*, there is a general consensus that states are prohibited from adopting discriminatory measures.[133] It is clear that the issue will be to explore whether the reasons for

130 "In the view of the Committee, article 26 does not merely duplicate the guarantee already provided for in article but provides in itself an autonomous right. It prohibits discrimination in law or in fact in any field regulated and protected by public authorities. Article 26 is therefore concerned with the obligations imposed on States parties in regard to their legislation and the application thereof. Thus, when legislation is adopted by a State party, it must comply with the requirement of article 26 that its content should not be discriminatory. In other words, the application of the principle of non-discrimination contained in article 26 is not limited to those rights which are provided for in the Covenant." *See* HRC, *supra* note 124, ¶12.

131 Olivier De Schutter, *L'interdiction de discrimination sur la base de la nationalité dans le Pacte International relatif aux droits civils et politiques*, *in* L'ETRANGER FACE AU DROIT 157 (Jean-Yves Carlier, Bruylant, 2010).

132 *Gueye et al. v. France*, Comm. No. 196/1983 (Apr. 3, 1989), U.N. Doc. CCPR/C/D/35/D/196/1985, the Human Rights Committee confirmed that any form of discrimination based on national grounds have to be prohibited on the basis of the criteria of "other status".

133 The interpretation adopted by the Human Rights Committee on "Arbitrary interference" is also significant: "The introduction of the concept of arbitrariness is intended to guarantee that even interference provided by law should be in accordance with the provisions, aims and objectives of the Covenant and should be, in any event, reasonable in the particular circumstances", *see* HRC, *supra* note 124, at 146–148.

discrimination are based on proportional and reasonable elements.[134] This is the approach developed by the Human Rights Committee.

For example, in the case, *Gueye et al. v. France*,[135] the applicants considered French national law to be discriminatory, in particular the provision that granted the right to a pension to retired French military veterans but not to Senegalese veterans who had fought for the French state. In this context the Committee made a finding of discrimination, based on the fact that the criteria adopted–different economic conditions and existence of administrative abuse to identify the potential holders in Senegal–were not reasonable to justify any different treatment.[136]

In addition the jurisprudence takes the position that not all differential treatments based on nationality may be sanctioned, but that the justifications for this treatment need to be founded on "*des considérations très fortes*".[137]

In its General Comment No. 15, adopted in 1986, the Human Rights Committee[138] explicitly states that all rights formulated in the

134 As discussed by Judge Tanaka in his dissenting opinion in the South West Africa case, I.C.J. Reports 1966, 313: "if individuals differ one from another [...] their needs will be different, and accordingly, the content of law may not be identical. Hence is derived the relativity of law to individuals circumstances [...] a different treatment comes into question only when and to the extent that it corresponds to the nature of the difference [...] the issue is whether the difference exists [...] different treatment must not be given arbitrarily; it requires reasonableness, or must be in conformity with justice."

135 *Gueye et al. v. France*, Comm. No. 196/1983 (Apr. 3, 1989), ¶9, U.N. Doc. CCPR/C/D/35/D/196/1985. In addition, other cases in discrimination based on nationality: *Simunek v. Czech Republic* (Jul. 19, 1995), U.N. Doc. CCPR/C/54/D/516/1992; *Adam v. Czech Republic* (Jul. 23, 1996), U.N. Doc. CCPR/C757/D/586/1994.

136 *See* De Schutter, *supra* note 131, at 151.

137 François Tulkens, *L'évolution du principe de non-discrimination a la lumière de la jurisprudence de la Cour Européenne des droits de l'homme*, *in* L'ETRANGER FACE AU DROIT 192 (Jean-Yves Carlier, Bruylant, 2010).

138 The Human Rights Committee is the body that monitors the implementation ICCPR. In addition, the Committee publishes several decisions and resolutions giving its interpretation on specific human rights provisions. MANFRED

Covenant need to be provided without distinction between citizens and non-citizens.[139] At the same time the Covenant lists two exceptions: 1) political rights, such as the right to vote, are recognized only to citizens; 2) freedom of movement,[140] including the right to establish residence, is not granted to irregular migrants. The ICCPR includes a clause of limited opening, Art. 12(4),[141] allowing a foreigner to enter "in his own country". According to the interpretation provided by prof. Nowak, this wording allows migrants who have a strong and intimate link with a state to consider it as "his own country", and to be allowed entry.[142]

The ICESCR gives a low level of protection compared to the ICCPR.[143] This is linked to those specific rights stated in this instrument, in particular Art. 2(1), that set out for a gradual implementation of these rights,[144] even if the ICESCR has pointed, as

---

NOWAK, U.N. COVENANT ON CIVIL AND POLITICAL RIGHTS: CCPR COMMENTARY XXIV (Arlington Publisher, 1993).

139 "The rights set forth in the International Covenant on Civil and Political Rights apply to everyone, irrespective of reciprocity, and irrespective of his or her nationality or statelessness [...] [T]he general rule is that each one of the rights of the Covenant must be guaranteed without discrimination between citizens and aliens". Human Rights Committee, *General Comment No. 15: The position of aliens under the Covenant*, U.N. Doc. HRI/GEN/1/Rev.6 (Apr. 11, 1986).

140 Art. 12 states the right "to liberty of movement and freedom to choose one's residence" to individuals "lawfully within the territory of a State".

141 Art. 12(4): "No one shall be arbitrarily deprived of the right to enter his own country".

142 *See* NOWAK, *supra* note 138, ¶9 and 10. Nowak specifies that foreigners it applies to foreigners: "above all, children of immigrants and alien workers who were born in the host country and no longer have a home in their country of nationality", and "immigrants who have lived many years in the host country and broken all ties to their home country but have not–for whatever reason–acquired the nationality off the host country".

143 *See* Flauss, *supra* note 125, at 64.

144 Art. 2(1): "Each state party to the present Covenant undertakes to take steps, individually and through International assistance and cooperation, especially economic and technical, to the maximum of its available resources, with a view to achieving progressively the full realization of the rights recognized in

a priority, to the obligations for states to guarantee the core rights the Covenant established.[145]

Second, Art. 2(3) admonishes states "with due regard to human rights and their national economy", to "determine to what extent they would guarantee the economic rights recognized to non-nationals". This specific exception, defined by several scholars as a kind of *carte blanche* for developing countries,[146] applies only to economic rights and not to civil and political rights. The principle of progressive implementation of socio-economic rights may be frustrated by the lack of proper economic means or opportunity, and this limitation has to be for a limited period of time. As stated by Prof. Tiburcio, even if resources are limited, states have the obligation to provide adequate measures, in terms of programme and policies to vulnerable categories of persons. In any case, there is a general obligation to respect and promote human rights of individuals once under the jurisdiction of signatory states.[147] In this regard the content of Art. 2(2) needs to be properly understood.

> The states parties to the present Covenant undertake to guarantee that the rights enunciated in the present Covenant will be exercised without discrimination of any kind as to race, colour, sex, language, religion, political or other opinion, national or social origin, property, birth or other status.

As illustrated by Prof. Nowak, until now human rights doctrine has hesitated to include nationality in the criteria listed in that article. For

---

the present Covenant by all appropriate means, including particularly the adoption of legislative measures". Elles discusses this discriminatory aptitude against foreigners "with the present wide disparities in economic and social development there is no reason to suppose that the progressive achievement of these standards implies equal and simultaneous progress for all individuals within the jurisdiction of the Member States, including aliens". *See* Sub-Commission on Prevention of Discrimination and Protection of Minorities, *supra* note 129, ¶43.

145 CESCR, *General Comment No. 3: The nature of States parties' obligations,* 86, U.N. Doc. E/1991/23 (1990).

146 *See* CHOLEWINSKI, *supra* note 115, at 58.

147 *See* TIBURCIO, *supra* note 104, at 145–147.

example, Prof. Lillich suggested that the list as formulated has to be considered not comprehensive, and at the same time it seems that within the ICESCR there are non-exhaustive formulations, as in the case of the ICCPR.[148] In the same vein Prof. Goodwin-Gill affirms that this provision is quite broad in order to integrate the prohibition of discrimination against foreigners, even if the content of Art. 2(3) may concretely affect the implementation of this principle.[149] Prof. Klerk is inclined to focus on textual analysis and to suggest that "as to", rather than "such as", is not sufficient to confirm the comprehensive capacity of the list in Art. 2(2).[150] Furthermore, Warzazi states that most of the negotiators were inclined to interpret the word "discrimination" in Art. 2(2) to create a pretext to justify any distinction between citizens and non-citizens in the enjoyment of specific rights, such as right to work and social rights.[151]

In addition to Art. 2(3) and the uncertainty that shrouds the concrete application of Art. 2(2), within ICESCR it seems impossible to identify other limitations and restrictions to the rights entitlements of non-citizens.

On top of these provisions, migrants may invoke legal protection granted by other specialized instruments. First, as set out in Article 1(2) and 1(3) of the International Convention on the Elimination of All Forms of Racial Discrimination,[152] the adoption of provisions

148 *See* LILLICH, *supra* note 114, at 47. See NOWAK, supra note 138.

149 Goodwin-Gill Guy S., *International Law and Human Rights: trends concerning International migrants and refugees*, 23 INTERNATIONAL MIGRATION REVIEW 526 (1990).

150 Yvonne Klerk, *Working paper on article 2(2) and article 3 of the International Covenant on Economic, Social and Cultural Rights*, 9 HRQ 250, 256 (1987).

151 Halima Warzazi, *Exploitation of Labour through Illicit Clandestine Trafficking*, ¶93, U.N. Doc. E/CN.4/Sub.2/351 (Jun. 1, 1974).

152 Art. 1(1) gives the following definition of racial discrimination: "the term racial discrimination shall mean any distinction, exclusion, restriction or preference based on race, colour, descent, or national or ethnic origin which has the purpose or effect of nullifying or impairing the recognition, enjoyment or exercise, on an equal footing, of human rights and fundamental freedoms in the political, economic, social, cultural or any other field of public life."

that might discriminate on the basis of nationality is prohibited.[153] The implementation of this instrument has been broadly discussed by the international community, in particular in case of racial aptitude developed over the years against irregular migrants.[154] Indicative in this context is the Durban Declaration adopted in 2001 by the World Conference against Racism, Racial Discrimination, Xenophobia, and Related Intolerance "xenophobia against non-nationals, particularly migrants, refugees and asylum seekers, constitutes one of the main sources of contemporary racism".

In this regard the Committee on the Elimination of Racial Discrimination (CERD) that monitors the implementation of the Convention through Recommendation XI, establishes the need to interpret its provisions on the light of human rights standards in a coherent and comprehensive manner.

> Article 1, paragraph 2, must not be interpreted to detract in any way from the rights and freedoms recognized and enunciated in other instruments, especially the Universal Declaration of Human Rights, the International Covenant on Economic, Social and Cultural Rights and the International Covenant on Civil and Political Rights.

In particular, CERD has explicitly declared that the use of the criteria of nationality or legal status may constitute discriminatory treatment if the principle of proportionality is not respected, or if it violates Article 1(4) of the Convention that requires taking specific measures, described as "affirmative actions".

153 This provision applies in the cases of discrimination against non-citizens: "this Convention shall not apply to distinctions, exclusions, restrictions or preferences made by a State Party to this Convention between citizens and non-citizens." Art. 1(3) and Art. 1(2) state: "Nothing in this Convention may be interpreted as affecting in any way the legal provision of State Parties concerning nationality, citizenship or naturalization, provided that such provisions do not discriminate against any particular nationality".

154 *Quereshi v. Denmark*, Communication No. 33/2003 (Mar. 9, 2005), U.N. Doc. CERD/C/66/D/33/2003. In this case the CERD invited the Denmark to monitor the use of racial speeches against migrants, even if no violations have been found.

CERD specifically examines periodic reports submitted by member states and examines of individual complaints and on several occasions raised attention on specific issues, including:

- Publicly condemning of acts of discrimination perpetrated against specific racial, ethnic, or religious groups,[155] and the need to develop common understanding of the principle of non-discrimination and the rights of non-citizens;
- Ensuring the principle of non-discrimination and the legal recognition of non-citizens;
- Raising attention in the critical areas in which the rights of non-citizens are at risk of not being respected, in particular the rights of access to education, employment, and housing;
- Guaranteeing specific rights to non-citizens, including the right to housing and access to social services;[156]
- Adopting all measures to combat any forms of discrimination against non-citizens in the field of labour,[157] including attitudes and behaviours towards non-citizens that may have discriminatory consequences in their practical implementation;[158]
- Applying international and regional standards for the protection of asylum seekers[159]and refugees, paying attention to the right to housing, education, and work.[160]

155 CERD, *Conclusions and recommendations of the Committee on the Elimination of Racial Discrimination, Canada*, ¶338, U.N. Doc. A/57/18 (2002).

156 CERD, *Conclusions and recommendations of the Committee on the Elimination of Racial Discrimination, Ukraine*, ¶266, U.N. Doc. CERD/C/304/Add.48 (1998).

157 CERD, *Conclusions and recommendations of the Committee on the Elimination of Racial Discrimination, Costa Rica*, ¶64–86, U.N. Doc. CERD/C/60/CO/3 (2002), and *Report of the UN Committee on the Elimination of Racial Discrimination, Sixtieth Session (4–22 March 2002) and Sixty-first Session (5–23 August 2002), Estonia*, ¶344–366, U.N. Doc. A/57/18 (2002).

158 CERD, *Conclusions and recommendations of the Committee on the Elimination of Racial Discrimination, China*, ¶248, U.N. Doc. A/56/18 (2001).

159 CERD, *Conclusions and recommendations of the Committee on the Elimination of Racial Discrimination, Sudan*, ¶215, U.N. Doc. CERD/C/304/add.116 (2001).

Recently, CERD has sent out General Recommendation XXX to formally invoke state responsibility for prohibiting discrimination and to identify five crucial areas for *non-citizens:* protection against racialist speech; access to citizenship; administration of justice; expulsions and deportation; economic, social, and cultural rights.[161]

It is relevant to highlight how:

- In the context of the administration of justice, CERD stresses that states have to take action to ensure access for the victims of ill-treatment to effective legal remedies and to combat racial discrimination against non-citizens, and to avoid arbitrary detentions;[162]
- It must be ensured that the non-citizens are not subject to collective expulsion and to "ensure that non-citizens are not subject to collective expulsion in particular in situations where there are insufficient guarantees that the personal circumstances of each of the persons concerned have been taken into account" (this issue will later be addressed extensively).

CERD urged states to devote particular attention to violations that could take place in the employment of migrants, as in point of fact the absence of clear measures results in the emergence of a growing number of discriminatory practices. For these reasons, CERD called upon states parties to the agreement to take all necessary measures to prevent *de facto* discrimination under working conditions.[163] In addition to these instruments, as will be described later, there are also specific instruments in the human rights framework.

---

160 CERD, *Conclusions and recommendations of the Committee on the Elimination of Racial Discrimination, Azerbaijan*, ¶497, U.N. Doc. CERD/C/304/Add.75 (2001).

161 CERD, *General Recommendation XXX, Discrimination against Non-citizens (Sixty-Fourth Session, 2004),* U.N. Doc. CERD/C/64/Misc.11/rev. 3 (2004).

162 *Id.* ¶18 and 19.

163 CERD, *Consideration of Reports submitted by states parties under article 9 of the convention Concluding observations of the Committee on the Elimination of Racial Discrimination, Concluding observations, United States,* U.N. Doc. CERD/C/USA/CO/6 (May 8, 2008).

In this context, the Convention on the Elimination of All Forms of Discrimination Against Women (CEDAW, 1979),[164] the Convention Against Torture (CAT, 1985),[165]and the Convention on the Rights of the Child (CRC, 1989) [166] are especially relevant. In particular, the principle of non-discrimination has been included in the CRC at Article 2.

2.2.2. Female migrants

In 1995, during the fiftieth session of the Commission for the Human Rights, the global community voiced the need for a comprehensive approach to deal with the situation of migrant women

> Migrant women face a triple discrimination as foreigners, economically underprivileged and subject to gender-specific oppression. Undocumented migrant women were especially vulnerable to violations of their basic human rights, including rape and other forms of sexual exploitation. The situation was exacerbated by the disintegration of traditional support structures and by the lack of culturally and linguistically appropriate services.[167]

The CEDAW has gained a peculiar role in ensuring the protection of the rights of women and girls who migrate. As other human rights instruments, this Convention does not list any explicit provisions on

164 Convention for the Elimination of All Forms of Discrimination Against Women (CEDAW) adopted on 18 December 1981, entered into force on 3 September 1981, U.N. GA Res. 34/180. This Convention defines several measures to assist and protect women who become victims of abuses: elimination of sexual discrimination (Art. 5), elimination of trafficking in women and prostitution (Art. 6), and the prohibition of all forms of discrimination that affect the equal enjoyment of rights at work or to acquire the nationality (Art. 3, 9 and 11).

165 Convention against Torture, adopted on 10 December 1984, adopted on 26 June 1987, U.N. GA Res. 39/46.

166 Convention on the Rights of Child of 1989, adopted on 2 September 1990, 1577 *UNTS* 3.

167 Commission on Human Rights, Session Fifty-One, U.N. Doc. E/CN.4/1995/SR.21 (Feb. 17, 1995).

migrants, but instead has a number of provisions that refer to the obligations of member states to protect women. In light of this, the CEDAW regulates specific sectors such as living conditions of women in domestic houses or family relationships in which they might be exposed to abuses or relegated to an inferior situation, under several different rubrics (legal, gender, economic). [168]

In addition, the CEDAW addressed specific sectors regulated by public authority, as *law enforcement* and *welfare support*, excluded for undocumented migrants; this is described as a case of double jeopardy.[169] In this regard, the Convention states at Article 6 the need to "suppress all forms of trafficking in women and sexual exploitation of women".[170]

The fourth Global Conference on Women in 1995 gave rise to the Beijing Platform for Action, which called for, *inter alia*, addressing these themes and promoting active programmes and policies to deal with prostitution and enslavement of migrants and asylum seekers.

The CEDAW recently adopted a General Recommendation on female migrant workers.[171] This instrument takes into account the situation of women who travel alone, to join families abroad, and the working conditions of undocumented women. This calls the attention to the fact that the phenomenon of migration cannot be considered "gender-neutral", and it states that "regardless of the lack of immigration status of undocumented women migrant workers,

168 ICHRP, *Irregular Migration, Migrant smuggling and Human Rights*, Geneva (2010), at 71.

169 *Id.* at 71. Margot Mendelson, *The legal protection of Identities: a narrative analysis of conversations with battered undocumented women*, 19 BERKLEY WOMEN'S LAW JOURNAL 139 (2004).

170 For the definition of the terms "trafficking in women" and "exploitation" see the CEDAW, *General Recommendation No. 19: Violence against women (Eleventh session, 1992)*, ¶14, U.N. Doc. A/47/38 (1993). This General Recommendation addresses all these practices, as prostitution, sexual trade, domestic slave, and arranged marriage that are in contrast with human rights of women and may compromise to their security.

171 CEDAW, *General Recommendation No. 26 on Women Migrant Workers*, U.N. Doc. CEDAW/C/2009/WP.1/R (Dec. 5, 2008).

States Parties have an obligation to protect their basic human rights."[172]

These obligations aim to ensure the protection and safeguarding of the rights of migrant women during the entire process, including access to justice, and the circumstances in which their life may be at risk, or if they are victims of inhuman and degrading treatments, if they lack access to medical care, and in all cases in which they are victims of sexual abuse.

2.2.3. Unaccompanied minors

The Convention on the Rights of the Child (CRC) is one of the most comprehensive treaties for the protection of children. The CRC provides civil and political as well economic, social, and cultural rights that states shall guarantee to all children within their jurisdiction. The strong impact of this instrument implies that national legislation and jurisprudence must take care of children *in primis* more than considering them as migrants.[173] International human rights instruments have addressed the specific needs of migrant children, with a focus on refugees and asylum seekers, whether on their own or not.[174]

Article 1 of the Convention defines a child as "every human being below the age of 18". Even if the phenomenon of migration is not addressed directly by the CRC and it does not provide any definition of migrant children, it reasonable to affirm that its provisions are the highest standard available for all children, including those moving across borders.[175] In particular, the

172 *Id.* at 4 and 8.

173 Paul Martens, *Restaient les étrangers*, *in* L'ETRANGER FACE AU DROIT 601 (Jean-Yves Carlier, Bruylant, 2010).

174 Jacqueline Bhabha, *Children, Migration and international norms*, *in* MIGRATION AND INTERNATIONAL LEGAL NORMS 203–204 (Alexander T. Aleinikoff & Vincent Chetail, Asser Press, 2003).

175 Art. 1:"[...] Unless, under the law applicable to the child, majority is attained earlier".

Convention is available to all children, irrespective of their nationality or migration status.[176] These preliminary considerations suggest the applicability of all rights stipulated in the CRC to children, irrespective of their immigration status. This principle has been echoed by the Committee on the Rights of the Child in its comment on unaccompanied children

> the enjoyment of rights stipulated in the Convention is not limitated to children who are citizens of a State party and must therefore, if not explicitly stated otherwise in the Convention, also be available to all children–including asylum-seeking, refugee and migrant children–irrespective of their nationality, immigration status or statelessness.[177]

The legal framework available to ensure a comprehensive and rights-based approach for the protection of migrant children includes several resolutions adopted by the Commission on Human Rights, the Human Rights Committee, and the General Assembly.

The Human Rights Committee in its resolution 9/5[178] highlighted that, taking into account the vulnerable situation of unaccompanied children, states have the obligation to protect, respect, and fulfil the rights of migrant children, with a key concern for the best interests of children and the protection of the right to a family unit.

Unaccompanied or separated children[179] are vulnerable to abuse and rights violations throughout the migratory process. In particular,

176 Art. 3 (1): "In all actions concerning children, whether undertaken by public or private social welfare institutions, courts of law, administrative authorities or legislative bodies, the best interests of the child shall be a primary consideration".

177 Committee on the Rights of Child, *General Committee No. 6: Treatment of unaccompanied and separated children outside their country of origin*, U.N. Doc. CRC/GC/2005/6 (Sep. 1, 2005).

178 HRC, *Protections of Migrants*, U.N. Doc. Res. 9/5 (Sep. 24, 2008).

179 See the definition adopted by the Committee on the Rights of Child in its General Comment, *See* CRC, *supra* note 177, ¶7–8. "Children referred to as 'unaccompanied' are those separated from parents or other relatives, or as not being cared for by an adult who, by law or custom, is responsible for doing

as stated by several Special Procedures, migrant children may be at risk of being deported without access to legal assistance or measures of protection. It has been reported that in most cases child victims of trafficking or smuggling are considered and treated as adults in an irregular situation.[180]

According to a recent study published by the High Commissioner for Human Rights "serious protection gaps for migrant children in every region of the world" [181] have been identified, which themselves lead to multiples cases of discrimination, abuse, and rights violations. "Often the object of suspicion, neglect and abuse, children are locked up in immigration detention centers, denied access to essential select because off their or their parents' status and subjected to the same regime of criminalization as adult migrants". [182] One of the main issues of concern is the absence of a clear distinction between adults and children in the migratory policy adopted at national level;[183] in fact in many cases specific regulations are absent.[184]

In the light of this, it appears more than relevant that the protection of children needs to be addressed within the phenomenon of migration, preventing states from limiting children's protection through the adoption of restrictive policies to control irregular migration. Clearly, the criminalization of irregular migration[185] can incentivize and legitimate the diffusion of inhuman treatments and

---

so"."Children referred as 'separated' are those that may be accompanied by adult family members or caregivers."

180 CHR, *Conclusions and recommendations of the Special Rapporteur on the sale of children, child prostitution and child pornography,* U.N. Doc. E/CN.4/1999/71 (1999).

181 HRC, *Study of the Office of the United Nations High Commissioner for Human Rights on challenges and best practices in the implementation of the International framework for the protection of the rights of the child in the context of migration,* U.N. Doc. A/HRC/15/29 (Jul. 5, 2010).

182 *Id.* at 3.

183 SRHRM, *Report of the Special Rapporteur on the human rights of migrants, Jorge Bustamante,* ¶45–80, U.N. Doc. A/HRC/11/7 (May 14, 2009).

184 SRHRM, *supra* note 13, ¶13–33.

185 *Id.* ¶30.

other kind of violations against migrants. This suggests that the rights of unaccompanied children may be negatively affected, for instance where irregular migration is sanctioned with detention or other criminal measures.

2.2.4. Trafficking and smuggling of migrants

The United Nations Convention against Transnational Organized Crime (UNCTOC) and its attendant Protocols adopted by the United Nations for fighting against these activities are a relevant point of reference for irregular migrants affected by trafficking or smuggling in persons. The UNCTOC was adopted to promote and coordinate global action against several criminal activities, such as corruption, terrorism, and illicit trafficking, with the aim of preventing all related activities. The Optional Protocols achieve these goals. Two protocols are of interest in the protection of migrants:

a) The United Nations Protocol to Prevent, Suppress and Punish Trafficking in Persons, Especially Women and Children: ratified by 111 states and entered into force on 25 December 2003;
b) The Protocol Against the Smuggling of Migrants by Land, Sea and Air, ratified by 105 states entered into force on 28 January 2004.

On the main achievements of the Convention and its Protocols was the adoption a legal definition of trafficking and smuggling.

States, therefore, that have ratified these instruments will have to take appropriate consideration of these definitions and must adopt national instruments to provide and guarantee full protection for victims of such crimes. In addition, cooperation activities among states and the dissemination and exchange of information may facilitate the effective implementation of these instruments. It is essential to make a reference to the Arabic terminology in this context, because the language adopted seems particularly complex:[186]

186 *See* IOM, supra *note* 55, at 16. (Translation provided by the author).

التجـــار بـــــالرقيق ألبيــــض (*al-Ittijar bi ar-Raqiq al-Abiad*): trafficking of white women, and is also used to indicate the prostitution and sex trades;
السـتـرقاق (*al-Istirqaq*): submission of white women to become concubines or slaves;
السـتعباد (*al-Isti'bad*): submission of black men; it could also refer to individuals who become slave because of a debt not honoured;
التجـــار بالبشـــر (*al-Ittijar bi al-Bachar*): trade of human beings.[...]
In the Moroccan dialect, there is a reference to exploitation (*al-Istirlal* تغالـل السـ), and rarely to other conditions *al-Isti'bad* (the African trade) understood as trade of human beings (*al-Ittijar bi al-Bachar*).

As highlighted by a report published by the IOM, this incoherent and inappropriate use of different terminology made a clear understand difficult. So to avoid this kind of confusion (between smuggling and trafficking) IOM suggests to adopt the following international definitions:

"Smuggling of Migrants: التجـــار بالبشـــر (*al-Ittijar bi al-Bachar*) to exploit migrants and reduce them as merchandize deprived of all rights"; and
"The trafficking of migrants: تهريــب البشـــر (*Tahrib al-Bachar*) refers to the organization of irregular border-crossings".

2.2.5. Refugees and asylum seekers

The United Nations Convention Relating to the Status of Refugees of 1951,[187] as amended by the 1967 Protocol Relating to the Status of Refugees,[188] defines the rights of individuals who leave their countries

187 The United Nations Convention Relating to the Status of Refugees 1951, adopted on 22 April 1954, 189 *UNTS* 150.
188 The 1967 Protocol Relating to the Status of Refugees of 31 January 1967, 606 *UNTS* 8791.

as a result of persecution or other threats to life, as well as the duties of host countries for protecting refugees when human rights are at risk. Without making a comprehensive analysis of international refugee law, it is useful to illustrate some preliminary reflections on the admission conditions and salient elements of refugee status.

The first concern of an individual at risk of persecution is to be able to get access to the territory of another state, and to be in the condition to get access to status determination procedures.[189] In this context the main challenges were historically linked to norms not being well established, and now they are protected against penalties for irregular entry according to Article 31.[190] This provision is complemented by the principle of *non-refoulement,* established by the Article 33 of the Convention, during the examination of the applicant's request.

As illustrated by prof. Chetail, once refugee status has been granted, refugees are entitled to specific rights, such as the prohibition of discrimination (Art. 3), access to education (Art. 22), the freedom of religion (Art. 4), and eligibility for identity documents (Art. 27).[191] The problem is that the temporary nature of the status affects the substance of this status that may result in a difference of treatment between the foreigner and the citizen. Taking as starting point the fact that international law recognizes refugee status as a *temporary* form of protection that is to come to an end when the migrant return to his or her country of origin.[192]

189 JEAN-YVES CARLIER, DROIT D'ASILE ET DES RÉFUGIÉS. DE LA PROTECTION AUX DROITS 9–354 (Recueil des Cours de l'Académie de droit international de La Haye, Tome 332, 2007).

190 They need to declare themselves immediately to the public authorities, to explain the reasons of their irregular stay, and to arrive directly from the country of origin.

191 *See* Chetail, *supra* note 104, at 106–119.

192 *See* Chetail, *supra* note 104, at 106–118.

2.3. The role of human rights mechanisms

2.3.1. UN mechanisms

Within the UN human rights system there are several instruments that over the last two decades have been involved in the protection of the human rights of migrants. This part will provide a general overview of the main mechanisms and then the analysis will focus on the role of Special Procedures, with the focus on the creation of the Special Rapporteur on the Human Rights of Migrants (SRHRM).

2.3.1.1. Treaty committees

A Committee has been created for each of the human rights treaties described above with the fundamental role of monitoring the implementation and facilitating the interpretation of the provisions set out in the treaties, as will be described in Chapter 4, and in this regard very innovative roles have been acquired in the migration field.

Among these committees are: the Human Right Committee (HRC), created with the adoption of the International Covenant on Civil and Political Rights, and the Economic, Social and Cultural Committee (CESCR), created through the International Covenant on Economic, Social and Cultural Rights. Then there is an additional group of committees concerning specific human rights treaties: the Committee for the Elimination of Racial Discrimination (CERD) monitors the International Convention on the Elimination of All Forms of Racial Discrimination; the Committee for the Elimination of Discrimination Against Women (CEDAW) watches over the Convention on the Elimination of All Forms of Discrimination Against Women; the Committee Against Torture (CAT) monitors the Convention Against Torture; the Committee for the Rights of Child (CRC) is answerable for the Convention of the Rights of Child; and the Committee for the Protection of the Rights of All Migrants Workers and Members of their Families (CMW), the most recently created committee, has been created with the entry into force of the

International Convention of the Rights of All Migrants Workers and Members of Their Families.

These bodies have several responsibilities. Most of them adopt General Comments and Recommendations, formulating authoritative interpretation, even if not binding, of the treaties' provisions, and they respond to violations thought the consideration of individual complaints.[193] In addition, the Human Rights Committee may receive complaints from states parties to its optional Protocol.[194]

2.3.1.2. The Special Procedures

Special Procedures have been created within the Human Rights Council, and these procedures allow the nomination of independent international experts mandated to monitor the implementation of specific human rights. The experts appointed have to act according to a Code of Conduct that describes their rules of engagement. Special Procedures deal with specific activities: reacting to individual or group complaints, making fact-finding missions to verify the situation in sensitive territory, conducting research activities, and providing technical support if demanded by signatory state.[195]

Special Rapporteur on the Human Rights of Migrants (SRHRM)

The mandate of the SRHRM is mainly relevant for the protection of human rights of migrants.

The Commission on Human Rights raised the need to ensure the "full respect of the human rights and fundamental freedoms of migrants", focusing on the vulnerability of their situation and the absence of proper mechanisms to address it.[196] For these reasons, in

193 DAVID WEISSBRODT, THE HUMAN RIGHTS OF NON-CITIZENS 10 (Oxford University Press, 2008).

194 999 *UNTS* 302, entered into force on 23 March 1976.

195 Taryn Lesser, *The role of United Nations Special procedures in protecting the human rights of migrants*, 4 REFUGEE SURVEY QUARTERLY 139, 141 (2010).

196 As observed by the Special Rapporteur the vulnerability of migrants is self-evident, and not a symptom of weakness, but "because of the special circumstances in which migration is now taking place, migrants are exposed to

1999 the Commission took the decision to create this mandate,[197] with the peculiar aim of overcoming all impediments to full and effective protection.[198]

Since 1999, the resolutions adopted by the Commission on Human Rights have been oriented to the conclusions and recommendations formulated by the SRHRM.[199] In light of this, the Commission has explicitly addressed the protection of people on the move,[200] regardless of their irregular status.[201]

---

smuggling and trafficking and may fall into the hands of organized gangs which take advantage of their need to find work in order to survive", SRHRM, *Migrant Worker-Report of the Special Rapporteur on the human rights of migrants, Ms Gabriela Pizarro* , ¶55, U.N. Doc. E/CN.4/2001/83 (Jan. 9, 2001).

197 The mandate of the SRHRM was created in 1999 for a period of 3 years. Among the main functions the SRHRM needed to adopt recommendations and legal strategies to deal with the international migration, focusing on the protection of their human rights protection. Gabriella Rodriguez Pizarro served as the first SRHRM (1999–2005), then J. Bustamante, and last year F. Crépeau, from Canada, were appointed.

198 "Examine ways and means to overcome the obstacles existing to the full and effective protection of the human rights of migrants, including obstacles and difficulties for the return of migrants who are undocumented or in an irregular situation." *See* SRHRM, *supra* note 196, at 4.

199 Among the main functions of the SRHRM: the collection of information concerning the situation of migrants and their access to protection safeguards, the adoption of recommendations to advocate the elimination of serious abuses and violations identified during its mandate at national, regional and international levels with a gender perspective, and the promotion of international standards. The activities of the SRHMR include several missions on the field. As stated by Cholewinski, the added value of SRHRM is to contribute to raising the attention of the international community to the situation of irregular migrants. Ryszard Cholewinski, *International labour law and the protection of migrant workers: revitalizing the agenda in the era of globalization*, *in* GLOBALIZATION AND THE FUTURE OF LABOUR LAW (John D.R. Craig & S. Michael Lynk eds., Cambridge University Press, 2006).

200 The following categories have been identified: "a) persons who are outside the territory of the state of which they are nationals or citizens are not subject to its legal protection and are in the territory of another state; b) persons who do not enjoy the general legal recognition of rights which is inherent in the granting by the host state of the status of refugee, permanent resident or naturalized person or of similar status; c) persons who do not enjoy either general le-

> Definitions that are related to the reasons why people leave their countries of origin are perhaps the least suitable kind of definition, except to the extent that they give access to legal protection and status in the host country, as in the case of refugees. In the light of the political, social, economic and environmental situation of many countries, it is increasingly difficult, if not impossible, to make a clear distinction between migrants who leave their countries because of political persecution, conflicts, economic problems, environmental degradation or a combination of these reasons and those who do so in search of conditions of survival or well-being that do not exist in their places of origin.[202]

In addition, taking into account the United Nations engagement to ensure the full protection of the human rights of migrants,[203] the Commission recalled the need to align national legislation to international standards[204] and to include protection mechanisms as integral part of migration policies.[205]

In particular, in 2004 Gabriela Pizarro reiterated the need for providing effective mechanisms of protection, including the vital role of the implementation of the principle of non-discrimination. States have to respect obligations that arise in international law and they have to play an active role in addressing the existing gap between the theoretical and practical level.[206]

---

gal protection of their fundamental rights by virtue of diplomatic agreements, visas or other agreements". *See* SRHRM, *supra* note 92, at 9.

201 *See* SRHRM, *supra* note 183, ¶40–42.

202 *Id.* ¶30.

203 *See* ¶14 of the UN Millennium Declaration (UNGA Res. 55/2, 8 September 2000): "To take measures to ensure respect for and protection of the human rights of migrants, migrant workers and their families, to eliminate the increasing acts of xenophobia in many societies and to promote greater harmony and tolerance in all societies"; *see* also the Durban Declaration.

204 *See* SRHRM, *supra* note 196, ¶16–34.

205 Gabriela Rodriguez Pizarro, *The role of the United Nations Special Rapporteur on the Human Rights of Migrants*, 38 INTERNATIONAL MIGRATION 73, 73 (2000).

206 SRHRM, *Report of the Special Rapporteur on human rights of migrants, Jorge Bustamante,* ¶74–85, U.N. Doc. E/CN.4/2005 (Dec. 27, 2004).

As stated by Bustamante in his first report, there is a dangerous relationship between the anti-immigrant discourses and the need of migrant workers.[207]

In addition to the SRHRM there are other Special Procedures with complementary functions. First, the SR on the trafficking of human beings,[208] particularly women and children, may play an active role, even if the terms of its mandate are not completely clear in light of increasing numbers of cases and the complexity of the trafficking phenomenon.[209] The SR on violence against women and its causes and consequences could also contribute to all cases of violence and discrimination against women in transit. Recently, the resolution adopted to renew this mandate included the theme of migrant women in detention among its priorities.[210] The Human Rights Committee has also created an SR on contemporary forms of slavery, including its causes and consequences,[211] and requested the expert to intervene in any circumstances. The same is the case for the mandate on the sales of children and prostitution, to address the situation of unaccompanied children on the move.[212] Finally, the mandate of the SR on contemporary forms of racism, racial discrimination, xenophobia and related intolerances, in addition to its focus on a wide range of discriminatory practices, may offer specific protection to the human rights of migrants.

The vulnerable situation of irregular migrants gives rise to a large number of cases of abuse, not only in the situations mentioned above, but also in terms of access to specific rights, including housing, health care, and education. For these reasons the mandates of SR on the adequate conditions of living, education, and the right to

207 SRHRM, *Report of the Special Rapporteur on human rights of migrants, Jorge Bustamante,* U.N. Doc. E/CN.4/2006/73 (Dec. 30, 2005); G.A., *Human Rights of Migrants*, ¶8–9, U.N. Doc. A/60/357 (Sep. 30, 2005).

208 CHR, U.N. Doc. Res. 2002/50 (Apr. 23, 2002).

209 *See* Lesser, *supra* note 195, at 143.

210 *See* CHR, *supra* note 208.

211 HRC, U.N. Doc. Res. 6/14 (Sep. 28, 2007).

212 CHR, U.N. Doc. Res. 1990/68 (Mar. 7, 1990).

health have gained significance in this context, as it will be described in detail in Chapter 4.

2.3.2. Regional mechanisms

There are also a series of relevant regional mechanisms that report on violations of irregular migrants' rights. The main regional organization is the Council of Europe, with its 47 member countries, that developed several mechanisms for the promotion and protection of human rights.[213] The European Convention on Human Rights is the international treaty under which the members of the Council of Europe adopted the specific provisions invoked on several occasions to protect migrants' rights. Recently the European Court of Human Rights has issued relevant jurisprudence on the application of the principle of non-discrimination and to prohibit collective expulsions.

Today, the main African body is the African Commission for the Protection of Rights of Human Beings and Peoples.[214] The role of this Commission could be reinforced and strengthened by the recent creation of the African Court for Human Rights, potentially playing a prominent in this context.

The Inter-American system consists of the Inter-American Commission for Human Rights, based in Washington, DC, and the Inter-American Court for Human Rights, which were both created by the Organization of American States.[215] These institutions has been solicited in several cases to deal with the protection the human rights of migrants.

213 Juan Antonio Carrillo Salcedo, *The European Convention on Human Rights,* in INTERNATIONAL HUMAN RIGHTS LAW IN A GLOBAL CONTEXT 631–644 (Gomez Isa Felipe & de Feyter Koen eds., Duesto University Press, 2009).

214 Christof Heyns & Magnus Killander, *The African Regional Human Rights System, in* INTERNATIONAL HUMAN RIGHTS LAW IN A GLOBAL CONTEXT 855–898 (Gomez Isa Felipe & de Feyter Koen eds., Duesto University Press, 2009).

215 Ludovic Hennebel, *The Inter-American System for Human Rights: operation and achievements, in* INTERNATIONAL HUMAN RIGHTS LAW IN A GLOBAL CONTEXT 805–852 (Gomez Isa Felipe & de Feyter Koen eds., Duesto University Press, 2009).

3. International labour mobility and irregular migration

The relationship between regular and irregular migration is characterized by close inter-linkages in the context of labour migration.[216] It is evident that the phenomenon of irregular migration cannot be regarded only as an issue of security or of law, but that the participation of irregular migrants in the labour market needs to be recognized.[217] In fact, there is a general agreement that migration, irregular and regular, is beneficial for the economic growth and well-being of developed and developing countries.[218]

This chapter looks at the genesis of relevant normative standards for migrant workers to identify the rights applicable to migrants in irregular status, in addition to the basic rights conferred by International Labour Organisation (ILO) standards. Irregular migrants represent a vulnerable population that have limited access to fundamental rights and protections, and in many receiving countries they do not receive satisfactory protection. As stated by the UN Commissioner on Human Rights: "Migrant workers face the gravest risks to their human rights when they are recruited, transported and employed in defiance of the law".[219] Many governments seem to ignore their entitlement to

216 *See* ILO, *supra* note 17, at 99–101; Piyasiri Wickramasekara, *Irregular Employment of Migrants: an ILO Perspective*, *in* ADDRESSING THE IRREGULAR EMPLOYMENT OF IMMIGRANTS IN THE EUROPEAN UNION: BETWEEN SANCTIONS AND RIGHTS 297–313 (Marek Kupiszewski & Mattila Heikki eds., IOM, 2008).

217 ILO, *Towards a fair deal for migrant workers in the global economy, Report VI, International Labour Conference, 92nd Session,* Geneva (2004), at 120.

218 Piyasiri Wickramasekara, *Globalisation, International labour migration and the rights of migrant workers*, 29 THIRD WORLD QUARTERLY 1247, 1248 (2008).

219 OHCHR, *The Rights of Migrant Workers*, Fact Sheet No. 24 (1994), at 7.

having these basic rights provided by destination countries, including labour standards set by the ILO and UN in this field.

3.1. Evolution of international labour standards and the role of the International Labour Organization (ILO)

Many scholars and governments consider the International Labour Organization (ILO) to have played a pioneering role in the establishment of internationally agreed standards to regulate economic migration and to cover the situations of migrant workers.[220] It has been observed that the so-called "core labour standards", contained in ILO Conventions and the Declaration on Fundamental Principles and Rights at Work, apply to all migrants, regardless their nationality and/or status.[221] Wickramasekara refers to the eight fundamental ILO Conventions in four key areas: forced labour, child labour, freedom of association, and the principle of non-discrimination.[222] The ILO Declaration states:

> 2. All member states even if they have not ratified the Conventions in question, have an obligation arising from the very fact of membership in the Organization, to respect, to promote and to realize in good faith and in accord-

220 *See* CHOLEWINSKI, *supra* note 115, at 90. For a detailed analysis of the historical evolution of the normative action of the ILO *see ex multis* Roger Bohning, *The ILO and the new UN Convention on migrant workers: the past and the future*, 4 INTERNATIONAL MIGRATION REVIEW 698 (1991); Piyasiri Wickramesekara, *Protection of Migrant Workers in an Era of Globalization: the role of International Instruments, in* COMPARATIVE LABOUR LAW AND INDUSTRIAL RELATIONS IN INDUSTRIALIZED MARKET ECONOMIES (Richard Blanplain ed., Kluwer Law International BV, 2010); PHILIP ALSTON (ED.), LABOUR RIGHTS AS HUMAN RIGHTS (Oxford University Press, 2005); ILO, *Travailleurs Migrants*, CIT, Eighty-Seven Session, Geneva (1999).

221 *See* Wickramasekara, *supra* note 220, at 244.

222 *See* Wickramasekara, *supra* note 216, at 298.

ance with its Constitution, the principles concerning the fundamental rights which are the subject of those Conventions.[223]

The Preamble to the Constitution of ILO states that "the protection of the interest of workers when employed in countries other than their own"[224] is one of the aims pursued by the Organization. In fact the drafters of the Treaty of Versailles[225] expressed concern at the precarious condition of migrant workers: they were at risk of exploitation and discriminatory treatments that could destabilize the global peace.[226] It is legitimate to suppose that the drafters of the treaty identified migrant workers as a vulnerable group that required protection against the exercise of sovereign power.

At the international level, the situation was evolving and the institutional frameworks of the League of Nations and the ILO had a pioneering role in the elaboration and adoption of common actions.[227] The ILO, with the adoption of the Declaration on the Aims and Principles of the Organization, better known as Philadelphia Declaration of 1944,[228] entered into a second phase for the Organization, expanding its objectives of action and establishing at third paragraph of obligations for states parties to provide workers with better conditions of employment and life.[229] To this end, the adoption of

223 ILO Declaration on Fundamental Principles and Rights at Work, 1998.

224 The text of the Constitution of the ILO, adopted 1919, has been subsequently changed, as follows: amendment of 1922, adopted 4 June 1934; amendment of 1945, adopted 20 April 1948; amendment of 1953, adopted on 20 May 1954; amendment of 1972, adopted 22 May 1963, and amendment of 1972 adopted 1 November 1974.

225 Part XIII of the Treaties of Versailles realized the foundation of ILO as international organization. Versailles, 28 June 1919, 13 A.J.I.L., Supp. (1919) 151 to 361.

226 *See* ILO, *supra* note 17, at 4.

227 *See* CHOLEWINSKI, *supra* note 115, at 90.

228 The Philadelphia Declaration concerning the aims and the objectives of ILO was adopted by the Twenty-sixth Conference of the ILO on 10 May 1944 and it has been added as an Annex to the ILO Constitution.

229 Third Paragraph: "The Conference recognizes the solemn obligation of the International Labour Organization to further among the nations of the world

measures in favour of migrant workers from their countries of origin to their countries of destination were incorporated.

These new constitutional provisions expanded the scope of action of the Organization, addressing not only the protection of the rights of migrant workers employed abroad but favouring their mobility for employment and inter-state coordination. In fact, at the end of Second World War the Organization faced a new political climate that allowed it to elaborate international standards to deal with the condition of migrant workers.[230]

As identified by Prof. Awad, the ILO followed three different approaches in its normative action.[231]

First, the ILO applied international labour standards to migrants employed abroad, including their interests. The adopted ILO Convention No. 2 (Concerning Unemployment) that obliges member

---

programmes which will achieve: (a) full employment and the raising of standards of living; (b) the employment of workers in the occupations in which they can have the satisfaction of giving the fullest measure of their skill and attainments and make their greatest contribution to the common well-being; (c) the provision, as a means to the attainment of this end and under adequate guarantees for all concerned, of facilities for training and the transfer of labour, including migration for employment and settlement; (d) policies in regard to wages and earnings, hours and other conditions of work calculated to ensure a just share of the fruits of progress to all, and a minimum living wage to all employed and in need of such protection; (e) the effective recognition of the right of collective bargaining, the cooperation of management and labour in the continuous improvement of productive efficiency, and the collaboration of workers and employers in the preparation and application of social and economic measures; (f) the extension of social security measures to provide a basic income to all in need of such protection and comprehensive medical care; (g) adequate protection for the life and health of workers in all occupations; (h) provision for child welfare and maternity protection; (i) the provision of adequate nutrition, housing and facilities for recreation and culture; j) the assurance of equality of educational and vocational opportunity." (Official English Text).

230 *See* Bohning, *supra* note 220, at 699.

231 *See* ILO, *supra* note 17, at 32; Ibrahim Awad, *International labour migration: Evolution of the multilateral policy framework*, *in* THE INTERNATIONALIZATION OF LABOUR MARKERS 107–115 (Christiane Kuptsch ed., ILO, 2010).

states to provide migrant workers with equal benefits and to adopt bilateral agreements between states of origin and states of destination to this end.[232] Other examples include the Convention on Social Policy (Non-Metropolitan Territories), the Convention on Social Security (Minimum Standards),[233] and the Convention on Social Policy.[234]

A second approach concerns the formulation of labour standards that apply to migrant workers in selective thematic areas. In this context, for instance, measures that regulate certain aspects of migration mobility, like the Inspection of Emigrants Convention.[235] In the field of social security, equal treatment, and other benefits, there are specific instruments, such as the Equality of Treatment (Accident Compensation),[236] the Convention on the Maintenance of Migrants' Pension Rights,[237] the Convention on the Equality of Treatment (Social Security) of 1962,[238] and the Convention on the Maintenance of Social Security Rights.[239]

232 Art. 3: "The Members of the International Labour Organisation which ratify this Convention and which have established systems of insurance against unemployment shall, upon terms being agreed between the Members concerned, make arrangements whereby workers belonging to one Member and working in the territory of another shall be admitted to the same rates of benefit of such insurance as those which obtain for the workers belonging to the latter". Convention on Unemployment (No. 2), 1919, entered into force 14 July 1921.

233 Convention on Social Security (Basic Standards) (No. 102), 1952, entered into force 18 June 1982.

234 Convention on Social Policy (No. 117), 1962, entered into force 23 April 1964.

235 Inspection of Emigrants Convention (No. 21), 1926, entered into force on 29 December 1926, since withdrawn.

236 The Equality of Treatment (Accident Compensation) Convention (No. 19), 1925, entered into force 8 September 1926.

237 Convention on the Maintenance of Migrants' Pension Rights (No. 48), 1935, entered into force 30 May 1937.

238 Convention on Equality of Treatment (Social Security) (No. 118), 1962, entered into force 25 April 1964.

239 Convention on the Maintenance of Social Security Rights (No. 157), 1982, entered into force 5 December 1981.

The third approach, finally, adopted general standards to cover migrant workers. There are three Conventions; one of them, Migration for Employment, 1939 (No. 66), was withdrawn in 2000.[240] Conventions in force are the Convention on Migrant Workers (Revised) of 1949 (No. 97) and the Convention on Migrant Workers (Supplementary Provisions) of 1975 (No. 143).

This analysis will proceed to illustrate these two instruments, with a brief outline of Conventions No. 97 and No. 66, to disclose the different ways in which they were drafted. Then I will elaborate the more recent instrument, of *soft law,* for the protection of migrant workers and endorsed by the governing body of ILO in 2006: the ILO Multilateral Framework on Labour Migration. This framework elaborated in 2006 embraced the Philadelphia Declaration's setting up of non-binding measures and mechanisms.[241] It seems that flexibility is a consistent element of a number of provisions addressing the governance of economic migration.[242] In this regard, my analysis proposes to review this presence of *souplesse* into labour migration instruments.[243]

Finally, the International Convention on the Protection of the Rights of All Migrants and Members of Their Families (ICMWR), adopted by the U.N. General Assembly in 1990 and entering into force in 2003, will be explored. According to the International Labour Conference, the provisions of the UN Convention complement existing ILO standards and, as highlighted by some scholars, these three instruments are identified as the pillars of a global scheme for the protection of migrant workers.[244] Nevertheless, this chapter proposes to discuss the different approaches adopted in the drafting

240 Migration for Employment Convention (No. 66), 1939.

241 *See* ILO, *supra* note 17, at 32.

242 *See* Awad, *supra* note 231, at 113.

243 ILO, *Protecting the rights of migrant workers: a shared responsibility,* International Migration Programme, ILO, Geneva (2009).

244 International Labour Conference, 92nd Session, 2004, *Une approche équitable pour les travailleurs migrants dans une économie mondialisée,* Geneva (2004).

process of ILO instruments and the ICMWR to articulate a comparative analysis.

3.1.1. The Migration for Employment Convention (Revised), 1949 (No. 97)

In the summer of 1948 the phenomenon of international migration became an issue of concern for many international actors, including the United Nations, the World Bank, and the High Commissioner for Refugees.[245] The ILO's predominant interest was to deploy an effective and comprehensive action to work in concert with states concerning measures to address the economic and moral pressures created by flows of migrant workers.[246] In this context the Permanent Migration Committee revised the Convention of 1939, which became the Convention No. 97 concerning Migration for Employment.[247] This Convention is accompanied by Recommendation No. 86 of 1949.[248] The Convention deals with the protection of migrant workers in the destination country and seeks to prevent any kind of discriminatory practice. In this regard, it is clear that the linkages with the scope of the previous Convention No. 66, mentioned above, were revised to strengthen labour standards in favour of workers employed abroad.[249]

As stated by Prof. Awad, this specific attention to the management of international labour mobility has it own logic. In fact the elaboration of this instrument took place in an historical context characterized by a relevant disproportionality between the demand

245 See Bohning, *supra* note 220, at 672.

246 *See* PLENDER, *supra* note 104, at 298.

247 Forty-nine states ratified this Convention. See the ILO website, *available at* <http://www.ilo.org/ilolex/english/index.htm> (last visited Jun. 20, 2012).

248 On the notion of recommendations I note than within the normative framework of ILO this instrument does not have legal force. The instrument aims to identify principles and measures to be implemented at national level.

249 ILO, *Migrant Workers*, General Survey on the Reports on the Migration for Employment Convention (Revised) (No. 97), and Recommendation (Revised) (No. 86) (1949).

for and the supply of labour.[250] On the one side, the war, causing a temporary arrest of migratory flows, deprived the New World of a large number of workers and, on the other side, the high demand for workers in the European states resulted from the demobilization of troops engaged in fighting during the first half of the 1940s, but also as a consequence of the destruction of their production apparatus.[251] So both sides had an undeniable interest in promoting labour mobility. For these reasons the regulation of these flows to facilitate the recruitment of migrant workers found a solid constitutional basis in the Philadelphia Declaration.[252]

A comparative analysis of the provisions contained in this instrument and in Convention No. 66, makes clear the innovative approach; in fact the Conventions deal with promotion of migrant workers by facilitating their departure, travel, and reception and through the conclusion of bilateral agreements between the countries of origin and destination.[253]

Convention No. 97 covers the protection of migrant workers in the three Articles related to the adoption of measures against the diffusion of malicious information concerning the migration and immigration process, supporting the principle of non-discrimination between regular migrant workers and citizens, and against the return of migrant workers and member of their families if unable to perform a remunerated activity due to illness or accidents occurred after entry into the state concerned.[254] This last provision applies only to regular migrant workers admitted non-temporarily.[255]

The key provision of the Convention is Article 6, which provides for the application of the Conventions "without discrimination in respect to nationality, race, religion or sex".[256] According to Prof.

250 *See* Awad, *supra* note 231, at 108.
251 *See* Awad, *supra* note 231, at 108.
252 *See* ILO, *supra* note 17, at 120.
253 *See* PLENDER, *supra* note 104, at 299.
254 *See* ILO, *supra* note 17, at 38.
255 *Id.* at 27.
256 *See* Wickramasekara, *supra* note 220, at 252.

Awad this explicit reference to the criteria of nationality endures as an innovative elaboration of the principle of non-discrimination, if compared with the latest adoption of Convention No. 111 of 1958,[257] which does not refer to national origin as criteria for discriminatory practices.[258]

The Convention has three Annexes: one concerning migration by individuals (recruitment and working conditions if employed on the basis of inter-state agreements), the second covering collective migration (recruitment and working conditions if employed on the basis of inter-state agreements), and the third dealing with the transfer of the personal belongings of migrants, their working tools, and equipment.[259] The interesting character of these instruments is their optional nature, as in fact each member can choose to ratify only the Convention or to include the ratification of one or multiple Annexes.[260] This structure is an interesting example of the flexible approach adopted to favour broad ratification.

3.1.2. The Migrant Workers (Supplementary Provisions) Convention No. 143, 1975

In 1972, during the drafting process of the future Plan of Action Concerning Migrant Workers by the ILO, a terrible accident occurred in Switzerland: a *camion* supposed to transport sewing machines had an accident and the public authorities discovered that the driver was illegally carrying 38 irregular migrants from Tunisia to France. The news echoed widely, ECOSOC adopted a resolution against the illicit and clandestine traffic of migrants, and it was impossible for ILO not to react. In the meantime, the international

257 Convention against Discrimination (Employment and Occupation) (No. 111), 1958, entered into force 15 June 1960.

258 *See* ILO, *supra* note 243, at 19.

259 ILO, *Migrant workers,* Report III (1B), International Labour Conference, 87th Session, Geneva, International Labour Organization (1999).

260 *See* Awad, *supra* note 231, at 109.

background had changed dramatically. In fact, since the Fifties, several countries decided to join international organizations, becoming active members of the international community. For instance, the member states of ILO increased from 62 in 1949 to 123 by 1975. The reconstruction of Europe permitted the absorption of the excess labour on its territory as well as recruiting workers from Eastern Europe and North Africa.[261] As mentioned above, reconstruction and the end of the colonization generated a constant flow of migrants from the "old" continent to the new countries.[262] Since the end of the Sixties, the global economy began to lose its propulsive force. In particular the first oil crisis was the first sign of arrest for economic growth, and several difficulties linked to unemployment started to emerge. In this context during the elaboration of the first report of the Migrant Workers Commission in 1975, some delegates described the negative effects of the economic crisis affecting the world, the Western countries, and the consequent impact on the employment situation.[263] The countries of Western Europe adopted a restrictive attitude on the development of labour migration policies and the first clandestine flows emerged.[264]

ILO adopted Convention No. 143 in 1975, a flexible instrument composed of two parts (migration in abusive conditions, and equality of opportunity).[265] This structure allows member states to decide which part to ratify, and in fact this was a compromise adopted after a complex debate during the International Labour Conference in 1975. Indeed, some delegates, in particular the governments of destination countries, preferred the adoption of two separate conventions

261 *See* Awad, *supra* note 231, at 109.

262 ILO, *Protecting the most vulnerable of today's workers, Tripartite Meeting of Experts on Future ILO Activities in the Field of Migration*, Geneva (1997).

263 ILC, 60th Session, Record of proceedings, Geneva (1975), 839 and 843.

264 *See* Bohning, *supra* note 220, at 670.

265 The flexibility in Convention No. 97 of 1949 concerned only the Annexes, while in Convention No. 143 of 1975, it includes the substantial contents of the instrument.

because the issues addressed were too different.[266] Instead, the representatives of workers, supported by most of the other governments, tried to reach a compromise between the effort to combat abusive migratory flows and the promotion of equal treatment. This matter was settled by vote during the Migration Workers Commission.[267]

According to Prof. Awad the Preamble of this Convention is different from previous ones and reflects a modern perspective.[268] Unlike Convention No. 97 of 1949, it clearly states the foundations for normative action and highlights the most urgent issues concerning the labour mobility. The first two paragraphs concern the protection of the interests of migrant workers abroad and the mobility of workers.[269] Furthermore, it highlights the need to reduce the growing and unchecked increase in migratory flows encouraging the transfer of remittances and know-how instead of workers. The Preamble elaborates also on the right of every individual to leave his or her country of residence and to enter into his or her country of origin, without making any explicit reference to the right of freedom of movement.[270] At the same time, the Preamble calls attention to two main issues: the illicit or clandestine traffic of labour and discriminatory attitudes against migrant workers. Indeed, the Preamble recalls that the term "discrimination" within the Convention on this issue,

266 *See* ILO, *supra* note 17, at 27.

267 International Labour Conference, 60th Session, *Report of the Proceedings*, Geneva (1975), 847.

268 *See* Bohning, *supra* note 220, at 675.

269 "Considering that the Preamble of the Constitution of the International Labour Organisation assigns to it the task of protecting 'the interests of workers when employed in countries other than their'. Considering that the Declaration of Philadelphia reaffirms, among the principles on which the Organisation is based, that 'labour is not a commodity', and that 'poverty anywhere constitutes a danger to prosperity everywhere', and recognises the solemn obligation of the ILO to further programmes which will achieve in particular full employment through 'the transfer of labour, including for employment [...]'".

270 "Considering the right of everyone to leave any country, including his own, and to enter his own country, as set forth in the Universal Declaration of Human Rights and the International Covenant on Civil and Political Rights".

adopted in 1958, does not extend its provisions to discrimination founded on nationality. Even if this clause may be considered a step back if compared with Convention No. 97, it is clear that its intent is to strengthen and extend the measures and mechanisms available to implement the principle of equality. Even with all measures adopted, it is not possible to identify, within the text of the Conventions, provisions to implement the objectives formulated by the Philadelphia Convention, as mentioned above, though the proceedings incorporate the intention of the negotiators to improve the conditions of migrant workers.[271]

Article 1 of the Convention lays down a general obligation to respect the fundamental human rights of migrant workers, regardless of status. This provision deals with illegally migrant workers, clandestine migrations, migrants in abusive conditions, and the organizers of illicit trafficking of migrants.[272] These concepts were adopted in the Preamble to the resolution concerning equal treatment for migrant workers of the International Labour Conference in 1972,[273] mentioned above, and Resolution 3224, adopted by the General Assembly as "*Mesures en vue d'améliorer la situation des travailleurs migrants*"

271 On the interpretive function of the Preamble in international treaties *see* Eric Suy, *Le préambule*, *in* LIBER AMICORUM–JUDGE MOHAMMED BEDJAOUI (Emile Yakpo & Tahar Boumedra eds., Kluwer Law International, 1999); PAUL YOU, LE PREAMBULE DES TRAITES INTERNATIONAUX, Thèse de Fribourg (1941), and the synthesis: *L'interprétation des traités et le rôle du préambule des traités dans cette interprétation,* Tome XX REVUE DE DROIT INTERNATIONAL, DE SCIENCES DIPLOMATIQUES ET POLITIQUES, 22 (1942).

272 Article 2: "1. Each Member for which this Convention is in force shall systematically seek to determine whether there are illegally employed migrant workers on its territory and whether there depart from, pass through or arrive in its territory any movements of migrants for employment in which the migrants are subjected during their journey, on arrival or during their period of residence and employment to conditions contravening relevant international multilateral or bilateral instruments or agreements, or national laws or regulations. 2. The representative organisations of employers and workers shall be fully consulted and enabled to furnish any information in their possession on this subject".

273 *See* ILO, *supra* note 17, at 28.

(Measures to improve the situation of migrant workers).[274] These resolutions moved to develop and elaborate normative action concerning the protection of human rights of migrant workers. The member states of ILO are obligated to eliminate the phenomenon of illegal employment of migrants, sanctioning those responsible of these practices and prosecuting crimes related to labour trafficking. Clandestine or illicit movements with the aim of employment are migratory flows where individuals are subjected, throughout the process and during employment, to abusive conditions in violation of international standards or domestic law.[275] The Convention contains a definition of illegal employment, and Part I addresses the fight against migration under abusive conditions and the adoption of measures to protect the victims of such abuses, as stated in Articles 8[276] and 9[277] of the Convention, which set the basis for further devel-

274 G.A., *Measures to improve the situation of migrant workers*, G.A. Res. 3224 (XXIX), 29th session, Geneva (1974).

275 *See* ILO, *supra* note 17, at 29.

276 Art. 8: "1. On condition that he has resided legally in the territory for the purpose of employment, the migrant worker shall not be regarded as in an illegal or irregular situation by the mere fact of the loss of his employment, which shall not in itself imply the withdrawal of his authorisation of residence or, as the case may be, work permit. 2. Accordingly, he shall enjoy equality of treatment with nationals in respect in particular of guarantees of security of employment, the provision of alternative employment, relief work and retraining".

277 Art. 9: "1. Without prejudice to measures designed to control movements of migrants for employment by ensuring that migrant workers enter national territory and are admitted to employment in conformity with the relevant laws and regulations, the migrant worker shall, in cases in which these laws and regulations have not been respected and in which his position cannot be regularised, enjoy equality of treatment for himself and his family in respect of rights arising out of past employment as regards remuneration, social security and other benefits. 2. In case of dispute about the rights referred to in the preceding paragraph, the worker shall have the possibility of presenting his case to a competent body, either himself or through a representative. 3. In case of expulsion of the worker or his family, the cost shall not be borne by them. 4. Nothing in this Convention shall prevent Members from giving persons who are illegally residing or working within the country the right to stay and to take up legal employment".

opments in the regulation of economic migrations. Article 8 states that a migrant worker cannot be considered irregular or in irregular status after the loss of his or her job, because this situation cannot imply the withdrawal of his or her permit to stay. Consequently, foreigners enjoy the same treatment as nationals, including to social security. In the case where a citizen crosses national borders in violation of the law in force, or if his or her employment relationship violates the applicable legal standards, the migrant worker and the members of his or her families are to benefit from equal treatment with respect to rights derived from employment (for instance remuneration, social security, or other benefits). Furthermore, in case of dispute on the enjoyment of these rights, the worker must have access to the judicial system to exercise those rights.

Part II deals with the principle of equality of opportunity and treatment for regular migrant workers employed in the territory of a state party to the Convention. As mentioned before, the Preamble of the Convention does not list the criterion of nationality among anti-discrimination criteria. Whereas Convention No. 97 of 1949 was limited to invoke non-discriminatory practices between migrants and citizens, this new Convention adopts a more dynamic approach. In particular Art. 10 provides for national policies in line with the principle of equal treatment for migrant workers and member of their families.[278] Equal treatment must include, at minimum, the field of labour, social security, cultural rights, and individual and collective liberties.

278 Art. 10: "Each Member for which the Convention is in force undertakes to declare and pursue a national policy designed to promote and to guarantee, by methods appropriate to national conditions and practice, equality of opportunity and treatment in respect of employment and occupation, of social security, of trade union and cultural rights and of individual and collective freedoms for persons who as migrant workers or as members of their families are lawfully within its territory".

Article 12[279] requires all member states to cooperate with trade unions and other institutions and mechanisms in place to provide equal treatment and opportunity at the national level. This article specifically covers measures to be adopted for the implementation of national migration policies, taking into account the protection of the national and ethnic identities of migrant workers and their family members, and to strengthen the linkages with their countries of origin (e.g. by ensuring the teaching of their mother tongue). Article 13[280], furthermore, regulates family reunification of all migrant work-

279 Art. 12: "Each Member shall, by methods appropriate to national conditions and practice: (a) seek the co-operation of employers' and workers' organisations and other appropriate bodies in promoting the acceptance and observance of the policy provided for in Article 10 of this Convention; (b) enact such legislation and promote such educational programmes as may be calculated to secure the acceptance and observance of the policy; (c) take measures, encourage educational programmes and develop other activities aimed at acquainting migrant workers as fully as possible with the policy, with their rights and obligations and with activities designed to give effective assistance to migrant workers in the exercise of their rights and for their protection; (d) repeal any statutory provisions and modify any administrative instructions or practices which are inconsistent with the policy; (e) in consultation with representative organisations of employers and workers, formulate and apply a social policy appropriate to national conditions and practice which enables migrant workers and their families to share in advantages enjoyed by its nationals while taking account, without adversely affecting the principle of equality of opportunity and treatment, of such special needs as they may have until they are adapted to the society of the country of employment; (f) take all steps to assist and encourage the efforts of migrant workers and their families to preserve their national and ethnic identity and their cultural ties with their country of origin, including the possibility for children to be given some knowledge of their mother tongue; (g) guarantee equality of treatment, with regard to working conditions, for all migrant workers who perform the same activity whatever might be the particular conditions of their employment".

280 Art. 13: "1. A Member may take all necessary measures which fall within its competence and collaborate with other Members to facilitate the reunification of the families of all migrant workers legally residing in its territory. 2. The members of the family of the migrant worker to which this Article applies are the spouse and dependent children, father and mother".

ers abroad and Art. 14[281], finally, deals with the principle of freedom of movement and free choice of employment, albeit that it subordinates the enjoyment of this rights to the recognition of professional qualifications acquired.

The Convention is accompanied by Recommendation No. 151. This instrument contains three sections: 1) measures to ensure an equal treatment, 2) measures on social policy, and 3) measures protecting the migrant workers in case of expulsion or loss of work.

Today only 23 states have ratified this Convention, even though it is relevant to highlight that several countries of destination in Europe, such as Italy, Portugal, Norway, Sweden, and Slovenia, have ratified it.[282]

The adoption of the Resolution "Towards a fair deal for migrant workers in the global economy" by the International Labour Conference in 2004 [283] focuses on legal gaps in the protection of irregular migrant workers, seasonal workers, and female migrant workers.

3.1.3. The ILO normative framework on labour migration

The international community faced significant gaps in the implementation of international labour standards and this required the opening

281 Art. 14: "A Member may: (a) make the free choice of employment, while assuring migrant workers the right to geographical mobility, subject to the conditions that the migrant worker has resided lawfully in its territory for the purpose of employment for a prescribed period not exceeding two years or, if its laws or regulations provide for contracts for a fixed term of less than two years, that the worker has completed his first work contract; (b) after appropriate consultation with the representative organisations of employers and workers, make regulations concerning recognition of occupational qualifications acquired outside its territory, including certificates and diplomas; (c) restrict access to limited categories of employment or functions where this is necessary in the interests of the State".

282 *See* ILO, *available at* <www.ilo.org/ilolex/english/index.htm> (last visited Jun. 20, 2012).

283 *See* ILO, *supra* note 17, at 11.

of a debate to address the identified failures in the normative framework, as the framework was not always able to provide sufficient protection. The Permanent Migrant Workers Committee underlined how it was "unacceptable for millions of migrant workers to remain excluded from international protection".[284] In addition the Committee drew attention to the growing number of irregular migrants "fuelled by the growth of informal forms of employment" and in view of these developments, the solution was either to maintain the existing framework or to explore the possibility of launching a new legislative process. [285] For this reason the Committee adopted a report that "requires a rights-based approach in accordance with existing international labour standards and ILO principles [...]".[286] It states that

> to adopt national policies aimed at equal treatment of migrant workers with nationals in respect of national labour laws and access to applicable social protections, combating the exploitation often associated with migrants in irregular status, and the promotion of basic human rights for all migrants.[287]

In light of the concerns raised by the Migrant Workers Committee, in 2004 the governments of ILO member states called for moving towards the elaboration of a new instrument to safeguard the interests of migrant workers. The decision was to adopt a non-binding text, the ILO Multilateral Framework on Labour Migration, not likely to give rise to legal obligations, as stated by Art. 19, paragraph 6 of the ILO Constitution.[288]

It is clear that since 1975, the international *milieu* has been characterized by the emergence of new challenges and unforeseen questions in the definition of migration policies: for instance, the ageing of the population in developed countries and the closer relationship

284 International Labour Conference, 92nd Session, Provisional Records 22, *Report of the Migrant Workers Committee* (2004), ¶664–665.

285 *See* International Labour Conference, *supra* note 284, ¶664–665.

286 *See* ILO, *supra* note 17, ¶ 10.

287 *Id.* ¶ 28.

288 *See* Awad, *supra* note 231, at 111.

between migration and development, including "brain drain" consequences and the costs of remittances.

This provided an opportunity to discuss how to deal with major issues faced by states of emigration and immigration and to supplement the existing legal frameworks,[289] and the outcome of this debate became an integral component of the resolution adopted by the International Labour Conference in 2004.

The resolution urged the ILO Framework to deal with these matters, showing a direct link between the socio-economic changes at the international level and the redefinition of both binding and non binding legal instruments.[290] In 2005, the ILO Framework was adopted by a tripartite meeting of experts, and approved for publication by the governing body in 2006. [291] The text of this Framework clearly appears to be the result of a technical and political convergence of practices and opinions of member states in the formulation of labour migration policies.[292]

The Preamble of the ILO Framework recognizes the need to adopt a rights-based approach in the context of economic migration, taking into account labour market needs, as stated by the Resolution of 2004.[293] The Framework is composed of nine sections and fifteen principles. The guidelines highlight the measures for giving effective implementation to the principles. In this context, many governments emphasize the useful role of this set of practical guidelines to normatively guide domestic legislators and policy actors in their actions.[294]

The first three sections demand special attention to opportunities to obtain decent work, to measures promoting international cooperation, and to the relevance of developing global knowledge of labour migration policies. The subsequent sections deal with the

289 *See* Wickramasekara, *supra* note 220, at 253.

290 *See* ILO, *supra* note 17, at 130.

291 ILO, Governing Body resolution, 295th Session, Geneva (March 2006).

292 *See* Awad, *supra* note 231, at 111.

293 *See* Preamble, ILO Multilateral Framework on Labour Migration.

294 ILO Governing Body, 289th Session, *Meetings of experts: Purpose, function and lessons learned*, GB.289/STM/2, Geneva (March, 2004).

protection of migrant workers, addressing relevant issues such as the prevention of abuse and the adoption of appropriate measures for the management of labour migration. In particular section IV (effective management of labour migration) makes clear the sovereign power of national governments to set migration policy.[295] This section, at principle 5, requires that the state make the effort to identify legal channels for economic migration, taking into account domestic labour needs. Sections VI (prevention of, and protection against, abusive migration practices) through IX (migration and development) look in more detail at issues described in the ILO Conventions, such as social integration, including for the first time the return and the reintegration of migrant workers. The last section, finally, underlines the role of national migration policy in strengthening the linkages between migration and development.[296]

Several principles refer to migrant workers in irregular situation; these principles are, in particular, contained in the sections dealing with the protection of rights of irregular migrant workers, the management of labour flows and the prevention of abuses. The next principles are relevant to ensure the application of international labour standards to *all* migrant workers. The last guideline calls attention to the need to develop and guarantee effective legal remedies in case of abuse or discriminatory practices.[297]

*** *** ***

As mentioned above, this instrument, due to its non-binding nature, is considered a "soft law" instrument. Several scholars, weighing the advantages against the disadvantages of the stipulation of these instruments, considered it a step back in the debate to improve labour migration policies, others, instead, argued its potential role and contribution to existing international standards.[298]

295 *See* ILO, *supra* note 17, at 131–132.
296 *See* Awad, *supra* note 231, at 112.
297 *See* Wickramasekara *supra* note 216, at 313.
298 *See* Wickramasekara, *supra* note 218, at 1250.

I agree with the view of Prof. Awad that identifies this instrument as the result of reciprocal "exchange that is in the interests of migrant workers and the countries of origin and destination".[299] In fact even if during the drafting process the delegates opted to not give it binding force, the sphere of activity was enlarged and the concept of protection understood in general terms. This broad interpretation allows the elaboration of specific measures that may orient member states at the domestic level. In addition, the adoption of a non-binding instrument does not preclude the future elaboration of a binding Convention, and this process may benefit from the use of the provisions and guidelines contained in the ILO Framework.[300] This positive aptitude is supported by the actual debate on the relevance of soft law instruments in international law, if compared with hard law treaties. In this context, Prof. Awad focuses the discussion on the juridical nature of soft law, the binding nature of hard law and the sanctions that may be applied in case of violations. According to Duplessis, the absence of legal force is not sufficient to deny the efficacy of these provisions.[301] Duplessis states that a provision is first of all an instrument able to provide a direction to the collective attitudes of the members of a defined group, apart from its *souple ou dure* (feeble or strong) force.[302]

Similarly, Prof. Awad supported the argument that the Organization demonstrated a positive improvement in promoting alternative mechanisms for protecting of the rights of migrant workers, without weakening the existing standards, considered as a "stern indicator of progress towards the achievement of ILO objectives, not through

299 Statement of Ibrahim Awad, former Director of International Migration Department, ILO, during the Expert Meeting on Linking human rights and migrant empowerment for development, (8 October 2009); *See* Awad, *supra* note 231, at 112.

300 *See* Awad, *supra* note 231, at 113.

301 "*L'élément de la contrainte n'épuise pas le droit dans son ensemble*" ("The 'binding' element is not the only element of law.").

302 Isabelle Duplessis, *Soft law et droit international du travail, Rôle, impact et avenir de la législation du travail,* EDUCATION OUVRIERE 42 (2006).

lip-service but in law and practice".[303] This point is well argued by Prof. Abi-Saab, who argued that legality is not limited to enforceable rights or obligations to be invoked by an international judicial authority or by other actors. [304] Prof. Abi-Saab clearly notes that soft law instruments are not to be understood as opposing or replacing hard law instruments. They "share a certain proximity to law and have a certain legal relevance, but at same time they are not legally binding *per se* as a matter of law".[305] The flexibility of the soft law approach may be more appropriate in case of political obstacles to negotiating new norms. In other words, a soft law approach allows experimentation with new field of legal action, and in some circumstances the elaboration of soft law measures may be a precursor of further elaboration of hard law.[306] Prof. Abi-Saab considered soft law as "law in gestation, not defective law". Finally, in some cases states may be reluctant to enter into new obligations, particularly where the subject under debate is controversial, and in these circumstances instead of adopting a binding instrument with a *mou* ("light") content, as "an empty shell", they may opt to adopt a relevant regulation (*dur* or "strong" content) included in a soft instrument, not binding. Identified as law in gestation, the soft law approach addresses the role of "social architecture" instead of "guardian of law".[307]

*** *** ***

This brief analysis of the development of international labour standards gave the opportunity to highlight how deeply the phenomenon

303 Report of the General Director, *Reducing the Decent Work Deficit: a Global Challenge* (2001), chapter 3.2.

304 "*Juridicité ne signifie pas nécessairement obligatoriété et pertinence ou effet juridique ne se réduit pas seulement à effet obligatoire*" (Legality does not necessarily imply binding and legal effect is not limited to binding effect). GEORGE ABI-SAAB, COUR GENERAL DE DROIT INTERNATIONAL PUBLIC, Recueil des cours, Hague Academy of International Law, 27 (1987), at 205–212; *See* Awad, *supra* note 231, at 293.

305 *See* Kalin & Schrepfer, *supra* note 34, at 73.

306 *Id.* at 73.

307 *See* ABI-SAAB, *supra* note 304, at 205–212.

of economic mobility and the changes that occurred in the political-economic scene have been interrelated in the last sixty years.

3.2. The International Convention on the Protection of the Rights of All Migrant Workers and Members of Their Families (ICRMW)

The adoption of the International Convention on the Protection of All Migrant Workers and Member of Their Families (ICMWR) is the result of a complex drafting process, with the adoption of several reports, recommendations, and *travaux préparatoires* over a period of ten years of negotiations.

The General Assembly of the United Nations had been expressing concern and urging the elaboration of a new international instrument to address the situation of migrant workers since 1972, when the Economic and Social Council (ECOSOC) adopted the resolution 1706 (LIII). The ECOSOC recognized the danger of illegal transportation of migrants through European Member States, and their exploitation in conditions similar to slavery.[308] The General Assembly, with the adoption of the Resolution 2920 (XXVII), called upon states to end abuses against migrants and to ensure the respect of decent standards for migrant workers.[309] In this context Halima Warzazi, the Special Rapporteur of the Sub-Commission on Prevention of Discrimination and Protection of Minorities, was mandated to produce a report on the "exploitation of labour through illicit and clandestine trafficking".[310] The report, adopted in 1996, recommended the adoption of a resolution to raise awareness of discrimi-

308 ECOSOC, Resolution 1706 (LIII) (28 July, 1972).

309 G.A., *Exploitation of labour through illicit and clandestine trafficking, Resolution 2920* (XXVII) (Nov. 15, 1975).

310 The Report has been mandated by the Sub-Commission against discrimination and for the protection of minorities. *See* Warzazi, *supra* note 151.

natory practices against migrant workers in the countries of destination and the diffusion of illicit and clandestine trafficking. The resolution adopted by the Global Conference Against Racism and Racial Discrimination in 1978,[311] and endorsed by Resolution 33/163 of the General Assembly [312] concerning "measures to improve the situation and ensure the human rights and dignity of all migrant workers". Then, the General Assembly adopted Resolution 34/172 on 17 December 1979, and established a working group to start the formulation of a new Convention. The final text of this instrument was completed by the working group in 1990, eleven years after the start of the process. Bohning stated that the "ink on ILO Convention No. 143 had hardly dried" when some countries (specifically Mexico and Morocco) concentrated their efforts to launch a negotiation process outside the normative action of ILO.[313]

The provisions of the ICMWR expanded and complemented existing international standards. In particular, Art. 1 of Convention No. 143 explicitly states that "each Member for which this Convention is in force undertakes to respect the basic human rights of all migrant workers", without giving a detailed description of these rights. From this perspective, the ICMWR adopts "a human rights approach to labour standards" formulating an innovative approach to the traditional distinction between rights enjoyed by regular and irregular migrant workers.[314]

311 Report of the World Conference against racism and racial discrimination, Geneva (Aug. 14–25, 1978).

312 G.A., *Measures to improve the situation and ensure the human rights and dignity of all migrant workers*, U.N. Doc. A/RES/33/163 (Dec. 20, 1978).

313 See Bohning, *supra* note 220, at 670. The author describes the disappointment of some developing states on the provisions of the Convention No. 143, concerning in particular irregular migration and the role of ILO in addressing related social dimensions.

314 Virginia Leary, *Labour Migration*, *in* MIGRATION AND INTERNATIONAL LEGAL NORMS 227–239 (Alexander T. Aleinikoff & Vincent Chetail eds., Asser Press, 2003).

Dr. Wickramasekara in his detailed analysis highlights the following innovations:[315]

- This is the first comprehensive international instrument that seeks to establish a set of rights for migrant workers and members of their families;[316]
- The Convention is based on modifying international standards and it "contains the most comprehensive definition of migrant workers and their families formulated to date and clearly applies to all migrant workers and their families".[317] The Convention in its normative actions includes a group of individuals not explicitly protected by ILO standards: frontier workers, itinerant workers, and self-employed workers;
- This instrument includes the rights of migrant workers in irregular situation, and at the same time aims to prevent the irregularity of their condition, broadening the scope of the ILO Convention No. 143. Furthermore, the Convention provides additional rights to regular migrant workers, even if these rights are expressly subjected to the sovereign prerogatives of states.[318]

The Convention entered into force on 1 July 2003, thirteen years after the adoption of the final text by the United Nations.[319] Forty-four states have so far ratified this instrument.[320] The number of ratifications continues to be low compared to other UN instruments,

315 *See* Wickramasekara *supra* note 220.

316 Juhani Lönnroth, *The International Convention on the Rights of All Migrant Workers and Members of Their Families in the context of international migration policies: An analysis of ten years of negotiations*, 4 INTERNATIONAL MIGRATION REVIEW 710, 711 (1991).

317 *See* CHOLEWINSKI, *supra* note 115, at 150. *See* Wickramasekara, *supra* note 220, at 256.

318 Linda S. Bosniak, *Human rights, State sovereignty and the protection of undocumented migrant under the international migrant workers Conventions*, 4 INTERNATIONAL MIGRATION REVIEW 737, 740 (1991).

319 U.N. G.A., Res. 45/158, Annex, 45 U.N. GAOR Supp. (No. 49 A), at 262, U.N. Doc. A/45/49 (1990).

320 *See* the Committee for Migrant Workers, *available at* <www2.ohchr.org/english/bodies/cmw/index.htm> (last visited Jun. 20, 2012).

and the European Economic and Social Council has explicitly called for the ratification by European countries.[321]

3.2.1. Structure

The scope of this Convention was to contain, in a single comprehensive document, all basic human rights established in previous instruments and to extend them to migrants, a category specifically not explicitly addressed in other treaties. To this end, the Convention establishes minimum standards to be provided to all migrants and members of their families.

The Convention comprises nine sections: 1) scope and definitions (Art. 1–6); 2) principle of non-discrimination (Art. 7); 3) human rights of all migrants (Art. 8–35); 4) other rights of migrant workers and members of their families who are documented or in a regular situation (Art. 36–56); 5) provisions applicable to particular categories of migrant workers and members of their families (Art. 57–63); 6) promotion of sound, equitable, humane, and lawful conditions in connection with international migration of workers and members of their families (Art. 64–71) application of the convention (Art. 72–78); 8) general provisions (Art. 79–84) final provisions (Art. 85–93).

3.2.2. Scope

The Preamble of the Convention emphasises the reasons for including all migrant workers in the scope of this instrument, regardless of status.[322] The definition adopted is broad and comprehensive if com-

321 ECSC, *Opinion of the European Economic and Social Committee on the International Convention on Migrants*, Resolution A5-0445.2003, SOC/173-CESE 960/2004 ES/JOD/ET/-EN/o-ES-ET/nm (Jun. 30, 2004).

322 "Aware of the impact of the flows of migrant workers on States and people concerned, and desiring to establish norms which may contribute to the harmonization of the attitudes of States through the acceptance of basic principles concerning the treatment of migrant workers and members of their fami-

pared to previous international instruments.[323] According to the first Article the Convention applies to

> all migrant workers and members of their families without distinction of any kind such as sex, race, colour, language, religion or conviction, political or other opinion, national, ethnic or social origin, nationality, age, economic position, property, marital status, birth or other status.

According to Article 2 "'migrant worker' refers to a person who is to be engaged, is engaged or has been engaged in a remunerated activity in a State of which he or she is not a national." Article 5, in particular, introduces the definition of migrant in irregular situation at point b): "Are considered as non-documented or in an irregular situation if they do not comply with the conditions provided for in subparagraph (a) of the present article". It appears difficult to formulate a comprehensive definition and art. 5 a) refers explicitly to national legal instruments to identify if a migrant could be considered documented or not.[324]

The extensive scope of the Convention is the result of a complex process resulting from the proceedings of the working group. It is clear that the delegates had several difficulties in elaborating and adopting a common definition, and this disagreement raised difficulties for its ratification and the implementation.

The detailed analysis of Bosniak gives an illustrative outline of the main issues raised during the proceedings, useful to identify the

---

lies [...] Considering that workers who are non-documented or in an irregular situation are frequently employed under less favourable conditions of work than other workers and that certain employers find this an inducement to seek such labour in order to reap the benefits of unfair competition".

323 OHCHR, *The International Convention on Migrant Workers and its Committee*, Fact Sheet No. 24, OHCHR, Geneva (2008).

324 Art. 5 a): "For the purposes of the present Convention, migrant workers and members of their families: (a) Are considered as documented or in a regular situation if they are authorized to enter, to stay and to engage in a remunerated activity in the State of employment pursuant to the law of that State and to international agreements to which that State is a party".

main elements of the debate and to contextualize them in the contemporary debate.[325]

Since the beginning of the negotiations the definition adopted in Resolution 3449 (XXX)[326] was taken as reference, suggesting the use of "undocumented migrant workers or in an irregular situation". Several delegations, in particular the governments of Denmark and the United States, were against extending the scope of the Convention to irregular migrants. They suggested elaborating a definition in line with the European Convention on the legal status of migrant workers.[327] This suggestion was clearly rejected as contradicting the mandate of the working group to establish a comprehensive instrument.[328] Furthermore, other delegations argued that by defining rights as applying to all migrant workers and their families, it risked being an incentive to increase migration flows, even if others argued that this innovation could keep employers from informing workers about recruitment and illegal practices. As recalled in the Preamble of the Convention "the recourse to the employment of migrant workers who are in irregular situation will be discouraged if the fundamental human rights of all migrant workers are more widely recognized".

It is clear that the compromise adopted more than twenty years ago was crucial to advance the protection of irregular migrants, introducing an explicit legal argument against human rights violations addressing this vulnerable group and contrasting the increasing conviction as illegal or criminal. The Committee on the Protection of the Rights of All Migrant Workers and Members of their Families (CMW

325 *See* Bosniak, *supra* note 318, at 741.

326 U.N. GAOR, *Report of the Open-ended Working Group on the Elaboration of an International Convention on the Protection of the Rights of All Migrant Workers and Their Families*, U.N. Doc. A/C.3/37/1 (1982).

327 U.N. GAOR, *Report of the Open-ended Working Group on the Elaboration of an International Convention on the Protection of the Rights of All Migrant Workers and Their Families*, U.N. Doc. A/C.3/39/1 (Jun. 14, 1984).

328 U.N. GAOR, *Report of the Open-ended Working Group on the Elaboration of an International Convention on the Protection of the Rights of All Migrant Workers and Their Families*, U.N. Doc. A/C.3/39/4 (Oct. 11, 1984).

hereinafter) urged member states to adopt at domestic level legislation in line with this terminology.

As furthermore noted in the recommendations addressed to the government of Algeria, the frequent use of the "criminalization–illegality" nexus risked depriving migrants captured under this definition of the measures of protection and rights guaranteed by the Convention.[329]

3.2.3. Principle of non-discrimination

Article 7 of the Convention provides the obligations for states parties to ensure the rights of migrants and their family members contained in this instrument.[330] This provision, as interpreted by standard doctrine, applies to the rights defined in the text.[331] In light of this, three categories are identified for implementing the principle of equality: between nationals and non-nationals, between men and women, and between regular and irregular migrants.[332] It is clear that the principle of non-discrimination requires an equal treatment between citizens and migrant workers within the jurisdiction of a state, but this description is not sufficient. The structure of the Convention, by making explicit the difference between rights recognized to all migrant

329 CMW, *Concluding observations of the Committee on the Protection of the Rights of All Migrant Workers and Members of Their Families, Algeria*, U.N. Doc. CMW/C/DZA/CO/1 (May 19, 2010).

330 Article 7: "Without distinction of any kind such as sex, race, colour, language, religion or conviction, political or other opinion, national, ethnic or social origin, nationality, age, economic position, property, marital status, birth or other status."

331 *See* Hune and Niessen, "the essence of the provision was the obligation of every state to apply every article of the Convention, without distinction of any sort". U.N. GAOR, *Report of the Open-ended Working Group on the Elaboration of an International Convention on the Protection of the Rights of All Migrant Workers and Their Families*, U.N. Doc. A/C.3/41/3 (Oct. 10, 1986).

332 *See* CHOLEWINSKI, *supra* note 115, at 156.

workers and only to regular migrant workers, is strongly related to their status in the countries of destination.

3.2.4. Implementation

After the entry into force of the Convention, the states concerned faced different difficulties with implementing its provisions, specifically the emergence of new realities in which the states involved implemented the Convention in a restrictive and inconsistent way. With the identification of so-called mixed migratory flows, some states refused to implement the Convention. For example, the government of Syria refused to apply the provisions to the asylum-seekers, in violation of Art. 2. The situation in Syria has been denounced by the CMW. Furthermore, the CMW encouraged states parties to adopt a broad interpretation to apply the rights contained in Part III of the Convention to all migrant workers[333]. This is emblematic of the evolution of migratory flows raising new challenges to the international community that is urged to protect these vulnerable groups.

3.2.5. The Committee for the Protection of Human Rights of Migrant Workers and Members of Their Families (CMW)

Article 72 established the CMW, a body in charge of monitoring the implementation of the Conventions by all signatories.[334] This mechanism is composed of ten independent experts, elected by the states parties. According to Art. 73 within one year of the entry into force of the Convention the states concerned have to submit a report de-

333 The Committee highlighted that "in accordance with the definition of "migrant workers" in article 2, paragraph 1, of the Convention, Part III of the Convention is to be applied to all non-nationals engaged in remunerated activity, including those in an irregular situation". CMW, *Concluding observations of the Committee on the Protection of the Rights of All Migrant Workers and Member of Their Families, Syria*, U.N. Doc. CMW/C/SYR/CO/1 (May 2, 2008).

334 *See* ILO, *supra* note 17, at 49.

scribing the measures adopted to give effect to the Convention's provisions, and the Committee formulates recommendations and comments to orient the normative and political action of the states concerned.[335] The Committee is allowed to receive individual communication under Art. 77 if the state party explicitly declares it recognizes the Committee's competence. Until now this procedure has not been activated.[336]

3.2.6. Practical issues concerning implementation

One of the main reasons this Convention is significant is the recognition for the first time of a set of rights for migrant workers contained in an international instrument.[337] At the same time, it is necessary to draw attention to persistent factors and obstacles that face irregular migrants, in order to implement specific provisions, such as the principle of non-discrimination or the right to education for their children.[338] A first consideration derives from the legal-political context in which irregular migrants are inserted, the exercise of their rights may be undermined and limited by the risk of being denounced, persecuted, and finally expelled. This fear is a sufficient reason to keep them from raising their voices against abuse or deprivation.

335 *See* OHCHR, *supra* note 323, at 11–13.

336 *Id.* at 11.

337 ILO, *Guide on ratification, International Convention on the protection of the rights of all migrants workers and members of their families*, The International Steering Committee for the campaign for ratification on the Migrants Rights Convention, Geneva, April 2009.

338 Several examples may be cited in this context. An interesting one is the analysis of Kitamura on Japan's legal framework, where he highlights how migration law obliges police to report the detection of irregular migrants. In light of this, migrant workers may refrain from reporting labour violations for the fear of being arrested and expelled. Yasuzo Kitamura, *Recent development in Japanese Immigration Policy and the United Nations Convention on Migrant Workers*, 27 UBC L. Rev. 113, 125 (1993).

As argued by several scholars, the negotiations missed the opportunity to include specific standards of protection to protect migrants who intend to denounce violations and abuses to the national authorities.[339] Instead the provisions of the Convention seem to take a different direction, if we look for instance at Art. 79, which recalls the principle of national sovereignty concerning the regulation of the admission of migrants and member of their status.

The existing antinomy between the protection of human rights and the principle of sovereignty strongly appears in this context. Even though the adoption of the Conventions has been positively welcomed for the undisputable role in removing the veil over the existence of irregular migrants and their legal protection, until now the innovative effort risked not significantly changing the *status quo*. Specifically, it is hard to identify efficient provisions able to force the states concerned to implement comprehensively the international human rights standards affecting the national sovereign prerogatives.[340]

3.2.7. Analysis of the Advisory Opinion on the Legal Status and Rights of Undocumented Migrants

The Inter-American Court (IACHR) in an Advisory Opinion, adopted on 17 September 2003, gave, as recognized by legal doctrine, an innovative and revolutionary interpretation of the principle of non-discrimination concerning irregular migrant workers and the determination of their rights.[341] This opinion was adopted at the request of the government of Mexico, which invoked the violation, by the United

339 Prof. Bosniak reported that in several cases at nation level there are similar provisions. Bosniak states that the US Immigration Reform and Control Act 1986 encloses a "confidential clause", to keep secret the information on the regularization procedure of irregular migrants and this information cannot be used. In case of violation, specific criminal sanctions are provided. *See* Bosniak, *supra* note 318, at 761.

340 *See* DAUVERGNE, *supra* note 18, at 28.

341 I/A Court H.R., *Juridical Condition and Rights of the Undocumented Migrants,* Advisory, Opinion OC–18 of 17 September 2003, Ser. A No. 18.

States, of the principles of non-discrimination and equal treatment as well as applicable labour standards to protect irregular migrant workers. According to the Mexican government, employers were not entitled to deprive irregular migrants access to effective legal remedies and protection measures with the effect of increasing the migrants' vulnerability and a total negation of their basic rights.[342] In the same period Mexico submitted the request for an interpretative opinion concerning ILO Convention No. 143 to the ILO Committee for Experts on the Application of Conventions and Recommendation.[343]

This opinion followed the sentence adopted by the US Supreme Court in the case *Hoffman Plastic Compounds v. National Labour Relations Board* in March 2002. In this case an employer fired a Mexican worker in irregular status for union-organizing activities. The US Supreme Court held that the decision of the employer was in violation of national provisions, but ruled that in the case of irregular stay in the US, the migrant worker was not allowed to get back pay for lost wages according to National Labour Relations Board rules. It is clear that the key element of *Hoffman* was the interpretation on the rights granted to migrants in irregular situation.

The reasoning the Court had to take under consideration was the structural relationship between the situation of migrant workers in irregular situation and the significance of the principles of equality and non-discrimination.

In primis, the Court accepted the vulnerability of this group–due to cultural, economic, and social conditions–as the main reasons for employers to discriminate against them, violating working conditions and denying them workplace protection. The Court acknowledged the obligations of states to guarantee migrant workers with all basic human rights, as an "*erga omnes* obligation". [344] Then the Courtfound that a different treatment between "documented" and "undocu-

342 *See* I/A Court H.R., *supra* note 341, ¶32.

343 The implications of the debate on irregular migrant workers were important because 2.5 million workers from Mexico were undocumented.

344 Sarah H. Cleveland, *Legal Status and rights of undocumented migrants*, 2 AJIL 460, 464 (2005).

mented" migrant workers needed to be "reasonable, objective, proportionate and do not harm to human rights" (¶119). The main interesting part of the decision is that once an employment relationship is in place with an irregular migrant "the migrant acquires rights as a worker, which must be recognized and guaranteed, irrespective of his regular or irregular status in the State of employment".[345] The states have to guarantee rights inherent to the working relationship (¶134–136), and at the same time they have a positive obligation to avoid any kind of violations by private actors (¶147–149). In particular, employers are not obliged to employ irregular migrants but if they do they have to honour all their rights.

On this point Cleveland argued that the Court failed to provide a list and definition of rights applicable in the working context, but it seemed to make an implicit reference to the ILO core rights (non-discrimination, prohibition of forced labour, prohibition of child labour, freedom of association, and to form unions).[346] The opinion of the Court is that these rights are fundamental and inalienable. In addition, the Court stresses the need to ensure access to safeguard mechanisms and procedures (¶159) and due process (¶119) if there are violations occurring at the workplace.

*** *** ***

In the light of this, as was highlighted on several occasion by legal doctrine, this opinion represents a relevant development of international law for two main reasons:[347]

- The broad interpretation of the principle of non-discrimination, affirmed for the first time as a peremptory norm "which impose obligation *erga omnes* on all states";[348]

345 *See* I/A Court H.R., *supra* note 341, ¶134.

346 *See* Cleveland, *supra* note 344, at 464.

347 For a detailed analysis see Michelangela Scalabrino, *Le travailleurs clandestins dans la jurisprudence de la Cour Inter américaine des droits de l'homme*, *in* MONDIALISATION, MIGRATION ET DROITS DE L'HOMME: LE DROIT INTERNATIONAL EN QUESTION 363–400 (Vincent Chetail ed., Bruylant, Vol. I, Bruylant, 2007).

348 *See* Cleveland, *supra* note 344, at 462.

- The affirmation of the rights of irregular migrant at work, addressing the existing normative gap at international level.

The Inter-American court, in its interpretation concluded that the principle of non-discrimination has the status of *jus cogens*, as follows:[349]

> Accordingly, this Court considers that the principle of equality before the law, equal protection before the law and non-discrimination belongs to jus cogens, because the whole legal structure of national and international public order rests on it and it is a fundamental principle that permeates all laws. Nowadays, no legal act that is in conflict with this fundamental principle is acceptable, and discriminatory treatment of any person, owing to gender, race, color, language, religion or belief, political or other opinion, national, ethnic or social origin, nationality, age, economic situation, property, civil status, birth or any other status is unacceptable. This principle (equality and non-discrimination) forms part of general international law. At the existing stage of the development of international law, the fundamental principle of equality and non-discrimination has entered the realm of *jus cogens.*

Dr. Hennebel, in her detailed analysis, showed that any difference of treatment justified by (ir)regularity of the migrants' stay may be overcome by a hypertrophy of the principle of non-discrimination as a norm of international law. The advisory opinion of the Inter-American Court goes the same way. This focuses predominantly on the situation of migrant as worker, regardless of his or her status: in this regard irregular migrant workers are entitled to workers' rights as basic social rights and protection. A constructive interpretation of the principle of non-discrimination may be the way the vulnerable situation of irregular migrant workers legitimates *ad hoc* protection mechanisms, despite jurisprudence developed by other bodies in the context of human rights.[350]

349 *See* Tulkens, *supra* note 137, at 194. Tulkens called the attention to the fact that the European Court of Human Rights in *Strain v. Romania*, 21 July 1995, n. 57001/00, began to recognize the principle of non-discrimination as a fundamental principle of the Convention.

350 Hennebel Ludovic, *L'humanisation du droit international des droits de l'homme– Commentaire sur l'Avis Consultatif n. 18 de la Cour Interaméricaine relatif au droits des migrantes,* 59 REV. TRIM. DR. H. 747, 757 (2004).

4. Implementing human rights: which protection?

The Global Commission on International Migration included "Protecting the rights of migrants" among its six principles of Action, formulated as follows: "The legal and normative framework affecting international migrants should be strengthened, implemented more effectively and applied in a non discriminatory manner, so as to protect the human rights and labour standards that should be enjoyed by all migrant women and men".[351]

The UN Dialogue on Global Migration and Development recognized the need to strengthen the protection of fundamental rights and liberties of all migrants to improve the global governance of migration.[352] As mentioned in the previous chapter, the way in which migrants are captured by categories created by governments in the elaboration of their migration policies affects their ability to enjoy their fundamental rights. It was shown that, firstly, the international standards need to be ratified by government to be invoked by individuals and secondly, migrants need to be associated with the definitions provided in these instruments.[353] As argued in the previous chapter, the recognition of these differences is not condemned by international legal instruments, but belonging to certain categories is recognized as a legitimate parameter to differentiate.

In this context, an interesting view put forward by Prof. Flauss is that of a progressive erosion of the difference in treatments benefiting the categories of migrants, identifying specific forms of protection reserved to certain groups of individuals and then extending

351 *See* GCIM, *supra* note 74, at 4.

352 G.A., *Summary of the High-level Dialogue on International Migration and Development: Note of the President of the General Assembly, New York, 61st Session,* U.N. Doc. A/61/515 (Oct. 16, 2006).

353 *See* CHOLEWINSKI, *supra* note 115, at 411.

them to other categories.[354] This growing and positive trend is tempered, however, by the preservation of a strong emphasis on the distinction between regular and irregular situation, as will be described later.

To point out the existing challenges in balancing the interests of states and the individual's interest in the enjoyment of human migrants, the focus of this chapter will be on the interpretation and application of international standards by different monitoring mechanisms existing at international level. At present, since a World Court of Human Rights is not in place,[355] the judicial systems at the international, regional, and domestic levels orient how international law should apply to the governance of migration.[356] Furthermore, given the relevance of human rights treaty organizations in assessing the interpretation of the provisions of the treaties, these bodies could also play a role in advancing the application of these general standards in the context of irregular migration.[357]

354 *See* Flauss, *supra* note 125, at 69.

355 *See* Chetail, *supra* note 104, at 55–56.

356 The analysis of Foblets highlights the significant role played by jurisprudence in the evolution of the legal condition of foreigners in terms of advancing the protection of their economic, civil, and social rights and recognizing minimum standards for irregular migrants. *See* Foblets, *supra* note 37, at 145.

357 The analysis makes reference to several decisions adopted by UN monitoring mechanisms, such as the Human Rights Committee and the Committee Against Torture, which developed relevant "jurisprudence". The term "jurisprudence" is used as described by prof. Chetail not "from an organic perspective (the ensemble of decisions adopted by a judicial authority) because these decisions do not have legal force, but from a substantive perspective, as consistent ensemble to identify a common position on identified legal matters". Vincent Chetail, *Le Comité des Nations Unies contre la torture et l'éloignement des étrangers: dix ans de jurisprudence (1994–2004)*, 1 REVUE SUISSE DE DROIT INTERNATIONAL ET DROIT EUROPEEN 63, 66–67 (2006). (Translation provided by the author).

4.1. *Universal right–inalienable*

The starting point of this analysis is a brief overview, not exhaustive, of the right to life. The rights are affirmed in international instruments and located, for instance, in Article 1 of the ILO Migrant Workers (Supplementary Provisions) Convention 1975 (No. 143) in the definition of "basic human rights".

4.1.1. *Right to life*

The right to life is recognized as fundamental by Article 6 of the ICCPR[358] and has attained the status of *jus cogens* in international law. As stated by Dr. Oleschak, this right cannot be derogated and it "has been characterized as the supreme right without which all other rights would be devoid of meaning".[359] The provision explicitly contains a positive obligation of member states to provide measures and mechanisms to ensure the exercise of this right. The Human Rights Committee interpreted the scope of this right from two perspectives: its application as an independent norm and as a consequence of the violation of other international standards (forced evictions, use of force by public authorities). The importance of this broad interpretation is to include an extra-territorial application of international standards on the protection of the right to life, beyond the national borders, as will be described later.[360]

358 Article 6: "Every human being has the inherent right to life. This right shall be protected by law. No one shall be arbitrarily deprived of his life."

359 REKHA OLESCHAK, THE INTERNATIONAL LAW OF DEVELOPMENT-INDUCED DISPLACEMENT 99 (Niedermann Druck, St. Gallen, 2009).

360 For example, in two cases against Canada (*Charles Chitat v. Canada*, Comm. n. 469/1991 (Nov. 5, 1991); *Keith Cox v. Canada*, Comm. No. 539/1993 (Oct. 31, 1992)), concerning the extradition of individuals who may be condemned to death, the Committee considered the Canadian policy not in violation of Art. 6, barring Canadian authorities from interfering with the domestic matters of third countries. Several judges and scholars contested this conclusion recalling

4.2. Economic, social, cultural, and political rights

References to ILO labour standards and the provisions of the ICMWR are a significant support to the implementation of those economic, social, and cultural rights claimed by irregular migrants in destination countries. The content of these rights to which irregular migrants are entitled is quite nebulous, as clearly admitted by the government of Morocco during Universal Periodic Reviews. Morocco stated that is not-self evident how to apply international human rights standards at the domestic level, especially referring to the realities which exist in developing countries where economic constraints risk compromising their full effectiveness.[361]

Observation No. 6 of the Committee that requires member states to adopt preventive measures to ensure the full protection of the right to life (*Barbarin Mojoca v. Dominicanan Republica,* Comm. No. 449/1991 (Jul. 15, 1994); *Nydia Erika de Arellona v. Colombia,* Comm. No. 563/1993 (Oct. 27, 1995); *Brasilio Lauren Aatachira v. Peru,* Comm. No. 540/1993 (Mar. 25, 1996). In this vein the ECHR issued several judgements (*Bader v. Sweden,* Nov. 8, 2005, Request No. 13284/04; *Ocalan v. Turkey,* May 12, 2005, Request No. 46221/99) invoking the violation of Art. 2 (right to life) in similar cases. The aptitude of the ECHR was to refrain to apply Art. 2 in cases of expulsion *(M.A.R. v. United Kingdom,* 16 January 1997, Appl. No. 28038/95; *H.L.R. v. France,* 29 April 1997, Appl. No. 24573/94; *D. v. United Kingdom,* 2 May 1997, Appl. No. 30240/96) preferring the application of Art. 3 (prohibition of degrading and inhuman treatments). In the case *Drodz and Janousek v. Spain and France,* 26 June 1992, A/240 the ECHR stated that the Conventions does not oblige states parties to apply its provisions to third countries. On this issue see the comprehensive analysis made by Evelien Browuer, *Extraterritorial Migration Control and Human Rights, in* EXTRATERRITORIAL IMMIGRATION CONTROL 199 (Bernard Ryan & Valsamis Mitsilegas eds., Martinus Nijoff Publishers, 2010).

361 HRC, *Report submitted by the Government of Morocco, on the basis of para. 15(A), annex to the resolution n. 5/1,* ¶21, U.N. Doc. A/HRC/WG.6/2/MAR/1 (Mar. 11, 2008).

4.2.1. Right to health

The SRHRM, in its annual report, raises concerns about the health of irregular migrants, because the vulnerable condition of this group can exacerbate difficulties with access to health services in countries of destination.[362] There are several circumstances in which they are potentially exposed to human rights abuses: at work, in poor working conditions; before removal, for arbitrary detention; or during the migratory process, in unsafe travel conditions.[363]

In their detailed analysis, Prof. Chetail and Dr. Giacca, rightly pointed out how the interlinkages between "the social reality of migration and its legal regulation" and the implications for the implementation of the right to health face increasing reluctance from member states that tend to promote security and a restrictive approach in their national migration policies.[364]

During its mission to Sweden the SRHRM elaborated on this issue affirming that:

> The right to health is to be enjoyed by all without discrimination. It is especially important for vulnerable individuals and groups. Asylum seekers and undocumented people are among the most vulnerable in Sweden. They are precisely the sort of vulnerable group that international human rights law is designed to protect.[365]

Article 12(1) of the ICESCR states "right of everyone to the enjoyment of the highest attainable standard of physical and mental health".

362 *See* SRHRM, *supra* note 2, at 7.

363 According to the World Health Organization the "exposure to risk associated with population movements also raises migrants' vulnerability to psychosocial disorders, drug abuse, alcoholism and violence. In addition, limited access to health care during the transit and early insertion phases of migration increases the resultant burden of untreated conditions." World Health Organization, *Health of migrants,* WHA A 61/12 (Jan. 24, 2008), ¶17.

364 *See* Chetail & Giacca, *supra* note 89, at 224–234.

365 G.A., *Report of the Special Rapporteur on the right of everyone to the enjoyment of the highest attainable standard of physical and mental health (Mr. Paul Hunt) Sweden,* ¶73, U.N. Doc. A/HRC/4/28/ Add.2 (2007).

The right to health embodies several specific elements: access to adequate health care, public health services, social security, and the need to respect the principle of non-discrimination.[366] Article 5(1) asserts that everyone should enjoy the right to health. In the interpretation of the scope of this provision, CERD, in its General Recommendation No. 30, explicitly refers to non-citizens and urges the states to "respect the right of non citizens to an adequate standard of physical and mental health by, *inter alia*, refraining from denying or limiting their access to preventive, curative and palliative health services."[367] In this context, the principle of non-discrimination acquires a broad significance, and is mainly understood to provide all migrants with the benefit of equal effective opportunities to access health care. [368] Particularly, the CESCR states that:

> any discrimination in access to health care and underlying determinants of health, as well as to means and entitlements for their procurement, on the grounds of race, colour, sex, language, religion, political or other opinion, national or social origin, property, birth, physical or mental disability, health status, sexual orientation and civil, political, social or other status, which has the intention or effect of nullifying or impairing the equal enjoyment or exercise of the right to health.[369]

In the text of the ICMWR, a clear distinction is made between the full applicability of the right of health to regular migrant workers

366 CESCR, *General Comment No. 14: The right to the highest attainable standard of health (Twenty-second session, 2000)*, U.N. Doc. E/C.12/2000/4 (2000). "This term is most commonly used at the international level. It clearly underlines the importance of recognizing not only the right to health care, which is a part of the right to health, but also a right to a certain number of underlying preconditions for health. These preconditions are: safe and potable water and adequate sanitation, an adequate supply of safe food, nutrition and housing, healthy occupational and environmental conditions, and access to health-related education and information, including with regard to sexual and reproductive health." IOM, *Migration and the right to health*, 2009, at 9.

367 CERD, *General Recommendation XXX: Discrimination against Non-citizens (Sixty-fourth session, 2004)*, ¶36, U.N. Doc. CERD/C/64/Misc.11/rev. 3 (2004).

368 *See* CHOLEWINSKI, *supra* note 115, at 120.

369 *See* CESCR, *supra* note 366, ¶12.

(Art. 43), which seems to reflect the content of international standards, and Art. 28[370], in which the Convention specifically mentions the right of access for irregular migrants only to urgent health care "for the preservation of their life or the avoidance of irreparable harm in their health". In its first draft the content of this provision was broader, to include also "or the restoration of their health", but this was firmly opposed by the delegate of United States, who asked to limit their access to medical care in urgent situations.[371] This restrictive approach makes difficult to identify the proper functional interpretation of this right, for instance. In fact Art. 70 seemed to provide only to regular migrant workers the need to be kept "with the standards of fitness, safety, health and principles of human dignity". The prevalent doctrine is more oriented to support a broad understanding of this right in line with Art. 81, which provides favourable international standards, where they exist, to all migrant workers.[372]

Another issue of concern in this analysis is the condition of child migrants. The Convention on the Rights of the Child entitles them to the highest attainable standards of health (Art. 24), the need to adopt specific measures to "to ensure that no child is deprived of his or her right of access to such health care services" and to benefit children with "necessary medical assistance and health care" and to ensure "appropriate prenatal and post-natal health care for mothers". As is

370 Art. 28 states: "Migrant workers and member of their families shall have the right to health, specifically accessibility to health care that is urgently required for the preservation of their life or the avoidance of irreparable harm to their health on the basis of equality of treatment with nationals of the state concerned. Such emergency medical care shall not be refused them by reason of any irregularity with regard to stay or employment".

371 U.N. GAOR, *Report of the Open-ended Working Group on the Elaboration of an International Convention on the Protection of the Rights of All Migrant Workers and Their Families*, U.N. Doc. A/C.3/42/1 (Jun. 21, 1987). Other delegates from Germany and Yugoslavia rejected the adoption of explicit provisions to define the principle of equality of treatment between migrant workers and citizens. *See* CHOLEWINSKI, *supra* note 115, at 161–167.

372 *See* Chetail & Giacca, *supra* note 89, at 224.

the case for other rights, the gap between the scope of this right and the realization of it in the case of children born from irregular migrants is significant. In practice, in many situations their parents, for fear of being arrested or denounced, refrain from accessing public health care services.[373] In this regard, as highlighted by Watter, is relevant to properly differentiate between "entitlement" and "access" to health care.

> The former relates to questions at a macro level concerning laws and policies and can be answered with reference to official literature. By contrast questions of access can only be answered adequately through investigating the implementation of laws and policies at 'street level'.[374]

In any case the CESCR adopted in its concluding observations a broad interpretation of the scope and the obligation of member states to extend the implementation of the rights to health to irregular migrants.[375]

4.2.2. *Right to housing*

Article 11 of the ICESCR recognizes the right to housing and Article 5 of the ICERD complements it by prohibiting any kinds of

373 Francois Crépeau, *Right and access to healthcare for undocumented children: addressing the gap between international conventions and disparate implementations in North America and Europe*, 70(2) SOCIAL SCIENCE AND MEDICINE 5 (January 2010). Of significant interest is the analysis of the criteria to be used to ensure the right to health of children migrants.

374 CHARLES WATTERS, REFUGEE CHILDREN: TOWARDS THE NEXT HORIZON 135 (Routledge, 2008).

375 CESCR, *Conclusions and recommendations of the Committee on Economic, Social and Cultural Rights, France*, U.N. Doc. E/C.12/1/Add.72 (2001). In its conclusions the Committee noted that even if the ICERD gives a broad definition of the right to health some groups of individuals, such as irregular migrants or asylum seekers, they experienced several difficulties and inequalities in their access to these rights. For this reason, a member state, on the basis of the General Comment No. 14, must formulate special measures to avoid denying them health care.

discrimination in its practical implementation at the national level.[376] General Comment No. 4 adopted by CESCR offers a preliminary interpretation on the scope of this right, exploring the significance of "adequacy" by articulating a list of seven criteria to formulate its definition.[377] This preliminary interpretation was advanced by the subsequent adoption of General Comment No. 7 in 1997, which dealt with cases of forced eviction and defined and elaborated requirements for domestic legislation to address this specific right.[378]

With regard to migrants, the SRHRM highlighted the relevance of the implementation of this right for the enjoyment of other rights, such as the right to health. It is evident that deprivation of adequate living conditions may generate mental illness or other problems linked, for instance, with the absence of fresh water. It should be acknowledged that despite the growing attention devoted by the international community to these challenges, a large gap between the theoretical and the practical level in the realization of human rights standards persists.[379]

Specifically, the vulnerable situation of irregular migrants impels states to elaborate national action plans to ensure the access to these rights, justifying any restriction or limitation to their enjoyment.[380] In fact the major issue of concern is that migrants may be discriminated against and disadvantaged with respect to the accessibility of ade-

376 Art. 11 of the ICESCR states that "The States Parties to the present Covenant recognize the right of everyone to an adequate standard of living for himself and his family, including adequate food, clothing and housing, and to the continuous improvement of living conditions. The States Parties will take appropriate steps to ensure the realization of this right, recognizing to this effect the essential importance of international cooperation based on free consent".

377 "(a) legal security of tenure including legal protection against forced evictions; (b) availability of services, materials, facilities and infrastructure; (c) affordability; (d) habitability; (e) accessibility for disadvantaged groups; (f) location and (g) cultural adequacy". CESCR, *General Comment No. 4: The right to adequate housing*, ¶8, U.N. Doc. E/1992/23 (1991).

378 CESCR, *General Comment No. 7: Forced evictions, and the right to adequate housing (Sixteenth session, 1997)*, ¶9, U.N. Doc. E/1998/22 (1997).

379 *See* SRHRM, *supra* note 2, ¶39.

380 *See* ICHRP, *supra* note 168, at 122, 127–130.

quate living conditions by the prerogatives of national member states in the elaboration of migration policies.

The living conditions of irregular migrant workers are exemplary in this regard. According with the description contained in the report of SRHRM, they live in inappropriate, overcrowded homes that do not meet minimum hygienic standards.[381] For instance, this situation may occur in contexts where irregular migration is criminalized and domestic legislation identifies it as a crime to rent homes to these groups of individuals.[382] Or, in other circumstances, administrative procedures require migrants to provide a work contract or residence permit to rent an apartment. Not surprisingly, migrants are directed to the informal housing market, where they "encounter in excessive rents and poor living conditions".[383]

In addition, the right to housing implies the prohibition of forced evictions, even in the case of accommodation occupied by irregular migrants,[384] unless they provide an alternative solution or allocate a public housing.[385]

The only reference to this right in the ICMWR is Art. 29, which states the need to provide adequate housing to migrant workers, stressing the "social significance" of this right, "for its plays a vital role in assisting the integration into the society of that country."[386] This

381 G.A., *Report of the Special Rapporteur on adequate housing as a component of the right to an adequate standard of living, Miloon Kothari, Spain,* ¶74, U.N. Doc. A/HRC/7/16/Add.2 (Feb. 7, 2008); *see* G.A., *Report of the Special Rapporteur on adequate housing as a component of the right to an adequate standard of living, and on the right to non-discrimination in this context, Raquel Rolnik, Addendum Mission to the United States of America*, U. N. Doc. A/HRC/13/20/Add.4 (Feb. 12, 2010).

382 *See* G.A., *supra* note 381, ¶89.

383 *See* SRHRM, *supra* note 2, ¶46–47; *see* CHOLEWINSKI, *supra* note 115, at 121.

384 Such practices are increasing against migrants and asylum seekers, as noted by the SRHRM: "There are many instances where migrants, most often vulnerable groups such as irregular migrants, asylum-seekers and unaccompanied children, are forcibly evicted from their homes without adequate notice, prior consultation or alternative accommodation." *See* SRHRM, *supra* note 2, ¶8.

385 *See* CESCR, *supra* note 377, ¶18. *See* ICHRP, *supra* note 168, at 129–130.

386 *See* CHOLEWINSKI, *supra* note 115, at 121.

provision is restricted to regular migrant workers.[387] Irregular migrants do not seem to be included in the scope of this article, even if a broad obligation is formulated in Art. 64, which mandates that signatories "consult and co-operate with a view to promoting sound, equitable and human conditions in connection with International migration of workers and members of their families". ILO instruments refer to adequate housing in Convention No. 97 and in Recommendation No. 15 accompanying Convention No. 143. The Recommendation, in paragraph 2(1), recalls the application of the principle of non-discrimination with respect to the enjoyment of adequate accommodation. In this regard, Prof. Cholewinski emphasize the relevance of elaborating proper national plans to implement equality effectively.[388]

4.2.3. Right to education

The ICESCR contains a provision to "recognize the right of everyone to education".[389] In the context of international standards, educa-

387 Article 43 highlights the need to provide equal access to housing and to legal remedies in case of abuse. *See* ICHRP, *supra* note 168, at 129–130.

388 *See* CHOLEWINSKI, *supra* note 115, at 121.

389 Article 13: "1. The States Parties to the present Covenant recognize the right of everyone to education. They agree that education shall be directed to the full development of the human personality and the sense of its dignity, and shall strengthen the respect for human rights and fundamental freedoms. They further agree that education shall enable all persons to participate effectively in a free society, promote understanding, tolerance and friendship among all nations and all racial, ethnic or religious groups, and further the activities of the United Nations for the maintenance of peace. 2. The States Parties to the present Covenant recognize that, with a view to achieving the full realization of this right:
(a) Primary education shall be compulsory and available free to all;
(b) Secondary education in its different forms, including technical and vocational secondary education, shall be made generally available and accessible to all by every appropriate means, and in particular by the progressive introduction of free education;

tion of migrants is a crucial right and its application does not allow limitation. This right benefits migrants and migrant children at the same time.

Before being a foreigner, an individual is a "*créancier d'éducation*" and according to the principle of non-discrimination migrants, regardless of their status, needs access to effectively equal opportunities and free education.[390] This principle is controversial, in fact, in a number of states, where the general opinion is to limit the access to this right to regular migrants.[391] The UNESCO Convention[392] and

---

(c) Higher education shall be made equally accessible to all, on the basis of capacity, by every appropriate means, and in particular by the progressive introduction of free education;

(d) Fundamental education shall be encouraged or intensified as far as possible for those persons who have not received or completed the whole period of their primary education;

(e) The development of a system of schools at all levels shall be actively pursued, an adequate fellowship system shall be established, and the material conditions of teaching staff shall be continuously improved.

3. The States Parties to the present Covenant undertake to have respect for the liberty of parents and, when applicable, legal guardians to choose for their children schools, other than those established by the public authorities, which conform to such minimum educational standards as may be laid down or approved by the State and to ensure the religious and moral education of their children in conformity with their own convictions.

4. No part of this article shall be construed so as to interfere with the liberty of individuals and bodies to establish and direct educational institutions, subject always to the observance of the principles set forth in paragraph I of this article and to the requirement that the education given in such institutions shall conform to such minimum standards as may be laid down by the State".

390 *See* Martens, *supra* note 173, at 601.

391 U.N. GAOR, *Report of the Open-ended Working Group on the Elaboration of an International Convention on the Protection of the Rights of All Migrant Workers and Their Families,* U.N. Doc. A/C.3/42/1 (Jun. 21, 1987); U.N. GAOR, *Report of the Open-ended Working Group on the Elaboration of an International Convention on the Protection of the Rights of All Migrant Workers and Their* Families, U.N. Doc. A/C.3/42/6 (Oct. 9, 1987).

the ICERD, however, clearly state that the scope of this right is to secure equality of treatment and opportunity of migrants with that of nationals, and specific measures have to taken to not compromise their access to this right.[393] It is relevant to highlight that the provisions of the UNESCO Convention refer to all migrants, without reference to their legal status.[394]

Another problem connected with the access to this right by irregular migrants is connected to the recent debate on the legality of adopting obligations at the national level for teachers to inform public authorities when irregular children are identified among their students. The elaboration of these measures is particularly dangerous for the establishment of a direct link between the elaboration of restrictive migratory policies that prevent the enjoyment of their rights and the vulnerability of their status. According to the legal system in place, these practices and policies have to be prevented and prohibited, and limited exceptions may be justified for national security concerns.[395]

4.2.3.1 Situation of children born from irregular parents

Article 7 of the Convention on the Rights of the Child explicitly addresses the situation of children born from irregular parents.[396] In general, the CRC states the principle that citizenship is acquired on the criteria of *jus soli* (the birth place) is recognized by international

---

392 UNESCO Convention against any forms of discrimination in the context of education, adopted by the International Conference of UNESCO 14 December 1960, entered into force 22 May 1962.

393 Article 3: "The States Parties to the present Covenant undertake to ensure the equal right of men and women to the enjoyment of all economic, social and cultural rights set forth in the present Covenant".

394 *See* ICHRP, *supra* note 168, at 135.

395 *Id.* at 135.

396 According to Art. 7, a migrant born from irregular parents: "shall be registered immediately after birth and shall have the right from birth to a name, [and] the right to acquire a nationality [...] States parties shall ensure the implementation of these rights [...] in particular where the child would otherwise be stateless".

law in the case of irregular born children migrants. Article 7 has to be read in accordance with other specific provisions, namely Article 8 (respect of identity, nationality, and names), Article 9 (prohibition of separating the child from his or her parents), and Article 20 (protection of children deprived of their familiar environment). The Committee on the Rights of Child, in its broad interpretation of the Convention, requires incorporating these rights with the general principles recognized by the Conventions, such as Article 2 (non-discrimination), Article 3 (the best interest of the child), Article 6 (right to development).

The need to promote and guarantee safeguards has been stressed by the SRHRM in several communications[397] and during its countries visits.[398] The Special Rapporteur brought attention to the serious

397 SRHRM, *Report of the Special Rapporteur on the human rights of migrants, Jorge Bustamante, Summary of cases transmitted to Governments and replies received*, U.N. Doc. E/CN.4/2005/85/Add.1 (Feb. 4, 2005); SRHRM, *Report of the Special Rapporteur on human rights of migrants, Jorge Bustamante, Burkina Faso,* U.N. Doc. E/CN.4/2006/73/Add.1 (Jan. 3, 2006); SRHRM, *Report of the Special Rapporteur on human rights of migrants, Jorge Bustamante, United States,* U.N. Doc. A/HRC/7/12/Add.2 (Mar. 5, 2008); SRHRM, *Report of the Special Rapporteur on human rights of migrants, Jorge Bustamante, Summary of cases transmitted to Governments and replies received*, U.N. Doc. A/HRC/11/7/Add.1 (May 20, 2009).

398 SRHRM, *Report of the Special Rapporteur on human rights of migrants, Gabriela Pizzarro, Mexico*, U.N. Doc. E/CN.4/2003/85/Add.2 (Oct. 30, 2002); SRHRM, *Report of the Special Rapporteur on human rights of migrants, Jorge Bustamante, Mexico*, U.N. Doc. A/HRC/11/7/Add.2 (Mar. 24, 2009); SRHRM, *Report of the Special Rapporteur on human rights of migrants, Jorge Bustamante, Guatemala*, U.N. Doc. A/HRC/11/7/Add.3 (Mar. 18, 2009); SRHRM, *Report of the Special Rapporteur on human rights of migrants, Jorge Bustamante, Burkina Faso*, U.N. Doc E.CN.4/2006/73/Add.2 (Jan. 5, 2006); SRHRM, *Report of the Special Rapporteur on human rights of migrants, Jorge Bustamante, Italy*, U.N. Doc E/CN.4/2005/85/Add.3 (Nov. 15, 2004); SRHRM, *Report of the Special Rapporteur on human rights of migrants, Jorge Bustamante, Spain,* U.N. Doc. E/CN.4/2004/76/Add.2 (Jan. 14, 2004); SRHRM, *Report of the Special Rapporteur on human rights of migrants, Jorge Bustamante, Ecuador*, U.N. Doc E/CN.4/2002/94/Add.1 (Feb. 18, 2002); SRHRM, *Report of the Special Rapporteur on human rights of migrants, Jorge Bustamante, United States*, U.N. Doc A/HRC/7/12/Add.2 (Mar. 5, 2008).

consequences of the progressive criminalization of irregular migrants and the vulnerable condition of irregular children migrants, who in most cases were not registered at birth due to the fear of their parents of being denounced to the local authorities and, consequently being deported.[399] As stated by the CMW

> State party take appropriate measures to ensure that access to education is guaranteed to all migrant children in accordance with article 30 of the Convention. Furthermore, the State party should intensify its efforts to guarantee that each child of a migrant worker shall have the right to a name and to registration of birth throughout the country, in accordance with article 29 of the Convention.[400]

Recently, the SRHRM dealt with a case against the government of Japan, concerning the situation of a thirteen-year-old child born to irregular migrant from Philippines. The government of Japan ordered the expulsion of the parents and as well as the child, even though she was born in Japan and speaks Japanese as mother tongue. In this case, the SRHRM declared the Japanese legislation to be in violation of the principle of non-discrimination because it adopted a measure of expulsion against the child on the basis of the irregular status of the parents.[401] The SRHRM urged the government of Japan to report on the situation of irregular migrant children as regulated by domestic provisions, to see whether the legislation in place was in line with international human rights standards. As stated by the Government of Japan

> According to the principle of customary international law, whether foreign persons are accepted in another state or meet the criteria for being accepted in a non-discriminatory manner is left entirely to the discretion of the legislative policies of each state. The International Covenant on Civil and Political Rights

399 UNICEF, *The "rights" start to life: A statistical analysis of birth registration,* UNICEF, 2005.

400 CMW, *Concluding observations of the Committee on the Protection of the Rights of All Migrant Workers and Members of Their Families, Ecuador*, ¶35 and 36, U.N. Doc. CMW/C/ECU/CO/1 (Dec. 5, 2007).

401 *See* SRHRM, *supra* nota 2, ¶263.

takes these principles as its premise and does not change the fundamental basis. 292. It is owing to their illegal stay that deportation procedures for the three C. family members are being carried out, and the decision of whether or not to grant them special permission to stay was made with overall consideration being given to a number of factors including the necessity for humanitarian consideration.[402]

According to Japan, the domestic migration fully respected the right of children migrants without any discrimination based on their legal status, and in this case the child was allowed to remain on the national territory, even if her parents were deported.[403]

In another case, *The Yean and Bosico children v. Dominican Republic*,[404] the Inter-American Court of Human Rights supported the obligation of states to ensure the registration of birth of all children of migrants, irrespective of status.[405] In its reasoning the Inter-American Court, on the basis of a previous opinion adopted in 2003,[406] rejected the

402 *See* SRHRM, *supra* nota 2, ¶432.

403 "In the case of a child born from foreign national parents in Japan, regardless of whether they are staying legally or illegally in Japan, the child can apply for acquisition of a status of residence to the Minister of Justice within 30 days of the child's date of birth if the foreign national child wishes to stay in Japan for over 60 days in accordance with Article 22–2 of the Immigration Control Act".

404 *The Yean and Bosico Children v. Dominican Republic*, Sep. 8, 2005, Inter-Am Ct. H.R., (Ser. C) No. 130 (2005).

405 The case concerned the juridical status of children born from mixed couples (such as a mother from Dominican Republic and a father of Haitian origin). According to domestic law, registration of their births was prohibited and this caused their "statelessness" and exposure to several violations. *See* the detailed analysis provided by Scalabrino, *supra* note 347.

406 "(a) The migratory status of a person cannot be a condition for the State to grant nationality, because migratory status can never constitute a justification for depriving a person of the right to nationality or the enjoyment and exercise of his rights; (b) The migratory status of a person is not transmitted to the children; and (c) The fact that a person has been born on the territory of a State is the only fact that needs to be proved for the acquisition of nationality, in the case of those persons who would not have the right to another nationality if they did not acquire that of the State where they were born". I/A Court H.R., *Juridical Condition*

justification that considered these children as "foreigners in transit", not entitled to enjoy national protection. In its statement the Court declared the national migration law in violation of the fundamental rights of children migrants (right to have a name, right to acquire a citizenship, right to education). Similarly, the UN treaty body stressed the need for all states to protect the right of migrant children due to the fact that their rights before the law could be severally constrained by the growth of discriminatory practices against them and the effect of restrictive migratory policies.[407]

4.2.4. Employment rights and work conditions

4.2.4.1. Access to work

Without doubt a fundamental challenge concerning the enjoyment of human rights by irregular migrants is their access to work and their ability to choose their employment without restrictions.[408] Even if Art. 23(1) of the UDHR seems to recognize for everyone "the right to work, to free choice of employment, to just and favorable conditions of work and to protection against unemployment" a preliminary interpretation of the use of term "everyone", on the basis of the *travaux préliminaires,* in the drafting process was restricted to migrants regularly present on the territory of the state concerned.[409] This re-

---

and Rights of the Undocumented Migrants, Advisory Opinion OC–18 of 17 September 2003, Series A No. 18, ¶134.

407 "In particular, concern [was] expressed about the situation of children of Haitian origin or belonging to Haitian migrant families whose right to birth registration has been denied in the State [... and, as a] result of this policy, those children have not been able to enjoy fully their rights, such as to access to health care and education". Committee on the Rights of the Child, *Concluding observations of the Committeee on the Rights of the Child for the Dominican Republic Initial Report, The Dominican Republic* ¶22 and 26, U.N. Doc. CRC/C/15/Add.150 (Feb. 21, 2001).

408 *See* ICHRP, *supra* note 168, at 123–126.

409 U.N. GAOR, *Report of the Open-ended Working Group on the Elaboration of an International Convention on the Protection of the Rights of All Migrant Workers and*

strictive interpretation has been extended by the adoption of Art. 6 of the ICESCR that imposes the obligation on states to "recognize the right to work, which includes the right of everyone to the opportunity to gain his living by work which he freely chooses or accepts". Quite obviously, the states contend that this right may be limited in time of economic crisis and by the need to accommodate the employment needs of nationals and foreigners according to their national labour markets needs.[410] In any case the states ratifying international human rights standards are obliged to protect rights pertaining to employment and work conditions (e.g. equal remuneration, rest periods, security of employment).[411]

Another fundamental aspect concerning the realization of this right is related to the national legal framework adopted at the domestic level, which in most cases manifestly differentiates between regular and irregular migrants workers, limiting and restricting the access of the latter to formal employment. As mentioned in chapter 2, the use of legal status as criteria to differentiate access to work it is very controversial, since may raise several concerns on the potential violation of Art. 2(1) of the ICCPR.[412] Not surprisingly, the ICMWR recognizes this right only to regular migrant workers, at Art. 52 and 53, as in fact most of the states preferred to maintain the exercise of their national prerogative on this sensitive issue.[413]

Their Families, U.N. Doc. A/C.3/38/5 (Oct. 11, 1983).

410 Art. 4: "The States Parties to the present Covenant recognize that, in the enjoyment of those rights provided by the State in conformity with the present Covenant, the State may subject such rights only to such limitations as are determined by law only in so far as this may be compatible with the nature of these rights and solely for the purpose of promoting the general welfare in a democratic society".

411 *See* CHOLEWINSKI, *supra* note 115, at 108.

412 CESLA AMARELLE & MINH SON NGUYEN, MIGRATIONS ET ECONOMIE-L'ACCES DES ETRANGERS A LA VIE ECONOMIQUE: LES NORMES ET LEUR APPLICATION 132–139 (Stämpfli Editions SA, 2010).

413 For instance excluding migrant workers from public-sector employment, *see* CHOLEWINSKI, *supra* nota 115, at 161–167.

4.2.4.2. Right to safe working conditions

It is well known that irregular migrant workers, in most cases, are employed in the informal labour market, where "general labour standards are rarely respected".[414] In many circumstances, the working conditions are very poor, even dangerous, and in the worst cases migrant workers are subject to slavery or slave-like conditions. This issue has been explicitly addressed by the European Court on Human Rights.[415] The legal invisibility of irregular migrants is exacerbated by their vulnerability to abuse.[416] As stated by Dr. Cholewinski

> National laws in [Council of Europe] Members States make access to many of these rights very difficult if not possible. Moreover, even where such access is not prohibited by the law and should be available, the very illegality of migrants' stay creates further legal and practical obstacles to the enjoyment of these rights.[417]

On the same vein also the ILO Committee recalled that

> The Committee is deeply concerned by these reports on violations of basic human rights, especially of undocumented migrants coming from Africa, Asia

414 *See* Chetail & Giacca, *supra* note 89, at 226.

415 In 2005 the European Court on Human Rights adopted a landmark decision on this issue, stating that an irregular migrant from Togo, informally employed in France, had been subjected to slave trade by employers, in violation of Art. 4 of the ECHR. The Court affirmed that "in interpreting Article 4 of the European Convention, the Court has in a previous case already taken into account the ILO conventions, which are binding on almost all of the Council of Europe's member States, including France, and especially the 1930 Forced Labour Convention" (*Van der Mussele v. Belgium*, Nov. 23, 1983, Series A No. 70, ¶32; *Siliadin v. France*, Jul. 26, 2005, No. 73316/01). Recently, in a case involving a young woman from Russia, presumably irregularly present in Cyprus, the Court found the national law in violation of the Convention for restraining the state to its obligation to adopt at the domestic level proper regulation in line with international human rights standards (*Rantsev v. Cyprus and Russia*, Jan. 7, 2010, No. 25695/04). *See* AMARELLE & NGUYEN, *supra* note 412, at 140–143.

416 *See* SRHRM, *supra* note 13, ¶13–59.

417 *See* CHOLEWINSKI, *supra* nota 115, at 90.

and Eastern Europe, and of an apparently increasing climate of intolerance, violence and discrimination against the immigrant population, especially the Roma of Romanian origin. As these matters have an impact on the basic level of protection of the human and labour rights and the living and working conditions of the immigrant population in Italy, the Committee considers that they raise serious issues of non-application of the Convention. The Committee recalls the Government's obligation under Article 1 of the Convention to respect the basic human rights of all migrant workers, irrespective of their migrant status. Moreover, under Article 9 (1), the Government has the obligation to ensure that migrant workers, even those illegally employed, are not deprived of their rights in respect of the work actually performed as regards remuneration, social security and other benefits.[418]

Article 25(1) of the ICMWR makes reference to the application of the principle of non-discrimination between migrant workers and citizens in the enjoyment of specific rights at work, such as the equal remuneration and other employment conditions. Within the expression "Other conditions of work" is included for instance holidays, security, health, and rest periods (Art. 25(1)(a)). These conditions needed to be transposed by national provisions without allowing any derogation by private law (Art. 25(2)).[419] During the drafting process of the Convention, the use of this broad formulation was very controversial; in particular the delegate from Germany considered it "would prove increasingly impracticable" to bring regular and irregular migrant workers onto the same level.[420]

4.2.4.3. Freedom of association

This right refers to the right to join trade unions provided to all migrant workers according to Art. 8 of ICESCR, Art. 22 of the ICCPR, and the ILO labour standards. In the ICMWR there are several pro-

418 CEACR, *Individual Communication on migrant workers, Italy*, 2009.

419 Article 81 prohibits any kind of derogations to the provisions listed in the Convention.

420 U.N. GAOR, *Report of the Open-ended Working Group on the Elaboration of an International Convention on the Protection of the Rights of All Migrant Workers and Their Families*, ¶196, U.N. Doc. A/C.3/42/1 (Jun. 21, 1987). *See* CHOLEWINSKI, *supra* note 115, at 161–167.

visions that address this issue, such as Art. 26(1)(b), which states "to seek the aid and assistance of any trade union [...]."[421] This provision, pertaining to Section III of the ICMWR, is probably applicable to all migrant workers, while the other provision, Art. 40, may only be invoked by regular migrant workers. The acceptable limitations to the implementation of these rights are those related to national security and public order. The decision to formulate distinct standards raised specific concerns on the basis of the existence of international labour standards on these issues at that moment.[422] In this regard, the practices developed at the national and international level have significantly contributed to the widening interpretation of this right. Specifically, the ILO Committee of Independent Experts on the Interpretation of Conventions and Recommendations notes the relevance of Art. 10 of Convention No. 143. It is affirmed that the status of an individual is not a legitimate reason to denying his or her access to human rights, including the enjoyment of rights derived from his or her work relationship.

On the right of freedom of association two relevant decisions have been issued.

The first was adopted by the ILO Committee on Freedom of Association in response to a question raised by the Spanish Trade Unions (UGT).[423] In this context, the trade unions contested a spe-

421 Art. 26 (1) states: "take part in meetings and activities of trade unions and of any other associations established in accordance with the law, with a view to protecting their economic, social, cultural and other interests [...]."

422 According to Hasenau, this provision clearly contravenes the existing international labour standards, in particular ILO Convention No. 87 on the freedom of association, which at Art. 2 considers illegitimate any kind of discrimination on the basis of nationality. He therefore finds it "a considerable depreciation of trade union rights of migrant workers in an irregular situation", U.N. GAOR, *Report of the Open-ended Working Group on the Elaboration of an International Convention on the Protection of the Rights of All Migrant Workers and Their Families*, ¶244, U.N. Doc. A/C.3/42/1 (Jun. 21, 1987).

423 Rebecca Smith, *Prosecute, Prevent, Protect: migrant labor, forced labor, and human rights*, *in* HUMAN RIGHTS IN LABOR AND EMPLOYMENT RELATIONS 165 (James A. Gross & Lance Compa eds., 2010).

cific provision formulated at the national level that permitted foreigners to join trade unions only "when they obtain authorization of their stay or residence in the country". The Committee recalled that Art. 2 of Convention No. 87 guarantees the right "of all workers without distinction whatsoever, to establish and join organizations of their own choosing".[424]

Similarly, as illustrated by Dr. Smith the courts in South Korea addressed this issue. In 2007 the Seoul High Court recognized the right of migrant workers to join trade unions and to exercise their trade union rights. In this case the government of South Korea prohibited exercise of this right to migrant workers and officially demanded a list of all union members, affirming that according to national provisions irregular migrants are not workers. In a first sentence, the Tribunal upheld as legitimate the decision of the Ministry of Labour to prohibit the exercise of this right, but the High Court reversed the decision, validating this right for irregular migrants.[425] The same interpretation has been adopted by the ILO Committee of the Freedom of Association in 2009.[426]

4.2.4.4. Role of labour inspections

Many states recognize labour inspections as playing the role of monitoring working conditions regularly, and in some cases identifying the legal status of migrant workers. To combat exploitation of migrant workers, high sanctions have been formulated against employers but from the information available, their effective impacts do not appear significant. In this regard, Dr. Wickramasekara raises the need to balance the adoption of these measures with safeguard-

424 ILO, Committee on the Freedom of Association, *Report n. 326–Spain*, Case No. 2121 (Mar. 23, 2001).

425 Seoul High Court decision 2006 NU 6774. The decision has been appealed and the final outcome is pending.

426 Amnesty Int'l, *South Korea: crackdown against migrants' trade union*, 3 December 2007; *Illegal Aliens Can Form Unions, High Court in Seoul Korea has ruled,* 2 Feb., 2007; ILO, Governing Body, Six item on the agenda, 353rd (Apr. 20, 2009). *See* Smith, *supra* note 423, at 165.

ing mechanisms that allows migrant workers to denounce the case of abuses and violations.[427]

In 2006 the ILO Committee of Experts on the Interpretation of Conventions and Recommendations, as the conclusion of a survey, recalled that the primary role of labour inspectors is to ensure the protection of the workers and not to implement national migration laws.[428] Also the CEACR has recalled in its individual communication submitted to the government of Cameroon that

> the fact that migrant workers are in an irregular situation will make it difficult to claim their rights, as the irregular situation may deter them from having recourse to the judiciary for fear of making their situation known to the authorities and hence incurring the risk of being expelled.[429]

At the same time, it must be considered that migrant workers become doubly vulnerable: they are at risk of losing their jobs and of being deported.

In light of this, the labour inspectors are identified as key actors in improving working conditions for this vulnerable group.[430] Even if the inclusion among their activities of monitoring legal status risks to undermining this role.. In particular the overlap between these different, and in a sense incompatible, functions may contravene the provisions of ILO Convention No. 181, on labour inspections.[431]

Finally, it is important to be mindful of the inefficacy of the sanction system in place, and to recall that "labour inspectors have a

427 *See* Wickramasekara, *supra* note 216, at 306–307.

428 ILO, *Labour Inspection: ILO Survey for the 96 Session of the International Labour Conference*, Geneva (2006).

429 CEACR, *Individual Communication on migrant workers, Cameroon*, 2009.

430 *See* Wickramasekara, *supra* note 216, at 306–307.

431 ILO, *Labour Inspection in Europe: undeclared work, migration and trafficking*, Geneva (2010), at 31. Among the guidelines adopted in this context: "Issues relating to migrant labour should be integrated in any definition or consideration of undeclared work. Undocumented migrant workers are a particularly vulnerable category of workers who often end up in undeclared situations. Labour inspectors should consult with migration authorities to guarantee the legitimate protection of migrant workers' rights–even in situations of illegal work".

key role to play to facilitate access for those workers and to collaborate with criminal justice authorities to adequately enforce sanctions".[432]

4.3. *Procedural rights*

4.3.1. *Due process*

Article 14 of the ICCPR provides that "all persons should be equal before the courts and tribunals" and by the virtue of this right "everyone shall have the right to recognition everywhere as a person before the law" (Art. 16). This right and the related obligations of governments necessitate the adoption of special measures to ensure that migrants have access to effective legal remedies and due process.[433] The ICMWR devoted Articles 18 and 24 to making this entitlement explicit. [434]

4.3.2. *Detention of irregular migrants*

At present, cases of arbitrary detention of irregular migrants during the migratory process or in their countries of destination have been recognized as among the main serious violations against and abuses

432 *See* ILO, *supra* note 431, at 17.

433 This provision has been violated in several cases; in particular the Human Rights Committee required the government of Jamaica to guarantee migrants with adequate access to national courts. Also several complaints were raised about the excessive length of proceedings in cases concerning the application of the death penalty (*Fuenzalida v. Equador* (Jul. 12, 1996), U.N. Doc. HRC 480/1991; *Barrosa Isidora v. Panama* (Jul. 19, 1995), U.N. Doc. HCR 478/1991; *Ben Said v. Norway* (Mar. 29. 2000), U.N. Doc. HCR 767/1997).

434 Art. 18 and art. 24.

of their right to liberty.[435] In the case of irregular migration, the majority of states have shown a clear tendency to prefer to detain irregular migrants or asylum seekers if they violate domestic migration law instead of considering alternative non-custodial measures.[436] In this context, it is relevant to highlight that the existing legal bases, both international and domestic, limit the discretionary authority of governments to legitimate the deprivation of individual liberty.

Article 9 of the ICCPR, reiterating what was previously formulated in Article 9 of the UDHR, [437] contains the fundamental principle that "everyone has the right to liberty and security of person. None shall be subjected to arbitrary arrest or detention. No one shall be deprived of his liberty except on such grounds and in accordance with such procedures as established by law." The provision formulates a non-exhaustive list of possible grounds for detention, but its content brings attention on two key criteria: any case of arbitrary detention is not permitted and the deprivation of liberty has to be in line with international standards.[438]

On the interpretation of these requirements

435 For a comprehensive analysis of this issue see GALINA CORNELISSE, IMMIGRATION DETENTION AND HUMAN RIGHTS (Martinus Nijoff Publishers, 2010).

436 SRHRM, *Report of the Special Rapporteur on the human rights of migrants, François Crépeau*, U.N. Doc. A/HCR/20/24 (Apr. 2, 2012).

437 Article 9: "No one shall be subject to arbitrary arrest, detention or exile".

438 This principle has been stated in several cases by the Human Rights Committee, see *Baban et al. v. Australia*, Comm. No. 1014/2001 (Aug. 2, 2003), U.N. Doc. CCPR/C/78/D/1014/2001. In this case an Afghan citizen and his son in irregular situation were detained in a prison in Australia for two years, and the Committee stated that "in the present case, the author's detention as a non-citizen without an entry permit continued, in mandatory terms, until he was removed or granted a permit. While the State party advances particular reasons to justify the individual detention [...] the Committee observes that the State party has failed to demonstrate that those reasons justified the applicant's continued detention in the light of the passage of time and intervening circumstances such as the hardship of prolonged detention for his son or the fact that during the period under review the State Party apparently did not remove Iraqis from Australia".

> (a) *Lawfulness* requires that detentions rest on such grounds and are carried out in accordance with procedure established by law. It transpires from the analysis of article 9, paragraph 1–and from all comparable provisions in the ICCPR–that the requirement, which a "law" has to meet, is that the national legislation must set down all permissible restrictions and conditions thereof. Therefore, the word "law" has to be understood in the strict sense of a parliamentary statute, or an equivalent unwritten norm of common law accessible to all individuals subject to the relevant jurisdiction. Hence, administrative provisions do not meet this requirement. Laws shall be couched in clear terms;
>
> (b) To comply with international standards it is not enough that the deprivation of liberty be provided by law; it must *not be arbitrary*, either. This requirement stems from article 9, paragraph 1, and its second sentence ("No one shall be subjected to arbitrary detention"). It transpires from all the ICCPR provisions making use of the term "arbitrary", or "arbitrarily", that the prohibition of arbitrariness shall be interpreted broadly. It is not possible, and in the view of the Working Group it is not necessary, to give an exhaustive list of arbitrary detention; arbitrariness must be assessed in the light of all the relevant circumstances of a given detention. The minimum requirement for respect by States of the prohibition of arbitrariness is that deprivation of liberty must not be manifestly disproportionate, unjust, unpredictable or discriminatory. Moreover, the detention is manifestly arbitrary if a person is deprived of his liberty on the pretext of his (alleged) mental disability, but it is obvious that he is detained on account of his political, ideological, or religious views, opinion, conviction or activity.[439]

The Working Group on Arbitrary Detentions recognized this provision as a principle of customary international law, applicable to all states.[440] This right also appears at Art. 5 of ICERD and Art. 16(1–4) of the ICMWR, which include the prohibition of the arbitrary arrest and deprivation of liberty of migrants, individually and collectively. Furthermore, a similar provision is of central importance in the protection of child migrants (Art. 37).[441] The SRHRM insisted that the

439 WGAD, *Report of the Working Group on Arbitrary Detention*, at 19, U.N. Doc. E/CN.4/2005/6 (Dec. 1, 2004). (Emphasis added by the author).

440 *Id.* at 17.

441 "No child shall be deprived of his or her liberty unlawfully or arbitrary. The arrest, detention or imprisonment of a child shall be in conformity with the

detention of migrant children, especially unaccompanied children, has to be considered as a measure of last resort.[442] The Committee on the Rights of the Child clarified that the best interest of the child must be the most important criterion in order to avoid detention of migrant children. In particular, the Committee on the Rights of the Child observed that their vulnerable situation requires the adoption of specific guarantees and conditions while detained to ensure the enjoyment of their fundamental rights (e.g. access to diplomatic protection, health care, and education).[443]

4.3.2.1. The Working Group on Arbitrary Detention (WGAD)[444]

The Commission on Human Rights, with the adoption of Resolution No. 1997/50, extended the mandate of the WGAD to monitor the detention of migrants and asylum seekers. On the basis of this decision (and even before), the WGAD gives a close attention to the situation of detained irregular migrants, to clarify matters of concern

---

law and shall be used only as a measure of last resort and for shortest appropriate period of time".

442 SRHRM, *Report of the Special Rapporteur on the human rights of migrants, Jorge Bustamante*, ¶45–80, U.N. Doc. A/HRC/11/7 (May 14, 2009).

443 *See* SRHRM, *supra* note 2, ¶62.

444 The Working Group on Arbitrary Detention has been created by the Commission on Human Rights with the adoption of the resolution 11991/42. The mandate of this body is to monitor cases of potential arbitrary detentions and deprivation of liberty. In light of its interpretation the following measures are considered arbitrary: "(i) When it manifestly cannot be justified on any legal basis (such as continued detention after the sentence has been served or despite an applicable amnesty act) (category I); (ii) When the deprivation of liberty is the result of a judgment or sentence for the exercise of the rights and freedoms proclaimed in articles 7, 13, 14, 18, 19, 20 and 21 of the Universal Declaration of Human Rights and also, in respect of States parties, in articles 12, 18, 19, 21, 22, 25, 26 and 27 of the International Covenant on Civil and Political Rights (category II); (iii) When the complete or partial non-observance of the international standards relating to a fair trial set forth in the Universal Declaration of Human Rights and in the relevant international instruments accepted by the States concerned is of such gravity as to confer on the deprivation of liberty, of whatever kind, an arbitrary character (category III)".

and to identify measures to avoid disproportional and arbitrary deprivation of liberty.[445] Several reports submitted by the WGAD to the General Assembly contain a specific section on immigration detention, and specific country visits have been made to investigate the situation of irregular migrants who are detained in the countries of destination or transit. The WGAD has developed substantial experience on this topic, explicitly addressed by its annual reports in 1998,[446] 2003,[447] 2005,[448]and 2008,[449] followed by the formulation of recommendations. In its last report the WGAD recalled that

445 WGAD, *Report of the Working Group on Arbitrary Detention–Malta,* at 23, U.N. Doc. A/HRC/13/30 (Jan. 18, 2010).

446 WGAD, *Report of the Working Group on Arbitrary Detention,* U.N. Doc. E/CN.4/1999/63 (Dec. 18, 1998).

447 The following recommendation has been adopted: "The Working Group considers that, even where illegal immigrants and asylum-seekers are concerned, any decision to place them in detention must be reviewed by a court or a competent, independent and impartial body in order to ensure that it is necessary and in conformity with the norms of international law and that, where people have been detained, expelled or returned without being provided with legal guarantees, their continued detention and subsequent expulsion are to be considered as arbitrary". WGAD, *Report of the Working Group on Arbitrary Detention,* at 23, U.N. Doc. E/CN.4/2004/3 (Dec. 15, 2003).

448 The following recommendation has been adopted: "With regard to detention of illegal immigrants and asylum-seekers, the Working Group urges Governments to ensure that the right to challenge the lawfulness of detention is, in practice, guaranteed to any foreign national detained under their immigration law. It further recommends that the detention of asylum-seekers remain exceptional and not mandatory and that, when detained, they be maintained separate from convicts". WGAD, *Report of the Working Group on Arbitrary Detention,* at 24, U.N. Doc. E/CN.4/2006/7 (Dec. 12, 2005).

449 The report allowed the raising of several concerns related to the length of immigration detention: "It was felt that States should be reminded that detention shall be the last resort and permissible only for the shortest period of time and that alternatives to detention should be sought whenever possible. Grounds for detention must be clearly and exhaustively defined and the legality of detention must be open for challenge before a court and regular review within fixed time limits. Established time limits for judicial review must even stand in 'emergency situations' when an exceptionally large number of undoc-

during the period reported upon, a development yet again towards tightening restrictions, including deprivation of liberty, applied to asylum-seekers, refugees and immigrants in an irregular situation even to the extent of making the irregular entry into a State a criminal offence or qualifying the irregular stay in the country as an aggravating circumstance for any criminal offence.[450]

In 1999 the WGAD adopted the Deliberation No. 5 on the detention of irregular migrants and asylum seekers into their normative actions.[451] In particular

> Principle 3: Any asylum-seeker or immigrant placed in custody must be brought promptly before a judicial or other authority; [...]
> Principle 7: A maximum period should be set by law and the custody may in no case be unlimited or of excessive length;
> Principle 8: Notification of the custodial measure must be given in writing, in a language understood by the asylum-seeker or immigrant, stating the grounds for the measure; it shall set out the conditions under which the asylum-seeker or immigrant must be able to apply for a remedy to a judicial authority, which shall decide promptly on the lawfulness of the measure and, where appropriate, order the release of the person concerned.[452]

*** *** ***

---

umented immigrants enter the territory of a State. Provisions should always be made to render detention unlawful if the obstacle for identifying immigrants in an irregular situation or carrying out removal from the territory does not lie within their sphere, for example, when the consular representation of the country of origin does not cooperate or legal considerations–such as the principle of *non-refoulement* barring removal if there is a risk of torture or arbitrary detention in the country of destination–or factual". WGAD, *Report of the Working Group on Arbitrary Detention*, at 23, U.N. Doc. A/HRC/10/21 (Feb. 16, 2009).

450 *Id.* at 23.

451 WGAD, *Deliberation No. 5: Situation regarding immigrants and asylum-seekers*, U.N. Doc. E/CN.4/2000/4 (Dec. 28, 1999). This deliberation contains ten principles divided into procedural guarantees for the arrest (1–5) and procedural guarantees for the detention (6–10). In addition, the report adopted on 15 January 2010 confirmed the need to identify alternative measures to detention among the main objectives of the WGAD.

452 *See* WGAD, *supra* note 451, at 22.

The following opinions adopted by the WGAD have been particularly relevant (37/2007,[453] 45/2006,[454] 18/2004,[455] and 34/1999[456]) in the interpretation of the criteria of proportionality and arbitrariness in the immigration detentions:

Opinion No. 37 of 2007 adopted against the United States. In this case a Thai citizen was put into detention for more than five years to decide his request for international protection as a refugee. He argued that this detention resulted in deterioration of his physical and mental health. With regard to the arbitrariness, the application of the principle of proportionality was invoked. There was insufficient justification for the duration of his detention: he was not a risk to the national public order and security, and he had not been condemned for any crime. According to the information provided, his request to be extradited to Thailand has been accepted, and it seemed that this administrative detention was justified until he was removed. Against this backdrop, the WGAD considered this detention as arbitrary.

Opinion 45/2006 against the United Kingdom. This case concerned the detention of a Somaliland citizen, an asylum seeker, who entered in the territory of the UK in 2002. During his stay he was arrested and condemned for the alleged rape of a child and the government, according to its migration law, detained him for the purpose of sending him back to his country of origin. He has been detained for four-and-a-half years. According to the circumstances of this case, the WGAD noted that the duration of the deprivation of his liberty appeared excessive and that the scope of this detention not appropriately justified. On this last point, it was clear that his return to Somalia was a "remote" hypothesis to make this condition as an

453 WGAD, *Opinion 37/2007, United States* (Feb. 4, 2009), U.N. Doc. A/HRC/10/21/Add.1.

454 WGAD, *Opinion 45/2006, United Kingdom and Northern Ireland* (Nov. 19, 2004), U.N. Doc A/HRC/7/4/Add.1.

455 WGAD, *Opinion 18/2004, United States* (Nov. 19, 2004), U.N. Doc E/CN.4/2005/6/Add.1.

456 WGAD, *Opinion 34/1999, United States* (Nov. 9, 2000), U.N. Doc E/CN.4/2001/14/Add.1.

indefinite deprivation of his liberty. In its conclusions the WGAD insisted that Art. 9 of ICCPR prohibited situations of indefinite detention as violating the criterion of proportionality, which requires a maximum period of time to set by national provisions.

Opinion 18/2004 against the United States. An Algerian citizen, who regularly entered the United States, asked for international protection as an asylum seeker and after the expiration of his residence permit tried to enter Canada. The American authorities arrested him and he was detained for nearly three years. In this period of time, he was charged with terrorism, even if there was not sufficient evidence to prove this crime, according to the WGAD. In addition, he was not able to get access to procedural guarantees, as to apply for remedy to a national judge. In light of the above, the Working Group considered the detention to be arbitrary and in violation of the provisions of Articles 9 and 14 of the ICCPR.

Opinion 34/99 against the United States. A Cuban citizen, a refugee, was condemned for drug possession to thirty-seven years imprisonment. After his time was served, the government decided to extend his detention based on domestic migration provisions. In this case it was impossible to return him to his country of origin, so the national authorities decided to continue his detention. The WGAD found this detention arbitrary given the length of the time (up to five years) and the absence of concrete chances of removal.

*** *** ***

In light of these cases, it is clear how discretionary use and normative gaps in the identification of conditions for immigration detention of irregular migrants may result in unlawful detention that violates detainees' fundamental rights.[457] The legal norms available do not pro-

457 According to the jurisprudence developed by the ECHR on the interpretation of Art. 5(f), the decision to detain an irregular migrant has to be taken after a deep evaluation of his/her individual case (*Saadi v. United Kingdom*, 11 July 2006, req. No. 1329/03; *Vasileva v. Denmark*, 25 September 2003, req No. 52792/99; *Jecius v. Lithuania*, 31 July 2000, req. No. 34578/97; *Mansur v. Turkey*, 8 June 1995, req. No. 16026/90; *Litwa v. Poland*, 4 April 2000, req. No. 26629/95). In the case *Ali v. Switzerland*, 5 August 1998, req. No. 24881/94,

vide any such limitation to the state's authority to "resort to immigration detention as such".[458]

At the same, the international community is devoting a growing attention to the need to identify and elaborate alternative measures, as highlighted by the SRHRM in his annual report,[459] to reduce and eventually abolish immigration detention. In this vein, several scholars argue that in the absence of criminal charges there can no longer be a justification for depriving migrants of their liberty. That said, the criminalization of irregular migration to legitimate these arbitrary practices goes far beyond national prerogatives and concerns the regulation of migratory flows. As clearly illustrated by Dr. Martens, this uncertain situation risks consolidating the emergence of a new category in addition to the detainee: the "*retenu*" (restrained). This individual is not suspected of criminal acts, but at the same time does not have access to the procedural safeguards related to his or her status as detainee.[460] The circumstances illustrated stress the need to respect the principle of proportionality in each case of arrest or detention of migrants. [461] At administrative level, governments have to

---

the Court found the use of detention to extradite a Somaliland national from Switzerland to Somalia non-proportionate, considering the political background, and did not allow extradition. Also in the case *Singh v. Czech Republic*, 25 January 2005, req. No. 60538/00, the Court found a violation of Art. 5(f) on the part of the Czech Republic for delaying contact with Indian authorities to get the necessary travel documents for deportation.

458 Shyla Vohra, *Detention of irregular migrants and asylum*, *in* INTERNATIONAL MIGRATION LAW, DEVELOPING PARADIGMS AND KEY CHALLENGE 49 (Ryszard Cholewinski, Richard Perrouchoud, & Euan MacDonald eds., Asser Press, 2007). *See* CORNELISSE, *supra* note 435, at 254.

459 SRHRM, *Report of the Special Rapporteur on the human rights of migrants, François Crépeau*, ¶ 48–67, U.N. Doc. A/HCR/20/24 (Apr. 2, 2012).

460 *See* Martens, *supra* note 173, at 606.

461 On the interpretation of the principle of proportionality *see* the Communication of the European Parliament concerning the situation of irregular migrants and the related adoption of the Return Directive 2008/115/EC on 16 December 2008: "Proportionality of detention (article 15). We would like to emphasize that irregular immigrants are not criminals. As a rule they should not be subjected to detention at all. States may only revert to detention as a

justify detention as a last resort and exclude the adoption of other alternative measures.[462] To this end, the Human Right Committee interpreted the concrete prospect of return as a tangible part of the principle of proportionality.[463]

In this context, the WGAD has observed during its mission how detention conditions are deteriorating in states that understand these measures as obligatory and apply them automatically. In addition, the conclusions adopted by the WGAD after its visit to Malta insisted on the vulnerable situation of irregular migrants and detainees in all circumstances (e.g. irregular entry or stay) without any distinction on individual basis.

> Vulnerable migrants in an irregular situation, such as families with children, unaccompanied minors, pregnant women, breastfeeding mothers, persons with disabilities, elderly persons, or people with serious and/or chronic physical or mental health problems, are also subjected to mandatory detention when arriving to Malta. They are released from detention under a fast-track procedure once the competent Government agency, the Organization for the Integration and Welfare of Asylum Seekers, has assessed their situation and determined that they are indeed vulnerable.[464]

---

measure of last resort pursuant to a strict application of the principle of proportionality". SRHRM, *Report of the Special Rapporteur on the human rights of migrants, Jorge Bustamante, Summary of cases transmitted to Governments and replies received*, 26, U.N. Doc. A/HRC/11/7/Add.1 (May 20, 2009).

462 "In the Committee's opinion, court review of the lawfulness of detention under article 9, paragraph 4, which must include the possibility of ordering release, is not limited to mere compliance of the detention with domestic law. While domestic legal systems may institute differing methods for ensuring court review of administrative detention, what is decisive for the purposes of article 9, paragraph 4, is that such review is, in its effects, real and not merely formal." (para. 9.5). *A v. Australia,* Comm. No. 560/1993 (Apr. 30, 1997), U.N. Doc. CCPR/C/59/D/560/1993. OHCHR, *Expulsion of Aliens in International Human Rights Law*, OHCHR Discussion paper, Geneva (September 2006).

463 *See* A v. Australia, *supra* note 462; *see* CORNELISSE, *supra* note 435, at 252.

464 WGAD, *Report of the Working Group on Arbitrary Detention, Malta,* ¶41, U.N. Doc. A/HRC/13/30/Add.2 (Jan. 18, 2010).

Another major issue of concern with the detention of irregular migrants is that these measures are exclusively at the mercy of the state authority and discretion. The WGAD insisted on the need to review domestic standards and to provide clear limitations to maximum periods of detention.

Finally, Art. 9(4) of the ICCPR explicitly illustrates the procedural guarantees that migrants detainees are to enjoy, in particular the right to access judicial remedies.[465] In several cases migrants reported that they lacked complaint mechanisms against unlawful detention decisions adopted by national authority. Due to the above-mentioned critical situations, there exists a need for the elaboration of coherent legal framework for avoiding human rights violations.

4.3.4. The principle of non-refoulement

The principle of *non-refoulement*, recognized as a cornerstone principle of humanitarian law and international refugee law,[466] is also a key component of the protection mechanisms in place under human rights law.[467] According to this principle states are obligated not to expel, return, or remove a migrant to his or her country of origin if there are "substantial grounds of believing" [468] that the individual

465 "Legal aid for migrants in an irregular situation exists in theory only. Public lawyers are available from a pool designated solely for the asylum procedure. For detention related challenges, there are a very limited number of civil society lawyers available. Legal aid for filing a case in court is virtually inaccessible to the detainees. Persons seeking legal aid have to present their case at the Office of the Advocate for Legal Aid, situated in the Law Courts, which is impossible for detainees. The few cases challenging immigration detention that have been brought before the courts to date were handled by civil society organizations without the benefit of a waiver of court fees". *Id.* ¶46.

466 Article 33 of the Refugees Convention 1958, and article 45(4) of the Geneva Convention Concerning the Protection of Civilians in Time of War, 1940.

467 *See* Chetail, *supra* note 104, at 79.

468 For a detailed analysis of this topic *see* Chetail, *supra* note 357, at 75–80.

could be subjected to torture or other inhuman treatments.[469] The prohibition and prevention of torture represents the privileged vector for affirming this principle in the context of human rights.[470] The principle of *non-refoulement* is also considered a part of customary international law. Article 3(1) of the Convention Against Torture and Other Inhuman or Degrading Treatment or Punishments provides the obligation not to return an individual to a country where he or she is at risk of being subjected to ill-treatment,[471] and also Articles 6[472] and 7[473] of the ICCPR. The CAT considers that

469 The African Commission on Human and Peoples' rights included the prohibition of expulsion of an individual to a country where he or she could be subjected to torture in the interpretation of the Art. 5 of the African Charter on Human and Peoples' Rights, *Modise v. Botswana,* Comm. No. 97/93 (1997 and 2000).

470 This is also in line with the jurisprudence developed by the European Court on Human Rights, in particular in the case *Soering v. United Kingdom,* 7 July 1989, the Court stated that the interpretation of Art. 3 do not allow expelling a migrant if he or she is at risks of degrading treatments, *see Cruz Varas et al. v. Switzerland,* 20 March 1991, A/201; *Chahal v. United Kingdom*, 15 November 1996, rep. 1996–V; *Mamaktulov and Abdurasulovic v. Turkey*, 6 February 2003, Commm. No. 46827/99 and 46951/99.

471 Article 3(1): "1. No State Party shall expel, return (*'refouler'*) or extradite a person to another State where there are substantial grounds for believing that he would be in danger of being subjected to torture".

472 Article 6: "1. Every human being has the inherent right to life. This right shall be protected by law. No one shall be arbitrarily deprived of his life. 2. In countries which have not abolished the death penalty, sentence of death may be imposed only for the most serious crimes in accordance with the law in force at the time of the commission of the crime and not contrary to the provisions of the present Covenant and to the Convention on the Prevention and Punishment of the Crime of Genocide. This penalty can only be carried out pursuant to a final judgment rendered by a competent court. 3. When deprivation of life constitutes the crime of genocide, it is understood that nothing in this article shall authorize any State Party to the present Covenant to derogate in any way from any obligation assumed under the provisions of the Convention on the Prevention and Punishment of the Crime of Genocide. 4. Anyone sentenced to death shall have the right to seek pardon or commutation of the sentence. Amnesty, pardon or commutation of the sentence of death may be

> [i]t would recall that the protection accorded by article 3 of the Convention is absolute. Whenever there are substantial grounds for believing that a particular person would be in danger of being subjected to torture if he was expelled to another State, the State party is required not to return that person to that State.[474]

All migrants, including irregular migrants, are entitled to invoke this principle. In addition, the CAT in several individual cases addressed the need to take under consideration the general socio-political context of the country of origin in views of factors that are particular to an individual request not to be returned. In this regard, the CAT considered as insufficient the occurrence of mass violations in the country of destination to limit the state's power to return an irregular migrant.[475] Finally, the CAT in the case *Mutombo v. Switzerland* affirmed that return decisions may not be carried out if there is a grounded

---

granted in all cases. 5. Sentence of death shall not be imposed for crimes committed by persons below eighteen years of age and shall not be carried out on pregnant women. 6. Nothing in this article shall be invoked to delay or to prevent the abolition of capital punishment by any State Party to the present Covenant."

473 Article 7: "No one shall be subjected to torture or to cruel, inhuman or degrading treatment or punishment. In particular, no one shall be subjected without his free consent to medical or scientific experimentation".

474 *Aemei v. Switzerland*, Comm. No. 34/1995 (May 29, 1997), U.N. Doc. CAT/C/18/D/34/1995.

474 *Mutombo v. Switzerland*, Comm. No. 13/1993 (Apr. 7, 1994), U.N. Doc. CAT/C/12/D/13/1993; *Arana v. France*, Comm. No. 63/1997 (Jun. 5, 2000), U.N. Doc. CAT/C/23/D/63/1997; *K.N. v. Switzerland*, Comm. No. 94/1997 (May 20, 1998), U.N. Doc. CAT/C/20/D/94/1997; *N.P. v. Australia*, Comm. No. 106/1998 (Jun. 3, 1999), U.N. Doc. CAT/C/22/D/106/1998; *M.S. v. Switzerland*, Comm. No. 156/2000 (Nov. 13, 2001), U.N. Doc. CAT/CC/267/ D/156/2000; *M.M.P.S. v. Australia*, Comm. No. 138 /1999 (Apr. 30, 2002), U.N. Doc. CAT/C/28/D/138/1999; *M.A.K. v. Germany*, Comm. No. 214/2000 (May 12, 2004), U.N. Doc. CAT/C/D/214/2000; *Brada v. France*, Comm. No. 195/2002 (May 17, 2005), U.N. Doc. CAT/C/D/195/2002; *Z.T. v. Norway*, Comm. No. 238/2003 (Nov. 14, 2005), U.N. Doc. CAT/C/D/238/2003; *Dadar v. Canada*, Comm. No. 258/2004 (Nov. 23, 2005), U.N. Doc. CAT/C/D/258/2004.

risk that the individual be subjected to torture if he/she is to be returned to his/her country of origin.[476]

Finally, the Human Rights Committee, in General Comment No. 15, considered a broad number of situations where the national power to expel foreigners is limited, but it did not allude to the principle of *non-refoulement.* Originally, the scope of the prohibition of inhuman and degrading treatment referred only to the right to entry and stay, before starting to elaborate its own jurisprudence.[477]

4.3.5. Expulsion and procedural guarantees

Expulsion measures have attracted growing attention at the international level, as many states have identified them as the most effective tool to prevent migration and to regulate international migration flows.[478] From a legal perspective, the challenge is to understand the impact on the growing discrepancy between the discretionary exercise of states' prerogatives to protect national interest and security and the difficulties migrants face in protecting their basic rights.

Preliminary, the term "expulsion" refers to the adoption by national authority of a judicial or administrative measure to oblige an individual to leave, through voluntary or coercive enforcement, the

476 *See* Mutombo v. Switzerland, *supra note 474,* ¶9–10. *See ex multis, Korban v. Switzerland*, Comm. No. 88 (1997), U.N. Doc. CAT/C/21D/88/1997; *Tebourski v. France*, Comm. No. 20/2006 (May 1, 2007), U.N. Doc. CAT/C/D/300/2006. In this case the applicant asked to be returned to a third country, not Tunisia, his country of origin, and France rejected his request. The HRC considered this rejection apt to increase the risk of a violation of Art. 3 refusing to adopt a common practice in similar cases.

477 HRC, *General Comment No. 15: The position of aliens under the Covenant*, U.N. Doc. HRI/GEN/1/Rev. 6 (Apr. 11, 1986).

478 Giorgio Gaja, *Expulsion of Aliens: some old and new issues in International Law, in* CURSOS EUROMEDITERRANEOS BANCAJA DE DERECHO INTERNATIONAL, Centro International Bancaja para la Paz y el Desarollo, Castello, Volume III (1999), at 289.

territory of the country concerned. According to Art. 13[479] of the ICCPR, the expulsion procedures require, above all respecting the dignity of migrants to be treated as human beings.[480] In that case it still has to be in line with several procedural guarantees, specifically the respect of due process,[481] and taking into consideration all individual circumstances (including health and the risk of being subjected to ill-treatment in the country of origin) that would justify not proceeding with return.[482] The Committee on Migrant Workers, in its concluding observations on the report submitted to the government of Colombia, insisted that any measures of expulsion need to be taken in full respect of procedural guarantees.

479 "An alien lawfully in the territory of a state party [...] may be expelled there from only in pursuance of a decision reached in accordance with law".

480 On this theme the ECHR established an extensive jurisprudence, giving a broad description of relevant principles and norms. Article 5(f) contains the possibility of detaining an individual before the removal. The formulation of this article is the result of the temptation to balance the principle of sovereignty and the right to liberty. In this regard the ECHR specified that safeguards and guarantees have to be in place to preserve the physical and psychological health of the detained (*Dougoz v. Greece*, Mar. 6, 2001, Report 2001-II, ¶46); to have access to judicial remedies (*Slivenko v. Latvia*, Oct. 9, 2003, Request No. 48321/99, ¶158); the detention procedure has to be proportional and lawful (*Chahal v. United Kingdom*, Nov. 15, 1996, ¶113; *Bozano v. France*, 18 December 1986, A/111, ¶54; *Shamsa et al. v. Poland*, Nov. 27, 2003, req. No. 45355/99 e 45357/99, ¶55–58); in addition the member states have to implement their obligation even the migrants are detained at the airport on an a transit area, because for these situations the principle of extra-territoriality could not be applied. (*Amuur v. France*, Jun. 25, 1996, rep. 1996–III, ¶52).

481 "[I]llegal entrants and aliens who have stayed longer than the law or their permits allow", *see* HRC, *supra* note 477, ¶9.

482 The HRC states: "if the legality of an alien's entry or stay is in dispute, any decision on this point leading an expulsion or deportation ought to be taken in accordance with article 13. It is for the competent authorities of the state party, in good faith and in the exercise of their power, to apply and interpret the domestic law, observing, however, such requirements under the Covenant as equality before the law (art. 26)". *See* HRC, *supra* note 477, ¶9.

(a)That, in all cases, interested parties have the right to submit the reasons why they should not be expelled and to have their case reviewed by the competent authority, unless compelling reasons of national security require otherwise;
(b)The right to seek a stay of the decision of expulsion, pending the review mentioned in the above subparagraph;
(c)The right to seek compensation if a decision of expulsion that has already been executed is subsequently annulled.[483]

As mentioned before, the ways in which migrants are arrested and then detained before expulsions[484] has called attention to the political and legal debates that formed as a reaction to the abusive practices developed by a number of states.[485]

Theoretically, the principle of the absolute prohibition of torture and any degrading and inhuman treatments, as illustrated by Art. 7 of ICCPR, limits the discretionary use of coercive measures of member

483 CMW, *Consideration of reports submitted by states parties under article 74 of the convention, Concluding observations of the Committee on the Protection of the Rights of All Migrant Workers and Members of Their Families, Colombia*, ¶28, U.N. Doc. CMW/C/COL/CO/1 (May 22, 2009).

484 On this issue the jurisprudence developed by the ECHR recognized the use of force by the police in case of arrests as circumstances integrating the hypothesis of inhuman and degrading treatments if they cause moral and physical suffering (*Ribitich v. Austria*, Dec. 4, 1995, req. No. 18896/91; *Hurtado v. Switzerland*, Jan. 28, 1994, req. No. 17549/90). As in the case *Selmouni v. France*, Jul. 28, 1999, req. No. 25803/94, the abuses of the police was retained as a violation of Art. 3.

485 The Committee Against Torture in its concluding observations raised several concerns on the mechanisms in place to monitor expulsion procedures and their effectiveness with regard to the respect of human rights. Similarly, the Migrant Worker Committee considered particularly serious the situation of migrants detained in Egypt, where they were "arrested without warrant and if they are unable to show valid identity documents, are detained by law enforcement officials and allegedly sometimes subjected to torture or ill-treatment". CMW, *Concluding observations of the Committee on the Protection of the Rights of All Migrant Workers and Members of Their Families, Egypt*, ¶29, U.N. Doc. CMW/C/EGY/CO/1 (May 25, 2007).

states.[486] This principle is also complemented by procedural guarantees provided by the ICCPR concerning the detention of migrants, as detailed above.

The Migrant Workers Committee has on several occasions stated that all public officers, especially those employed in prisons, have to be trained on human rights standards and on the respect of the principle of non-discrimination on the basis of ethnic and racial origins.[487] This would reinforce the protections of the right of child migrants not to be deported, unless the best interest of the children requires it.[488]

4.3.5.1. Prohibition of collective expulsions of migrants

Collective expulsions are expressly prohibited by international law. The general principle requires that during expulsion procedures, the personal circumstances of each individual have to be taken under consideration.[489]

This principle is contained in Art. 22 of the ICMWR.[490] This provision adopts an innovative perspective to call attention to the

486 The Human Rights Committee states: "States parties must not expose individuals to the danger of torture or cruel, inhuman or degrading treatment or punishment upon return to another country by way of their extradition or *refoulement*", HRC, *General Comment No. 7: Article 7 (Prohibition of Torture or Cruel, Inhuman or Degrading Treatment or Punishment)*, U.N. Doc. HRI/GEN/1/Rev.6 (May 30, 1982).

487 *See* CMW, *supra* note 485, ¶29.

488 *See* Eur. Ct. H.R., *Mubilanzila Mayeka and Kaniti Mitunga v. Belgium* (No. 13178/03, 12 October 2006). In this case the Court issued that the expulsion procedure needs to respect the fundamental rights of migrants. In particular to take under consideration the risk of ill-treatment for children to be deported and detained before removal in a detention centre without any support. In this case the Court found that the Belgian legislation was not in line with the international human rights principles.

489 OHCHR, *Expulsion of aliens in international human rights law*, OHCHR Discussion paper, Geneva (September 2006).

490 Article 22: "Migrant workers and members of their families shall not be subject to measures of collective expulsions. Each case of expulsion shall be examined and decided individually".

vulnerable situation of irregular migrants. During the expulsion proceedings, all migrants must be informed of their rights and the procedural guarantees that proceedings be held before a judge to decide on the lawfulness of the expulsion, and that the migrants be allowed to be in contact with their national diplomatic authorities.

On this issue the Inter-American Commission on Human Rights adopted two measures, on 18 August and 12 November 2000,[491] in response to the request by the Commission to urgently react against the Dominican Republic concerning the collective expulsion of irregular Haitian workers and irregular Haitian-origin Dominicans. The case concerned the massive expulsion of more than 100,000 individuals. The deportations were made at night, without following any legal procedures for identifying the victims of these orders. The expellees were deprived of the possibility of informing their families or bringing their belongings with them. When confronted with these serious abuses, the Dominican Republic invoked economic reasons to justify the adoption of these measures and relied on its sovereign authority to execute such expulsions. The Court rejected the claims of the government on the principle of sovereignty, declaring that the adoption of such an order of expulsion can only be made by a competent authority. The formulation and execution of national migratory policies cannot be conducted in violation of the principle of non-discrimination based on the colour or the race. It was clear in this case the only criteria adopted was the colour of their skin; under the circumstances being "black" was considered sufficient to declare them to be Haitian or of Haitian origin and therefore to be irregularly present in the territory of the Dominican Republic.[492] Similarly the

491 Inter-American Court of Human Rights, *Dominical Republic case. Case of Haitian and Haitian-Origin Dominican Persons in the Dominican Republic (Provisional Measures requested by the Inter-American Commission on Human Rights in the matter of the Dominican Republic)*, 18 August and 12 November 2000.

492 *See* Scalabrino, *supra* note 347. *Andric v. Sweden*, Febr. 23, 1999, req. No. 45917/99. In the *Conka* case the Court found a violation of Art. 4, Additional Protocol No. 4, on the basis that the measure of expulsion was adopted without ensuring all safeguard procedures and taking under consideration the individual situation. *Conka v. Belgium*, Feb. 5, 2002, req. No. 51564/99.

International Law Commission stated that "the expulsion of aliens who are minor children, particularly those who are not accompanied by family members, has raised serious concerns in the International community. The expulsion of such aliens may be prohibited, or permitted on very limited grounds".[493]

4.3.5.2. Readmission agreements

Readmission agreements are important instruments of the European Union's border strategy for addressing "illegal" migration, involving undertakings, presumably reciprocal ones, by the European Union and third countries to facilitate the return of irregular migrants to their countries of origin or transit.[494] The main objective is to "facilitate and expedite the enforcement of return decisions in respect of irregular migrants and may also function as an incentive for countries of origin or transit to enhance their migration control".[495]

493 International Law Commission, *Expulsion of Aliens: Memorandum by the Secretariat*, ¶826, U.N. Doc. A/CN.4/565 (August, 2006). On this point, *see* also the Inter-American Court "any decision pertaining the separation of a child from his or her family must be justified by the best interest of the child". I/A Court H.R, *Juridical condition and Human rights of child, Advisory opinion OC-17/02*, 28 August 2002, Inter-Am. Ct. H.R., No. 17 (2002), ¶71.

494 Marion Panizzon, *Readmission Agreements of EU Member States: a case for EU Subsidiarity or Dualism*, 31(4) REFUGEE SURVEY QUARTERLY (forthcoming 2012); NILS COLEMAN, EUROPEAN READMISSION POLICY THIRD COUNTRY INTERESTS AND REFUGEE RIGHTS (London, Martinus Nijhoff Publishers, 2009); Catherine Withol De Wenden, *Les enjeux fondamentaux du renvoi de étrangers dans une perspective européenne et internationale*, *in* LES RENVOIS ET LEUR EXÉCUTION. PERSPECTIVES INTERNATIONALE, EUROPÉENNE ET SUISSE 4 (Cesla Amarelle & Minh Son Nguyen eds., Stampfli, 2011); Jean-Pierre Cassarino, *Readmission Policy in the European Union*, Directorate General for Internal Policies, Policy Department C: Citizens' Rights and Constitutional Affairs, Civil Liberties, Justice and Home Affairs, Brussels, European Parliament, Sep. 2010, *available at* <http://cadmus.eui.eu/bitstream/handle/1814/14957/EP_ReadmissionPolicy_en.pdf?sequence=4> (last visited Jun. 20, 2012); STEVE PEERS, EU JUSTICE AND HOME AFFAIRS LAW 586-589 (Oxford University Press, 2011).

495 Parliamentary Assembly, *Readmission agreements: a mechanism for returning irregular migrants*, Resolution 1741 (2010), adopted on 22 June 2010 (22nd Sitting).

Since 2007, European Union has started to conclude and negotiate readmission agreements that include third-country nationals. In this analysis, it is relevant to focus on the rights of these third-country nationals.[496] A particular question that I would like to discuss is whether the conclusion and implementation of readmission agreements could raise human rights concerns when applied to this group.[497] In fact, returning irregular migrants to countries other than their countries of origin might risk exposing them to violation of their human rights or leaving them unable to claim their specific rights and placing them in a vulnerable situation.[498]

Most readmission agreements contain "non-affection clauses" which provide that this particular instrument "shall be without prejudice to the right, obligations and responsibilities of the Community, the Member States and [the partner] arising from International Law".[499] Since 2004, the Commission reworded the original clause[500] to include explicit reference to international human rights instruments, such as the European Convention on Human Rights and the 1984 United Nations Torture Convention.

496 Kay Hailbronner, *Readmission Agreements and the obligations on States under Public International Law to Readmit their Own and Foreign Nationals*, 57 ZEITSCHRIFT FÜR AUSLÄNDISCHES ÖFFENTLICHES RECHT UND VÖLKERRECHT 1 (1997); Francesco Maiani, *Le droit communautaire et l'éloignement des ressortissants de pays tiers– vers des procédures de retour communes?*, *in* JAHRBUCH FÜR MIGRATIONSRECHT 2006/2007 69–96 (Alberto Achermann, Maria Caroni, Astrid Epiney, Walter Kälin, Minhn Son Nguyen & Peter Übersax eds., Stämpfli, 2007).

497 Gregor Noll, *Readmission Agreements, in*, IMMIGRATION AND ASYLUM: FROM 1900 TO PRESENT 495–497 (Matthew Gibney & Hansen Randall eds., ABC-CLIO, 2005).

498 This particular issue was raised by the European Commission, *Communication from the Commission to the European Parliament and the Council-Evaluation of EU Readmission Agreements*, COM(2011) 76 final, 23 Feb. 2011.

499 Carole Billet, *EC Readmission Agreements: A prime instrument of the external dimension of the EU's fight against irregular immigration. An assessment after ten years of practice*, 12 EUROPEAN JOURNAL OF MIGRATION AND LAW 72 (2010).

500 In the first clause, included in the first three agreements, no specific instruments were enumerated and this clause seemed to be too general.

This aspect must to be considered if the readmitting state fails to respect its international obligations, as highlighted by Tineke Strik, Rapporteur of the Committee on Migration, Refugees and Population:[501] "A starting point should be that sending countries make sure, when negotiating readmission agreements, that the relevant international instruments are ratified by receiving countries, but also that they are correctly implemented."

In this regard, it is interesting to recall the specific provisions adopted by Resolution 1741 (2010), titled "Readmission agreements: a mechanism for returning irregular migrants", which at Article 6 explicitly call for concluding readmission agreements only with countries "that comply with international human rights standards". These would include *inter alia* the 1951 Geneva Convention Relating to the Status of Refugees and the obligations established by the European Convention on Human Rights; to avoid the risk of breaching international standards, the sending countries also have the responsibility to evaluate the situation in receiving countries, for example if they might return irregular migrants to a country where they would lack access to the asylum procedure.[502] It would be helpful to recall also the extraterritorial effect of the provisions included in international human rights instruments, such as the International Covenant on Civil and Political Rights that arise when a state party adopts measures having an effect on individuals in the territory of another state.[503] As stated by McGoldrick, in the case of a state party deporting or expelling an individual within its territory to a state where there is a risk that the expellee would face treatment contrary to the provisions of the Covenant, this action can

501 Parliamentary Assembly, Committee on Migration, Refugees and Population, *Report, Readmission agreements: a mechanism of returning irregular migrants*, Doc. 12168 (Mar. 16, 2010), ¶37.

502 Nazare Albuquerque Abell, *The Compatibility of Readmission Agreements with the 1951 Convention relating to the Status of Refugees*, 11(1) INTERNATIONAL JOURNAL OF REFUGEE LAW 60 (1999); *See* Noll, *supra* note 497, at 496.

503 *See* for a comprehensive analysis BERNARD RYAN & VALSAMIS MITSILEGAS (EDS.), EXTRATERRITORIAL IMMIGRATION CONTROL, LEGAL CHALLENGES (Martinus Nijhoff Publishers, Leiden/Boston, 2010).

be a violation of the state party's own obligations under the Covenant,[504] as affirmed by the Human Rights Committee: "if a state party extradites a person within its jurisdiction in such circumstances, and if, as a result there is a real risk that his or her rights under the Covenant will be violated in another jurisdiction, the State party itself may be in violation of the Covenant."[505]

504 Dominic McGoldrick, *The European Convention on human rights and extraterritorial jurisdiction: a comment on life after Bankovic*, *in* EXTRATERRITORIAL APPLICATION OF HUMAN RIGHTS TREATIES 54 (Fons Coomans & Menno T. Kamminga eds., Intersentia, 2004).

505 *Kindler v. Canada*, Comm. No. 470/1991, ¶13.2, (Jul. 30, 1993), U.N. Doc. CCPR/C/48/D/470/1991.

Section II
The irregularity of migration issues in Morocco

5. Contextualization of migration issues in Morocco

This section attempts to provide a comprehensive introduction, not from an exclusively legal perspective, of the dynamics and challenges raised by migration in Morocco.

The first section comprised a detailed analysis of the influence of international law on the protection of human rights with respect to migration issues. As noted above, despite the protection of such rights being entirely subject to the state authority, today there hardly seems to be any sovereign principles without limits in this context. Gradually the migrant as individual has become a subject of rights and this erosion of sovereignty, as introduced above, has affected many normative and political aspects of migration. What is of interest is to deeply understand and to explore the effective role of domestic law, questioning the national reality in the context of Morocco as a state and identifying in what form the principle of national sovereignty, with respect to control of migration, is diminished by the resistances that exist in the protection of the migrant rights.[506]

506 *See* preliminary observations conducted by the Intergovernmental Working Group of Experts on the Human Rights of Migrants: "With regard to the measures being taken on the rights of migrants, a distinction should be made between legal/judicial measures and other measures. The trends indicated that in general, most legislation in this area was recent or even still in the process of being drafted, and that legislation tended to be framed in general terms and was compartmentalized. Not all States had the same position with regard to international law. Some States were very open to incorporating international law into domestic legislation, whereas others remained committed to a focus on their own domestic legislation." Commission on Human Rights, 54th Session, *Report of the working group of intergovernmental experts on the human rights of Migrants Measures to improve the situation and ensure the Human Rights and Dignity of all Migrant Workers*, ¶67, U.N. Doc. E/CN.4/1998/76 (Mar. 10, 1998).

In fact the mutual limitations that exist in the relationship between domestic and international law may not be easily identified, even if the latter has direct effects within the national context. As described by Prof. Sarolea, it is possible to discover that national sovereignty is present and has direct implications in migration law at the same time that its legitimacy is controversial.[507]

Inspiration comes from the question posed by Prof. Sarolea, whether the principle of sovereignty is a representation that serves as a useful fiction or a real element with practical implications for law, which she notes as: "*La souveraineté relève sans doute du mythe par la fragilité de ses fondations juridique, mais elle imprime la réalité.*"[508]

This discussion will be a cross-cutting theme on the protection of human rights and the irregularity of migration, as a dynamic process, intending to take under consideration the examination of the evolution of the socio-economic context and the progressive (re)definition of the legal framework.

As mentioned in the previous section, irregular migrants, as non-citizens, have particular difficulties in accessing their basic rights; they are placed in a sort of limbo, with a limited freedom of movement, a serious absence of legal protection, and a high degree of vulnerability to exploitation and deportation.[509] For instance, when they first arrive as workers without documents, they represent a cheaper and more easily exploited workforce.

Several states of the Maghreb, as is well known, are at the same time a source of migrants and a place where migrants are received,

507 Sylvia Sarolea, *La souveraineté en droit belge: mythe et réalité*, *in* L'ETRANGER FACE AU DROIT 75–122 (Jean-Yves Carlier ed., Bruylant, 2010).

508 (Sovereignty undoubtedly depends upon the myth of the fragility of its legal foundations, but it has an effect on reality.–Translation provided by the author). *Id.* at 75.

509 Driss Benzekri Foundation for Human Rights and Democracy, *Universal Periodic Review, Morocco July 2012*, Joint report, 2011, at 10.

thus these migrants come in contact with the two faces of the same coin.[510]

Morocco was chosen for several reasons. First and most importantly is that Morocco has in recent years suddenly changed its socio-geographical identity, despite having a peculiar role in African migratory routes that have earned it the categorization as a so-called transit country.[511] This is because many migrants arriving in Moroccan territory ultimately intend to reach Europe, and once passed the border into Morocco they find it impossible to continue their journey, often because they lack necessary documents or are unable to obtain a visa to enter Europe.[512]

This destines them to be put into an undefined legal status.[513] Thus Morocco had recently provided an articulated legal and institutional framework that could resolve, or at least provide an aid to, the needs of migrants under its jurisdiction.

This specific role taken on by Morocco over the years attained meaning especially for the consequences migrants faced passing into its territory and the alarm raised by the spread of cases of abuse and rights violations against them, as will be further analysed. Considering what is claimed by Jorge Martin, head of mission for Doctors Without Borders in Moroccan territory: "*Le Maroc est devenu un pays de transit, mais aussi un pays ou les gens restent longtemps, ce qui engendre frustrations, incertitudes et violence*".[514]

I would also like to emphasize, as it will further the discussion, that Morocco, despite having assumed an active role in the context of human migration, only recently came across the phenomenon of

510 Philippe Fargues, *Afrique du Nord et Moyen-Orient: des migrations en quête d'une politique*, 4 POLITIQUE ETRANGERE 1017, 1017 (2006).

511 Khachani Mohamed, *Maroc, Migration, marché du travail et développement*, ILO, 2010, at 27.

512 *See* PAPADOPOULOU-KOURKOULA, *supra* note 70, at 105.

513 GADEM, *The Human Rights of Sub-Saharan Migrants in Morocco*, 2010, at 5–6.

514 ("Morocco has become a transit country, but also a country where people remain for a long time; this produces frustration, uncertainty, and violence"– Translation provided by the author). MSF, *International Report, Morocco 2008*, Doctors Without Borders, August 2009, at 34.

irregular migration and this may be directly or indirectly attributable to internal and external events and elements.

In particular, the geographic location of Morocco and its proximity to the European continent have certainly had an impact on the role the migration issue has assumed with the European Union in recent years, to the point of being a recurring topic in political discussions, with the ill-concealed risk of sacrificing Morocco's own interests in favour of supporting European security concerns.[515] In this case the reference is directly to the "outsourcing" of European migration policy that many academics regard as one of the defining elements of the current domestic regulatory regime.[516]

For this reason, the analysis attempts to include some general considerations on the meaningful influence exercised by the European Union and the possible risks related to it in the frame of the protection of human rights.

This is not the place for going into detailed socio-political analyses, since the focus will be specifically to understand if the many complaints by irregular migrants of violations against them can arise from pressures determined by the confluence of multiple legal and institutional instances, creating artificial situations in which migrants themselves do not find suitable space.

This will give some answers to frequently asked questions, such as how the different categories of migrants can coexist and how they are protected; whether this categorization process is totally arbitrary; what forms of protection can be implemented; whether irregularity of status is the product of security issues.

515 Mehdi Lahlou, *The Current State and Recent Trends in Migration between Maghreb States and the European Union, in* MEDITERRANEAN TRANSIT MIGRATION 109 (Ninna Sorensen ed., DIIS, 2006).

516 Hassen Boubakri, *Le Maghreb et les migrations en transit: le piège?*, 107 MIGRATION SOCIÉTÉ: REVUE BIMESTRIELLE 86 (2006).

5.1. The nature of, and reasons behind, the phenomenon

Morocco has been a country of emigration throughout history. Today, more than 3 million Moroccans have migrated to other countries in Europe, North America, and the Middle East.[517]

Emigration is part of the country's history, though it began increasing rapidly from the 19th century onwards and still more so with the establishment of the French Protectorate of Morocco in 1912.[518] Subsequently, after achieving independence in 1956, emigration of Moroccan citizens initially to France, and later to other European countries, was a regular and frequent occurrence until the 1970s.[519]

Legal migration has been interrupted since 1970, and evolved mainly along the line of family reunification, only gradually becoming sadly characterized as irregular migration to Europe. The phenomenon worsened in the Nineties with the requirement of entry visas for Moroccans crossing the border. Add to this that at the same time, Morocco historically was also affected by migration and transit experiences linked to trade or within the *tijan* community in between Morocco and Senegal.[520]

517 Anna Di Bartolomeo, Tamirace Fakhoury & Delphine Perrin, *Morocco* (CARIM-Migration Profile, RSCAS, 2009).

518 For an historical overview *see* Ozge Bilgili & Silja Weyel, *Migration in Morocco: History, Current Trends and Future Prospects* (Paper Series: Migration and Development Country Profile, Maastricht Graduate School of Governance, December 2009); GADEM, *Le cadre juridique relative à la condition des étrangers*, January 2009, at 8.

519 The Fifties were characterized by a great demand for workers coming from North Africa to the states of Western Europe. Thanks to the fact that they were few in number, they were protected and appreciated. *See* Moha Ennaji, *Patterns and Trends of Migration in the Maghreb*, in *Migration and the Maghreb*, Viewpoints, The Middle East Institute, Washington DC, May 2010, at 7.

520 "Tijanism or tidjanism is a branch of Islam, derived from Sufism, that was founded by Ahmed Tijani in 1782; he died in Fes on September 22, 1815. Tijanism is widespread in the states of the Maghreb and sub-Saharan Africa (Mali, Niger, Libya, Ghana, Nigeria, Mauritania) and includes as a common

Only since the Nineties has Morocco, as one of the larger emigration states, begun to be affected by the arrival of increasing numbers of migrants, with significant consequences.[521] In fact, with the introduction of ever greater barriers to entry into Europe, the countries of Europe's so-called near abroad have witnessed the arrival of an ever growing number of people in search of a better life, believing in the possibility of identifying alternative ways to pass into Europe.

Significant migration flows have been seen from sub-Saharan countries, as well as other flows from Sierra Leone, Nigeria, and Côte d'Ivoire, following the domestic political and economics situations in those countries. Today, the main countries of origin for irregular immigrants in Morocco are Guinea-Bissau, Mali, Liberia, Sierra Leone, Nigeria, Guinea, Senegal, and Algeria.[522]

It is important to remember that the entrance to the interior of the Maghreb had not been a problem up to then, nor a social obstacle. The creation of the Arab Maghreb Union (AMU) in 1989 introduced the free movement of citizens within the AMU. Despite a recognized paralysis of the Union at the political level, at least it was an attempt to create a space to implement the free movement of people, with the exception of the Moroccan–Algerian frontier.[523]

---

worship practice the pilgrimage of the followers in Fes". GADEM, *Note à l'intention du Comité de lutte contre les Discriminations Raciales*, August 2010, at 5.

521 Some scholars, including Aderanti Adepoju, argue that this change coincided with the fact that Libya in that historic moment changed its political role, an adjustment caused by the embargo by the West up until the beginning of 2000, which led to neighbouring African countries to receive the lion's share of sub-Saharan migrants. Since 2000 the climate in Libya has completely changed, taking a hostile attitude toward the same migrants that before were previously accepted, and this has inevitably led to the identification and exploration of new routes and an attempt to migrate into Europe in a makeshift fashion. Adepoju Aderanti, *The challenge of Labour Migration Flow between West Africa and Maghreb*, International Migration Papers, Geneva, ILO (2006), at 11.

522 Mohamed Khachani, *La question migratoire au Maroc: données récentes* (CARIM Notes d'analyse et de synthèse 2001/11, 2011).

523 The AMU is located next to another space of free movement, the Economic Community of Development of the Western African Countries, which includes 15 countries. The citizens of a member state can move freely within

The entry into the countries of the Maghreb had not been a problem until then, though it entry in the European area became more and more difficult.[524]

Turning our attention to the last few years, irregular migration appears to affect all the major Moroccan towns, with strong echoes in the newspaper of arrests by the Moroccan authorities or tragic deaths occurring at the strait of Gibraltar. The extra-legal sub-Saharans are often arrested, judged, and expelled by Moroccan and Spanish authorities.[525]

To mention just a few sources, in 2003 the daily newspaper *Liberation* shows that more than 6,100 irregulars were arrested between 1 January and 14 July 2003 by the Spanish authorities, among which a significant number were sub-Saharan.[526] Between January and August 2003 in Taza Province alone (in the north of Morocco and a crucial transit point), the Moroccan authorities arrested 2,347 sub-Saharan irregular migrants of different nationalities, including 335 women.[527]

Migrants who find themselves in irregular status in Morocco have two options: using Moroccan territory as a temporary stop to reach Europe, or, in the hypothesis that they are unable to cross Gibraltar strait, remaining in Morocco because the situation they left

---

the identified space. There are walkways that allow passage between the two zones; for instance, citizens of certain sub-Saharan neighbour countries are exempted from visa requirements, provided their stay does not exceed three months. This is the case with Mali and Nigeria, whose citizens may enter Morocco without the need of a visa.

524 In this regard, Boubakri speaks of a double *piège* imposed on each of the transit countries of the Maghreb, including Morocco, because they faced not only the restrictive policies adopted by the EU in reference to this phenomenon, but they also have had to reconsider the existing relations with sub-Saharan countries. *See* Boubakri, *supra* note 516, at 86.

525 Mehdi Lahlou, *Undocumented Migration. Counting the Uncountable. Data and Trends accross Europe. Country report Morocco* (Report for the research project CLANDESTINO, 2008).

526 "*Plus de 6100 clandestine arrêtés sur les cotes espagnoles*", in Libération, 29 July, 2003, 4.

527 "*Immigration clandestine*", Le Matin du Sahara, 8 September, 2003, 4.

behind in their home countries is often linked to socio-economic factors and to a political situation worse than that one encountered in the host country.[528]

As a result, a growing number of potential migrants in these areas are not able to reach their planned destinations, remaining in a sense trapped in a poorly-defined situation, assuming the role of irregular migrants.[529]

Furthermore, it often occurs that migrants in transit are regarded as "unwanted newcomers" because they raise attention to several problems of the receiving state: for instance, at the administrative level (as it is traditionally a country of origin, Morocco found an absence of institutions at national level and legal instruments specifically to regulate the entry and stay of foreigners), or/and at the economic level (taking into consideration the critical situation that exists at the level of the domestic labour market).[530]

Until recently, available data on the extent of the phenomenon of migration across the Mediterranean were limited.[531] . Despite this introduction, the situation has begun to change and a growing number specific research projects are dedicated to this topic.

Well-known academics have since 2000 conducted specific studies, doing numerous interviews with sub-Saharan migrants in transit to Rabat, Tangier, and Casablanca.[532]

Although this was a qualitative study and devoid of the pretence of providing a comprehensive picture, certainly it was among the first to provide data pertaining to the origin of migrants, the routes they used, and the reasons underlie their departure.[533] These interviewed

528 SRHRM, *Report submitted by Ms. Gabriela Rodriquez Pizarro, Special Rapporteur on the human rights of migrants, Morocco*, U.N. Doc. E/CN. 4/2004/76/Add.3 (Jan. 15, 2004).

529 *See* PAPADOPOULOU-KOURKOULA, *supra* note 70, at 105.

530 *See* NYBERG SORENSEN, *supra* note 12, at 129.

531 *See* Kachani, *supra* note 522.

532 Lucile Barros, Mehdi Lahlou, Claire Escoffier, Pablo Pumares & Paolo Ruspini, *L'immigration irrégulière subsaharienne à travers et vers le Maroc,* Cahiers de Migrations Internationales, No 54 F, ILO, Geneva (2002).

533 *See* Betts, *supra* note 17, at 657.

migrants have different origins; they came from Nigeria, the Democratic Republic of the Congo, Senegal, Mali, Ghana, Sierra Leone, Gambia, Liberia, Sudan, Central Africa, Congo Brazzaville, Cameroon, and Côte d'Ivoire. As stated by Dr. Betts, it is interesting to focus on the fact that although several of those migrants interviewed would have had to rely on the protection provided by the 1951 Convention on Refugees, for most of them legislative and bureaucratic barriers provided material obstruction to the provision of those protections, as will be described subsequently.[534]

As pointed out by Dr. Betts, the picture that emerges from the analysis, although partial, certainly does not seem easy to read; in fact it is not enough to realize a simple dichotomy between voluntary and forced migration to identify the legislative regime that is to be implemented. If the majority of migrants make the decision to migrate because of the need to escape from dangerous situations, nevertheless political and economic reasons can provide additional intentions. "Poverty, drought, unemployment, civil war, ethnic conflict, political instability, and the inability to support their family, were amongst the factors cited".[535]

According to Dr. Betts, the conclusions of this survey were confirmed by subsequent studies published by the organization CIMADE on transit migrants in Morocco.[536]

Some recent studies have shown that a significant fraction of migrants have ever-higher levels of education and come from families of medium-high background.[537] One recent change taking place is the ever-growing presence of women, and sometimes even unaccompanied minors, who begin the long migratory route.

534 *See* Barros, Lahlou, Escoffier, Pumares & Ruspini, *supra* note 532, at 22. *See* Betts, *supra* note 17, at 657.

535 *See* Barros, Lahlou, Escoffier, Pumares & Ruspini, *supra* note 532, at 35. *See* Betts, *supra* note 17, at 657.

536 CIMADE, *La situation alarmante des migrants sub-sahrariens en transit au Maroc et les conséquences des politiques de l'Union Européenne,* 2004.

537 *See* Kachani, *supra* note 522, at 11.

The cost of the trip is generally borne by several family members, if not the entire community of origin; even if the journey is a personal project, the collective dimension is important. Furthermore, considering that migrants after their arrival in Morocco may remain for months, if not years, in a completely precarious situation in Morocco.[538]

Finally, in light of the above, one of the problems of particular concern for NGOs is the rising of migration of a mixed nature: in fact, among the people who arrive in Morocco, it is extremely difficult to distinguish asylum seekers and refugees on the one hand from migrants that we could define as "economic", a circumstance accentuated by the fact that they use the same migration routes. In addition, the personal reasons at the root of the decision to migrate may combine both economic and political factors, and even change during the migratory journey.[539]

5.2. The migratory routes

Migratory routes, with the exception of those taken by migrants from Iraq, mainly concern crossing the border between Morocco and Algeria.[540] Most of the migrants, asylum seekers, or refugees, arrive in a town located on the border between Algeria and Morocco: Oujda.[541]

Once across the border, they are in a "no-man's land" with indefinable contours. This area, arid and next to the desert, is also plagued by gangs of traffickers, including those engaged in smuggling of human beings, a phenomenon that, as I shall describe later, occurs to a certain extent within Morocco also. Traffickers take advantage of

538 Mohamed Mghari, *L'immigration sub-saharienne au Maroc* 5 (CARIM notes d'analyse et de synthèse 2007/77, 2008).

539 *See* Fargues, *supra* note 51, at 1.

540 *See* PAPADOPOULOU-KOURKOULA, *supra* note 70, at 94.

541 *See* SRHRM, *supra* note 528, at 12.

the extremely insecure condition of migrants, who are completely unaware of what awaits them.[542]

In particular, for those blocked into this border zone, it is extremely difficult to survive. They live in huts or precarious accommodation without suitable hygienic and sanitary conditions.[543]

All the others that faithfully carry out their original intent to continue immediately to Europe (either by immediately reaching the Spanish towns of Ceuta and Melilla, or by sailing in small boats to reach the Canary islands, or by going to the south of the European coasts), are able to reach some of the main towns in Morocco where the hope of survival at least appears to be greater.[544]

5.3. The volume and composition of irregular migrants

As described above, it is by definition difficult to have accurate and realistic estimates of the total size of irregular migration. Often the only data available are related to the number of arrests of migrants made, or similarly the number of migrants intercepted by the police, returned at the border, or prevented from leaving their country of origin.[545] Or in other circumstances, an approximation (even if not always reliable) can be inferred from the number of regularizations of status made, a tool that has not yet been used in Morocco.

According to information provided by Moroccan authorities, approximately 8,700 migrants were involuntarily repatriated to their countries of origin (especially Mali and Senegal) between 2004 and

542 Ryszard Cholewinski & Kristina Touzenis, *Irregular Migration into and though Southern and Eastern Mediterranean countries: legal perspective* 12 (CARIM, Analytic and Synthetic Notes 2009/01, CARIM-AS 2009/01, 2009).

543 *See* PAPADOPOULOU-KOURKOULA, *supra* note 70, at 105.

544 *Id.* at 110.

545 *See* SRHRM, *supra* note 528, at 12.

2008.[546] According to the same information, more than 65,000 people were intercepted, either at the border by the police or in an attempt to leave Moroccan territory in an irregular manner.

Moreover, between 2007 and 2008 it seems that the total population of asylum seekers decreased by 48 per cent (from 671 to 346). In 2010 the United Nations High Commissioner for Human Rights followed up on 999 applications for the recognition of refugee status (665 in the first instance and 334 appeals), of which 114 were recognized in the first instance and only a few after appeal.[547]

Thus the UNHCR, upon examination, rejected 551 initial requests and 334 in the second instance. In total the recognition corresponded to 11 per cent of the cases examined. At the end of 2008, the total number of refugees living in Morocco was modest (750); they were predominantly from Côte d'Ivoire (36 per cent) and from the Democratic Republic of Congo (42 per cent).[548]

According to the survey conducted by the Moroccan Association for Studies and Research on Migration (AMERM), currently 76 per cent of migrants are in irregular situation; 22 per cent have submitted an application for recognition of refugee status and only 2 per cent have obtained a favourable outcome.[549]

5.4. Institutional framework

There are specific institutions created to strengthen the operational and institutional framework dealing with migration policy in Mo-

546 Angela Li Rosi & Alanna Ryan, *Refugee Protection and international migration: a review of UNHCR's role and activities in Morocco*, UNHCR, March 2010, at 11.

547 *Id.* at 15.

548 UNHCR, *Morocco Fact Sheet*, July 2010.

549 Data divulged during the Meeting of the Global Group on International Migration, Geneva, 27–28 May 2010.

rocco.[550] The Ministry of the Interior has the main responsibility for the management of migration flows. In this context, the Ministry of the Interior is charged with rationalizing and implementing national initiatives to "combat illegal migrant flows and trafficking networks".[551]

At the institutional level, two institutions were established to coordinate government action with respect to migration problems:[552]

- *Department of Migration and Border Surveillance (DMBS)* is in charge of operationalizing the strategy to fight against irregular migration and related networks for trafficking in human beings, as well as the surveillance and control of national borders. The Directorate is divided into the Division of Research and the Division of Logistics.
- *Migration Observatory*, created in 2004, has as its primary mission the coordination of all national activities and strategies to monitor and reduce the pressure of immigration.

On this subject, Morocco adopted a first national strategy in 2003 for the period between 2003 and 2007 to raise awareness of irregular migration and to promote initiatives in regions that attract growing numbers of foreigners. It provided for the adoption of new of legislative measures to update domestic laws, to fight against the networks of traffickers of human beings and drugs, to improve the institutional and normative framework, and to strengthen the capacities of the national authorities.[553]

In 2007, a preliminary evaluation of this strategy was carried out. The Ministry of the Interior evaluated the impact of the different

550 Fatima Sadiqi, *Migration-Related Institutions and Policies in Morocco* (Analytic and Synthetic Notes 2004/05, RSCAS, 2004).

551 GADEM, *Rapport relatif à l'application par le Maroc de la Convention international sur la protection des droits de tous les travailleurs migrants et les membres de leur famille*, February 2009, at 11.

552 *See* Sadiqi, *supra* note 550, at 10.

553 *See* GADEM, *supra* note 551, at 11.

innovations positively, especially given the relative decline in irregular migration.[554]

Based on these results, it seems that Morocco will develop its migration policy focusing on three axes: 1) the prevention of irregular migration; 2) the fight against human trafficking; and 3) the protection of victims of trafficking. The Observatory for Migration will ensure the practical coordination of those activities, even if according to official information it is not sufficiently reliable and credible in its role for its direct link with the Ministry for the Interior.[555]

5.5. Relations between Morocco and European Union in the field of migration policy

The geographical position of Morocco and its current status as a country of origin and of transit has undoubtedly played a leading role in its relations with the European Union, influencing and in a certain way conditioning its evolution.[556]

As recognized by different authors, the relationship between Morocco and the EU starts to grow since the Sixties and reached particular force in the Nineties.[557]

554 *Id.* at 11.

555 *See* Li Rosi & Ryan, *supra* note 546, at 17.

556 *See* Barros, Lahlou, Escoffier, Pumares & Ruspini, *supra* note 532, at 110.

557 Summarizing the evolution of the Euro-Mediterranean relationship of the recent years, briefly and from a historical point of view: after the adoption of the Treaty of Maastricht in 1992 that marked the beginning of a political Europe within which citizens, goods, and services can freely move in implementation of the Single European Act of 1986, there was an evident need to implement a harmonization at the legislative level also on asylum and immigration issues in order to strengthen the common external border. From that moment, therefore, the European Union has attempted to establish a collaboration with the member states on their external borders, from Central and Eastern Europe. In 1995, with the adoption of the Barcelona process, a major

In fact, in 1995 the conclusion of Euro-Mediterranean Partnership Agreement was reached and it was signed at the Barcelona Conference in 1995, enhancing the relation between the EU–Morocco not only from an economic point of view, but also politically, starting to lay the foundations for the recognition of an advanced constitution for Morocco.[558]

In October 1999, the European Council adopted the Action Plan for Morocco arranged by the High Level Working Group on Asylum and Migration,[559] which contains several measures affecting migration. In addition, within the European Neighbourhood Policy, Morocco was chosen as one of the few countries for which a National Plan was developed and adopted.[560] Among the specific objectives of this Plan, it is important to mention the prevention and control of "illegal migration" to and from Morocco, in addition to the development of legislative tools for the implementation of international standards. In relation to this, another element of particular interest is the importance of the adoption of readmission agreements placed at the base of the last negotiations between Morocco and the EU.[561]

---

effort has been pronounced to strengthen the cooperation with the South Mediterranean countries in order to involve them in the management of external borders. In the meantime, the entry into force of the Amsterdam Treaty in 1999 represented a new stage in this process by integrating the Schengen Agreement within the EU, and giving the track to the so-called communitarization of European migration policies. *See* the detailed analysis of Delphine Perrin, *La nouvelle politique juridique de l'Europe en matière de contrôle et de limitation des migrations*, 137 L'ANNEE DU MAGHREB 117 (2004).

558 ABDELKRIM BELGUENDOUZ, POLITIQUE MIGRATOIRES IN MAROC (D'hier à l'horizon, Salé, 2007).

559 The High-Level Working Group on Asylum and Migration works under European Council supervision and was created to adopt an action plan for the countries of origin and transit, addressing all issues related to asylum seekers and migrants. The Action Plan shows the political and economic order and the human rights protection and situation in the states of origin, providing an analysis of the causes and consequences of the phenomenon of migration.

560 Abdelkrim Belguendouz, *Le Maroc et la migration irrégulière: une analyse sociopolitique* (CARIM 2009/07, 2009).

561 Maria-Teresa Gil-Bazo, *The Practice of Mediterranean States in the context of the*

In fact, up to now the process of consultation and coordination undertaken was oriented by the intention to operate a migratory control by the countries of origin. As stated by Prof. Gil-Bazo one of the main relevant results of the inclusion of migration matters into the EU external relations has been the "export of restrictive EU migration control policy to third countries with the adoption of more legislative response to EU's demands."[562]

5.5.1. Readmission agreements

After having dealt in general terms with the thematic of the readmission agreements in Chapter 4 in the specific case of Morocco, it must be stressed that in recent years, several member states of the EU have undertaken negotiations in order to conclude specific readmission agreements with Morocco, with the specific aim of repatriating foreigners found to be in irregular situations.[563]

The negotiation of such agreements seems to be governed by the exchange of specific benefits, in fact, through the provision of technical support, infrastructure, and specific tools for the control of the phenomenon of migration; the agreements seem to be aimed at transforming Morocco into a "buffer zone"[564] in order to reduce the pressure on the regions of destination.

Since 2000 the EU has also undertaken several negotiations to conclude a readmission agreement with Morocco, by placing a strong

European Union's Justice and Home Affairs External Dimension. The Safe Third Country Concept Revisited, 18 INTERNATIONAL JOURNAL OF REFUGEE LAW 571, 586 (2006).

562 *Id.* at 587.

563 For an inventory of the readmission agreements signed between the member states of the European Union and Morocco, see the following website, *available* at <www.mirem.eu/donnees/accords/maroc> (last visited Jun. 20, 2012).

564 Jean-Pierre Cassarino, *Informalizing readmission agreements in the EU Neighbourhood,* 179 THE INTERNATIONAL SPECTATOR 2 (2007).

emphasis on the role that such an agreement could also play in promoting political relations between the two partners.[565]

At the beginning, Morocco showed a more receptive attitude, namely that it has sorely suffered as a result of the exponential increase in sub-Saharan migrants that were passing through its territory. Even so, the increasing costs associated with the real implementation of such an agreement have considerably slowed down the works.[566] The European Commission is pushing Morocco forward in the negotiation and conclusion of a valid instrument for external relations in the field of migration. In this context the European Union does not seem to take into consideration the compatibility between such an instrument and the human rights concerns mentioned above.[567] A specific reference should be made to the national legal framework adopted by the government of Morocco in 2003. As described later, leaving Morocco irregularly is a punishable crime and the consequence is that the readmitted person risks being imprisoned or penalized with heavy fines upon return to the transit country. The Rapporteur of the Parliamentary Assembly of the Council of Europe expressed her concern about enforcing readmission agreements "to countries in which these scenarios [i.e., punishment for irregular emigration upon readmission] are likely to occur", affirming that readmission should not be used in such cases.[568] Past experience has highlighted how the proposed incentives often are not sufficient to encourage the conclusion of readmission agreements, and especially their concrete implementation, as represented by the case of the agreement between Spain and Morocco, which was not until now fully implemented for many reasons, including the detrimental im-

565 *See* Gil-Bazo, *supra* note 561, at 580.

566 *See* Cassarino, *supra* note 564, at 3.

567 Hicham Rachidi, *Accords de réadmission ou chantage à l'expulsion*, Rencontre internationale sur les accords de réadmission, 27 Novembre 2009.

568 *See* Parliamentary Assembly, *supra* note 501, ¶63.

pact that would have on the local economy and the unpopularity it found at the national level.[569]

Morocco had actually concluded a readmission agreement with Spain on 13 February, 1992.[570] The signature approving such an agreement on the part of Morocco was determined by the aim of eventually acquiring advanced status in its political and economic relations with the European Union, as mentioned above. Both contracting parties left some crucial elements to the concrete reality of the agreement underdeveloped, such as the precise procedures for identifying the nationality of origin to which intercepted migrants were to be repatriated, or what protocol to use in determining the origin of the migrants from Morocco and then be returned to that country.[571]

The superficiality of the wording of the provisions in the agreement impedes their implementation, to the point that today only 65 migrants of the 600 that were intercepted have actually been repatriated, rejecting the option of repatriation for the others because of the absence sufficient evidences to permit implementation of the repatriation terms in the agreement itself. [572]States in North Africa have progressively grown to understand the critical role that they are capable of assuming in this context, and this cannot avoid drawing attention to the fact that the role assumed affects the way in which the issue of cooperation in the field of readmission is considered, configured, and encoded. [573]As proficiently pointed out by Dr. Cassarino, the need to formulate and adopt a response to migration flows

569 *See* Rachidi, *supra* note 567; *See* Barros, Lahlou, Escoffier, Pumares & Ruspini, *supra* note 532, at 120.

570 Agreement between Spain and Morocco on movement of people, transit, and readmission of foreigners who have entered illegally. B.O., 25 April and 30 May, 1992.

571 El Arbi Mrabet, *Readmission Agreements. The case of Morocco*, 5 EUROPEAN JOURNAL OF MIGRATION AND LAW 379 (2003).

572 *See* CHOLEWINSKI, *supra* note 115, at 77.

573 Jean-Pierre Cassarino, *An overview of North African Countries' Bilateral Cooperation on the Removal of Unauthorized Migrants: drivers and Implications*, in *Migration and the Maghreb*, Viewpoints, The Middle East Institute, Washington DC, May 2010, at 36.

does not only focus on the operative implementation of the agreements, which often do not seem to be guided by criteria of transparency and respect for international commitments.[574] This situation does not of course originate from a lack of knowledge of international principles that govern the rights of migrants, asylum seekers, and refugees, but it mainly comes from what Dr. Cassarino refers to as the "prioritization of operable means of implementation".[575] The need to operationalize these agreements not only threatens to jeopardize respect for existing rules in the context of respect for human rights, but also at the same time can alter the true concept of effectiveness. In fact, in order to be effective such agreements must firstly be feasible, but respect for international standards does not seem to be a priority for states.[576]

574 *See* Cassarino, *supra* note 564, at 181–182.
575 *See* Cassarino, *supra* note 573, at 36.
576 *See* Mrabet, *supra* note 571, at 383.

6. National legal framework for the protection of irregular migrants

This part addresses the implementation at the national level of international standards meant to guarantee the basic rights of irregular migrants, highlighting the emerging implications for this group for being considered part of mixed migratory movements.

First of all, it is important to keep in mind that, as illustrated in the previous section, in principle all migrants enjoy the protection of international law regardless of status. International law in this field is well developed, and there are international standards that deal directly with migrants, as well as those that deal with wider human rights questions that directly or indirectly affect migrants.

In order to assess the exact scope and impact of the legal dimension of irregular migration, this chapter examines the normative frameworks in place by focusing on two levels:

1– The international approach, undertaking an examination of the international instruments ratified by Morocco in the field of human rights, migration, and refugee law. This legal background, as will be shown, is part of an on-going active debate on the way to effective shape the national regulatory process.

2– The domestic approach, situating the recent adoption of Law No. 02/03, the evolution of migration law generally, and the overall scope of migration regulation. This instrument, in particular, reveals the ambivalent nature of Moroccan legislation: on one hand, it permits innovation in the normative and administrative machinery to overcome the fragmentary nature of the instruments in place, but on the other hand, it reflects a securitarian approach in the context of migration to restrict the entry and stay of irregular migrants.

6.1. International standards and their implementation

As early as 1990, Morocco demonstrated a deep commitment to the protection and promotion of human rights. Morocco has been especially affected in the first place by the socio-economic changes that occurred on the international level, described by several scholars as "democratic proselytism", and secondly, the progressive reconfiguration of the principle of sovereignty in regard to the affirmation of human rights standards.[577] To this end the government of Morocco has voluntarily assumed several engagements and taken concrete actions at various levels to set up the institutions and the administrative machinery necessary for the protection and promotion of human rights, while gradually updating its legislation in force and introducing appropriate policies since King Mohammed VI acceded to the throne.

At the international level, Morocco is party to the most important international human rights instruments.[578] This gave rise to a period of intense reforms to gradually align its normative and administrative apparatus to international standards.[579]

577 Hamid Rbii, *Droits de l'homme et souveraineté: réflexions sur le cas du Maroc*, 32 REMALD 37 (2002).

578 Morocco has ratified in full: the Convention Against Torture and other Cruel, Inhuman or Degrading Treatment or Punishment; the International Covenant on Civil and Political Rights; the International Covenant on Economic, Social and Cultural Rights; the Convention on the Elimination of All Forms of Discrimination Against Women; the International Convention on the Elimination of All Forms of Racial Discrimination; the Convention on the Rights of the Child; the Optional Protocol to the Convention on the Rights of the Childs on the Sale of Children, Child Prostitution and Child Pornography; and the Optional Protocol to the Convention on the Involvement of Children in Armed Conflict.

579 M'chichi Houria Alami, *Les migrations maghrébines en Europe et la question de droits de l'homme*, 43 REVUE MAROCAINE DE DROIT ET D'ECONOMIE DU DEVELOPPEMENT 117, 119 (2000).

Moving from this perspective, it is more than relevant to examine the role that international provisions play at the national level, to move forward in the understanding of the mechanisms available for invoking these rights, for instance access to national judicial authority in case of violations of human rights provisions. The analysis to this end will give a brief illustration of the main provisions of the Constitutional Chart and of other legislative instruments and the role played by jurisprudence in this process.

A preliminary concern is the correct understanding of the harmonization of national law with the international instruments to which Morocco is a party. In fact the provisions enshrined in the Moroccan Constitution are particularly weak.[580]

First, it is not clear from a preliminary reading of the Moroccan constitution, adopted in 1972,[581] whether international law prevails upon national law. In this regard, the interpretation of constitutional provisions appears confusing,[582] and it is impossible to compare it with the content of the constitution of France, which for instance in Art. 55 establishes the primacy of international law, even though the French model is recognized by several scholars as the Moroccan constitution's original inspiration.[583] The only article that formulates an explicit reference on this point is Art. 31(2),[584] which states: "Treaties to modify constitutional provisions have to be approved according the procedures provided by the Constitution."[585] In particular, the Constitution has been the object of several revisions, in 1992 and in

580 *See* Rbii, *supra* note 577, at 140. Hamid Rbii, *La loi 02/03 relative à l'entrée et au séjour des étrangers au Maroc, à l'émigration et l'immigration irrégulières: contrôles des flux migratoires et droits des étrangers*, 17 LA GAZETTE DU PALAIS: REVUE TRIMESTRIELLE D'ETUDES ET DE DOCUMENTATION JURIDIQUES 29 (2007).

581 Morocco Constitution adopted in 1996.

582 *See* Rbii, *supra* note 577, at 142.

583 *See* GADEM, *supra* note 518, at 10.

584 In fact Art. 31 has not changed. The last version of its content was formulated in the provision adopted 19 September 1996, Chadi Ouazzani, *L'article 31 de la Constitution de 1972 et le droit des traités*, 1 REVUE MAROCAINE DE DROIT ET D'ECONOMIE DU DEVELOPPEMENT 87, 88 (1982).

585 (Translation provided by the author.)

1996, but the main changes have influenced in particular the structure and content of its preamble. The main result is that the new formulation explicitly highlights the international principle of human rights and their relevance at national level. The Preamble to the constitution states: "The Kingdom of Morocco, conscious of the need to place its actions in the context of the international bodies of which it is an active and dynamic member, subscribes to the principles, rights and obligations stemming from the charters of those bodies and reaffirms its commitment to human rights as universally recognized", but the Constitution does not explicitly affirm the primacy of international provisions over national regulations in case of direct conflict.[586]

This requires developing a few preliminary considerations on the legal implications of the choice made by the Moroccan legislation to include this reference in the Preamble, considering its non-binding nature, instead of elaborating upon a specific provision.

In this regard the doctrine has adopted controversial and opposed approaches.

Some authors, such as Prof. Naciri, argued that:

> It is not a symbolic term, because the legislature knows very well the meaning of the words used, [...] including this provision in the Preamble give to its content a privileged place. It is not necessary to emphasize the legal nature of the Preamble, because, as it well known, it is an integral part of the Constitution in a comprehensive and coherent perspective. Since its entry into force, national legal framework has had to respect and to implement the human rights provisions.[587]

586 It should further be noted that several statutes and regulations explicitly recognize the primacy of international norms over national law, for example the new Code of Criminal Procedure, which regulates the practice of the legal profession, as well as the Nationality Code.

587 Khalid Naciri, *Aspects du renforcement de l'Etat de droit dans la nouvelle Constitution, in* REVISION DE LA CONSTITUTION MAROCAINE, ANALYSE ET COMMENTARIES 100 (Driss Basri, Michel Rousset & Georges Vedel eds., Imprimerie Royale, 1992) (Translation provided by the author).

Other authors, such as Prof. Menouni, claimed that several interpretative doubts persist to challenge the "legal impact of this normative change"; in fact, the preamble cannot be considered a binding provision.[588] This issue was raised also by the Human Rights Committee in its concluding observations on the report submitted by Morocco. This body urged the government of Morocco to explicitly clarify the nature of the relationship between international standards and domestic legal frameworks. Similarly, CERD raised specific concerns on the lack of clear direction explaining how to address this interrelationship.[589] In any case, the emphasis on international human rights, even if only in the preamble, represents an innovative approach requiring the adoption of several provisions which have a direct effect of improving "the rule of law and coordinate a specific legal framework based on the principle of democracy as the primacy of law, separation of powers and principle of majority".[590] Furthermore, this element contributes to the increasing relevance of international legal standards, and in particular it appears that "the Constitution, in its new formulation, gives the opportunity to integrate international laws at the national level".[591] As stated by Prof. Chahdi, this is the first step in recognizing the prevalence of international law over national law for all actors implied, both the national regulation and the judicial authorities.[592]

This argument is supported also from other national instruments. In particular, Art. 1 of the *Dahir* (Decree) of 6 September

588 *See* Rbii, *supra* note 577, at 150–156.

589 CEDAW, *Concluding observations of the Committee on the Elimination of Discrimination against Women, Morocco*, ¶14 and 15, U.N. Doc. CEDAW/C/MAR/CO/4 (2008); *see* CERD, *Concluding observations of the Committee on the elimination of racial discrimination, Reports submitted by States Parties under article 9 of the Convention Seventeenth and eighteenth periodic reports of States parties due in 2006, Morocco*, U.N. Doc. CERD/C/MAR/CO/17-18 (Aug. 27, 2010).

590 *See* Rbii, *supra* note 577, at 150–156. (Translation provided by the author).

591 René Dupuy, *La Constitution marocaine et les relations internationales, in* REVISION DE LA CONSTITUTION MAROCAINE , ANALYSE ET COMMENTAIRE 273 (Driss Basri, Michel Rousset & Georges Vedel eds., Imprimerie Royale, 1992).

592 *See* OUAZZANI, *supra* note 584.

1958 on the Nationality Code states: "treaty provisions and international agreements ratified and published prevail on the national instruments". Also, domestic migration law establishes that "under the effect of ratified international conventions, national law regulates the entry and the stay of foreigners to Morocco".

In this regard judicial interpretation, not supported in its work by the wording of national provisions, contributes to advancing the common understanding of these interpretative challenges, and clarifies the possible outcomes of this tension, for instance in case of conflict between provisions.[593]

At the beginning, the first cases issued had the effect more of jeopardizing than coordinating the creation of legal doctrine on this issue. In fact, different opinions have been issued affirming, on one side, the primacy of domestic instruments[594] and, on the other side, the overruling nature of international standards, and the Supreme Court tried to identify a possible compromise to these divergent opinions.[595] The first approach of judicial authorities was to affirm that "national tribunals have to apply the provisions of civil or penal

593 Hamid Rbii, *Le juge marocain face aux conventions internationales des droits de l'homme liant le Maroc: méconnaissance ou reconnaissance?*, paper presented at an international conference held in Marrakesh, "La protections de droits de l'Homme entre la législation interne et le droit international", 21 and 22 January 2002, published in REMALD (January 2001), at 137–163. *See* Rbii, *supra* note 577, at 156–161.

594 Tribunal of Rabat, *Alla Abdellah v. Bellat Ahmed*, REVUE MAROCAINE DE DROIT, No. 15 (1987), at 308–310. For instance, the Tribunal of Casablanca had to decide if the creation of the Communist Party is to be considered compatible with Islamic rules and the constitutional monarchy, on the basis of the freedom of liberty and association. The Tribunal in its decision found no violations of international standards, but the Court of Appeals found a threat to public order and it maintained that it was necessary to disband the party. In particular, the Tribunal stated: "the action of the Tribunal must be to prioritize protecting the national public order, founded on common principles, even it is has to consider that Morocco is part of the main international standards, as the UN Chart and the Declaration on Human Rights" (Translation provided by the author).

595 Supreme Court, *Azdad Haj Mohammed v. Salmi Mostafa*, 9 April 1997.

procedural codes, on the basis that domestic instruments are progressive and oriented to improve human dignity, taking under considerations the ICCPR standards".[596] This orientation has been supported most of all by the scarce knowledge and understanding of international standards by individuals. Then, the government of Morocco and its main actors acquired a strong awareness of the impact of international standards at national level, and in applying the provisions of international conventions Moroccan courts have confirmed the primacy of international human rights law in a number of judicial decisions. Thus, the Supreme Court has endorsed the primacy of international norms in several decisions such as Judgment No. 426 of 22 March 2003, in which the Court applied Article 11 of the International Covenant on Civil and Political Rights (which prohibits imprisonment in connection with a contractual obligation).[597]

At this point, a few preliminary remarks are necessary to introduce the socio-political structure and the main rules of the Moroccan community. Several scholars, in particular Prof. Rbii, have identified a few main reasons that could clarify why Morocco has difficulties in implementing and adopting international standards. First, the government of Morocco argued that it would prefer to improve its judicial and administrative system, instead of recognizing the role of international monitoring mechanisms. Second, the political system in Morocco is conceived and implemented as a monarchy based on a *makhzen* structure, which means that a strong relationship of obedience and respect is in place between individuals and the government.[598] In the *makhzen* system the government prevails over indi-

596 HRC, *Consideration of Reports submitted by States parties under Article 40 of the Covenant–Second periodic report of Morocco,* 5, U.N. Doc. CCPR/C/SR.1032 (Nov. 12, 1990).

597 *See* Rbii, *supra* note 577, at 156–161.

598 "*Monarchie califale appuyée sur une structure makhzénienne, fondée sur une relation de crainte et d'obéissance des sujets et constitutionnalisée dans un objectif institutionnel et juridique combiné à des principes d'inspiration formellement libérale. La contrainte autoritaire du modèle makhzenien l'emporte cependant sur la potentialité libérale du dispositif institutionnel et juridique mis en place*". ("Caliphal monarchy dependent upon a *makhzen* structure, founded on a relation of fear and obedience of the subjects and

viduals. It seems unconceivable to allow mechanisms that are not part of the national system to interfere with sovereign authority, specifically in the context of human rights. This could be an act of "revolt" against the state.[599]

In any case, because it ratified these standards the government of Morocco must periodically submit several reports to the UN monitoring bodies, as described above, giving rise to a mechanism of "protection by investigation". In addition, these reports are discussed at the national and international levels, and the debate itself is a useful instrument for acquiring specific information about the domestic environment in the context of human rights protection for irregular migrants–even if the following analysis will describe some of the main obstacles to a full and coherent interpretation of those international standards. In particular, several scholars raised the need to adopt specific measures for the full application of these principles and to prevent cultural specificities from affecting their universality.[600]

6.1.1. Irregular migrants workers

Even if Morocco it is not party to the ILO Conventions on this topic,[601] it participated actively in the process of drafting and adopting the International Convention on the Protection of the Rights of All Migrant Workers and Their Families (ICRMW) and ratified it on

constitutionalized into institutional and juridical objectives, combined into principles formally liberal in inspiration. The authoritarian constraint of the *makhzen* model prevails upon the liberal potential of the institutional and legal disposition in place."–Translation provided by the author). *See* Rbii, *supra* note 593, at 51.

599 *See* Rbii, *supra* note 593, at 51.

600 "*Les spécificités culturelles ne pouvaient remettre en cause l'universalité des droits de l'homme, qui demeurait inaliénable et non négociable, ni empêcher l'adaptation des mesures appropries*", CEDAW, *Report of the CEDAW, Official Records–Fifty-Second Session, Supplement No. 38*, ¶64, U.N. Doc. A/52/38/Rev.1 (Aug. 12, 1997).

601 *See* Aderanti, *supra* note 521, at 14.

21 June 1993[602] with a Declaration on Article 92(1).[603] Morocco was an initiator of the Convention, the first country to ratify it, and Moroccan delegates, with Mexico, were the only ones to be involved during the entire time span of the negotiating process (11 years) until the adoption of the Convention. It played an important role in the entire process.

Initially, Morocco, as a source country of migration, was interested in the articles contained in Part VI of the Convention, concerning the promotion of sound, equitable, humane, and lawful conditions in connection with international migration of workers and members of their families, to guarantee the protection of its emigrants. As described above, Morocco, however, became a transit country for migration into Europe, a situation that led to the presence of migrants in irregular status. This new perspective and its practical consequences have influenced Morocco's implementation of the ICRMW, and it is no coincidence that the initial report on implementation of the Convention has been long overdue since 2004.[604]

602 Dahir No. 4 93-5, 14 June 1994.

603 "*Le gouvernement du Maroc ne se considère pas lié par le paragraphe 1 de l'article 92 de cette Convention qui dispose que tout différend entre plusieurs Etats parties concernant l'interprétation ou l'application de la présente Convention sera soumis à l'arbitrage, à la demande de l'un d'entre eux. Le gouvernement du Royaume de Maroc considère que cet différend de ce genre ne peut être soumis à l'arbitrage qu'avec le consentement de toutes les parties en conflit*". ("The government of Morocco does not consider itself bound by Article 92(1) of the Convention which provides that all disputes among States parties concerning the interpretation or the application of the present Convention shall be subject to arbitration should one or the other of them demand it. The government of the Kingdom of Morocco considers that disputes of this kind cannot be subjected to arbitration without the consent of all parties involved in the conflict."–Translation provided by the author).

604 Paul de Guchteneire & Antoine Pecoud, *Migration, Human Rights and the United Nations: an investigation into the obstacles to the UN Convention on Migrant Workers' Rights*, 24 WINDSOR Y. B. ACCESS JUST. 241, 263 (2006). The report has been submitted last November 2012 (CMW, *Rapport initial de l'Etat partie devant être soumis en 2004*, *Maroc*, U.N. Document CMW/C/MAR/1 (Nov. 1, 2012)) and it will be reviewed during the next CMW session in April 2013.

I would like to dwell on the relevance of this instrument and the position of irregular migrants with regard to access to human rights, in particular to equal working conditions and social rights, because the ICRMW explicitly grants rights to undocumented migrants and irregular migrants workers. In official responses to the communications sent out by the Special Rapporteur, the government of Morocco stated without exception the non-applicability of the provisions of the Convention to migrants in irregular situation, claiming that they are not addressed by the specific provisions of the ICRMW.[605]

This attitude is confirmed also by Dr. Cholewinski and Dr. Touzenis, who recognize that a number of sub-Saharan migrants in transit to Europe fulfil the conditions of the ICRMW for protection but are without any form of safeguards and subject to sanctions and expulsion. In fact, in excluding the application of the ICRMW "certain migration officials in Morocco declared, on the basis of interviews, sub-Saharans transiting the country are not migrant workers, that they only seek to access to Europe in order to work there and that they have no interest in contacting the Moroccan authorities".[606] This understanding, even if not universal, could be a starting point in need of more attention in demonstrating that the level of implementation is not satisfactory, and that a substantial gap exists between the commitments made by Morocco and the application of those commitments to migrants in irregular status. In particular there is an absence of interpretation and application of these norms to irregular migrants.

605 "Concerning the alleged violation of the ICMWR Convention, the government of Morocco ratified this Convention according to *Dahir chérifien* No. 4 93-5 of 14 June 1994. This instrument provides protection to migrant workers and members of their families in irregular situation. This Convention cannot be applied to irregular migrants who illegally entered national territory to join Europe". SRHRM, *Report of the Special Rapporteur on the human rights of migrant workers, Ms. Gabriela Rodriquez Pizarro, Addendum–Communications sent to Governments and replies received*, U.N. Doc. E/CN.4/2005/85/Add.1 (Feb. 4, 2005). (Translation provided by the author; emphasis added by the author).

606 *See* Cholewinski & Touzenis, *supra* note 542, at 27.

6.1.2. Asylum seekers and refugees

Concerning the refugee protection regime, Morocco acceded to the 1951 Convention on 7 November 1956 and to the 1967 Protocol on 20 April 1971.

Morocco adopted a Royal Decree on 29 August 1957, agreeing to the modalities for the implementation of the 1951 Convention.[607] This Decree established the Refugee Office and the Asylum Appeal Instance within the Ministry of Foreign Affairs. [608] The Decree stipulates that the Refugee Office recognizes as a refugee each person accepted under the mandate of UNHCR or the by the virtue of the criteria of the 1951 Convention (Art. 2).[609]

The adoption of the Decree, however, has not resulted in the establishment of a national asylum procedure and it is has not estab-

607 B.O. No. 2341 of 6 September 1957, at 1161–1162.

608 Decree of 29 August 1957 fixing the rules on the implementation of the Conventions relating to the Status of Refugees, signed in Geneva on 28 July 1951.

609 Article 1 states that: "*La protection juridique et administrative des personnes visés par la Convention de Genève du 28 juillet 1951 relative au statut des réfugiés est assurée par le bureau des réfugiés et apatrides, placé sous l'autorité du Ministre des affaires étrangers*". ("The judicial and administrative protection of persons provided by the Geneva Convention of 28 July 1951 concerning the status of refugees is assured by the Refugee and Stateless Persons Office, placed under the authority of the Minister of Foreign Affairs.") and Art. 2 : "*Le bureau des réfugiés et apatrides: – reconnaît la qualité de réfugié à toute personne qui relève du mandate du Haut Commissaire des Nations Unies pour les réfugiés ou qui répond aux définitions de l'article premier de la Convention de Genève signée le 28 juillet 1951;–délivré aux personnes ci-dessus vises les pièces nécessaires pour leur permettre soit d'accomplir les divers actes de la vie civile, soit de faire appliquer les dispositions de la législation interne ou des accords internationaux qui intéressent leur protection*" ("The Refugee and Stateless Persons Office: recognizes refugee status to all persons who fall under the mandate of the United Nations High Commissioner for Refugees or who meet the definitions in the first article of the Geneva Convention signed 28 July 1951; provides the above persons with the necessary documents to permit them to participate in civic life and/or to apply the provisions of domestic law or international agreements which concern themselves with their protection."–Translations provided by the author).

lished a comprehensive legal framework, nor a functional procedure to deal with matters pertaining to asylum and refugees, nor has it developed the necessary institutional and administrative capacities to address these challenges effectively.

In its absence, UNHCR has been undertaking refugee status determinations in Morocco for the past forty years.[610]

In 1959, the government of Morocco, together with the government of Tunisia, was the first country to welcome a delegation from the UNHCR on its territory.[611] Several years later, in 1965, it authorized the creation of an official seat in Casablanca; until this moment there were very few cases of applications for refugee status in Morocco.[612] Only in 2004, when the migratory flows started to increase at the borders with the Spanish enclaves of Ceuta and Melilla, the seat was moved to Rabat, the capital.[613] The bilateral agreement between the government of Morocco and the UNHCR to formalize the latter's legal status was signed only in 2007, to clearly recognize the fundamental value of UNHCR's presence and work. In fact the government of Morocco was in need of external support in dealing with the increasing number of applications.[614]

In this situation there is no guarantee that persons recognized as refugees under the UNHCR mandate will benefit from a legal status permitting them to exercise their rights and have formal access to basic services.[615] In fact, refugee documents issued by the UNHCR do not yet in practice provide legal protection against arrest and *refoulement*, as will be discussed later.[616]

610 *See* UNHCR, *supra* note 548.

611 *See* Li Rosi & Ryan, *supra* note 546, at 15.

612 *Id.* at 15.

613 *Id.* at 12.

614 *Id.* at 15.

615 UNHCR, *Submission by the UNHCR for the OHCHR Compilation Report, Universal Periodic Review*, Morocco, 2011.

616 G.A., *Compilation prepared by the Office of the High Commissioner for Human Rights in accordance with paragraph 5 of the annex to Human Rights Council resolution 16/21*, Morocco, 9, U.N. Doc. A/HRC/WG.6/13/MAR/2 (Mar. 12, 2012).

6.2. Introduction to the national legal framework: from an historical perspective

It is important to highlight that the ratification of international instruments represents a first step, but their effective implementation would guarantee fulfilment of their provisions at the national level. In this context, a brief overview of the existing legal background in Morocco regarding the entry into the territory of foreigners and the residence helps to assess the level of implementation and to focus on how Morocco incorporated international standards into its domestic legislation.[617]

A new immigration law was adopted on November 2003, Law No. 02/03 (*Loi 02/03 relative à l'entrée et au séjour des étrangers au Royaume du Maroc, à l'émigration et à l'immigration irrégulière*, concerning entry into the Kingdom of Morocco, the stay of foreigners, emigration, and illegal immigration) to deal with this issue. This new regulation represents a comprehensive reform of the legal framework for migration, which had been previously adopted under the French Protectorate.[618] It aims at updating the existing legal framework and establishing and defining precise categories of offences related to illegal emigration and trafficking in migrants through effective oversight. In particular, the law incorporates the hierarchy of the basic principle of international law, inasmuch as all its provisions are to be applied subject to International Convention ratified by Morocco (Art. 1).[619]

This text represents a valuable update of the existing legal instruments that dated back to the colonial era and in particular to 1914 and 1950. The first instrument was adopted two years after the

617 *See* Alami, *supra* note 579, at 117.

618 *See* GADEM, *supra* note 518, at 11.

619 *Dahir* No. 1.03.196 of 11 November 2003 on the adoption of Law 02/03 on the entry and stay of foreigners in the Kingdom of Morocco, and the regular migration and immigration, B.O. No. 5162 of 20 November 2003, 1295–1302.

institution of the French Protectorate and the second six years later the independence proclamation.[620]

The main text was the Law of 1914, later modified in 1915, which applied to the foreigners who entered and stayed in the territory of the *sharif*.[621] Later, according to an order adopted in 1915, entry into the territory was subject to the possession of a valid passport and a visa, unless the foreigner was exempt through the application of bilateral agreements between his or her country of origin and Morocco. In case of violation of these provisions, the immediate deportation or extradition of the foreigners was prescribed.

6.2.1. Law No. 02/03 adopted in 2003

It is relevant to highlight that the adoption of this law occurred almost simultaneously with the adoption of similar provisions in other countries of North Africa (Tunisia, Algeria, and Libya).[622] This illustrates the increasing need to respond to the growing pressure of migratory flows by promoting normative frameworks. In this regard, several scholars considered these changes more as due to European countries gaining horizontal harmonization of provisions in place and transposing principles inspired by European migration policy.[623]

The main objective of this analysis is to examine whether and to what extent Law 02/03 may be considered as a migration instrument

620 *See* Lahlou, *supra* note 515, at 40.

621 First article: *"Toute personne débarquant dans un port devra justifier devant l'autorité locale qui sera déléguée à cet effet, de son identité, de son dernier domicile, de ses moyens d'existence et de motifs de sa venue".* ("Every person arriving at a port of entry must show the appropriate national authority his identity, his last residence, the existence of sufficient economic means, and the reasons of his stay"– Translation provided by the author). *See*, GADEM, *supra* note 518, at 11.

622 Delphine Perrin, *Sémantique et faux-semblants juridiques de la problématique migratoire au Maghreb*, 123 MIGRATIONS SOCIETE 19 (2009).

623 Delphine Perrin, *La nouvelle politique juridique de l'Europe en matière de contrôle et de limitation des migrations*, 137 L'ANNEE DU MAGHREB 1 (2004).

apt for regulating and promoting migration, or instead as a repressive instrument adopted on the only basis of opposing irregular migration.

6.2.1.1. Legal framework on the entry and stay of foreigners in Morocco

Law 02/03 was adopted on 20 November 2003, the date of its publication in the Official Journal, as established by Art. 58. Its text is composed of three chapters: 1) Entry and Stay of Foreigners in the Kingdom of Morocco; 2) Penal Sanctions in the Context of Irregular Migration and Immigration; 3) Provisional Rules.

A review of the terminology in the text indicates a distinction between "the entry and stay of foreigners in Morocco" (which could be in some circumstances in irregular situation) and "irregular emigration and migration", which implies a different set of conditions and sanctions. In the first place this distinction is not really clear, because the emphasis on irregular migration presumes the existence of this phenomenon. Secondly and in contrast, specific provisions devoted to irregular migrants risk stigmatizing this vulnerable group.[624] This appears to be part of a campaign started in the political sphere and exacerbated by the media. As stated by Prof. Lahlou, the notion of irregularity did not exist for the population, "the Moroccans in general consider sub-Saharan Africans as them, which are in territory where they are free to be, as they are considered themselves free everywhere outward journey in the remainder of Africa. The irregularity/illegality appeared with the public speech to accompany the official policy change occurred after 2003".[625]

Field of application

According to Art. 1, "any foreigner disembarking or arriving on the Moroccan territory must report to the competent authorities, in charge of control at the border crossings, in possession of a passport issued by the State of which he or she is a national, or any other valid

624 *See* Perrin, *supra* note 622, at 19.

625 *See* Lahlou, *supra* note 515, at 13.

document recognized by the Moroccan State as a valid and subsisting travel document and provided, where relevant, with the required visa, issued by the administration" (Translation provided by the author). The criteria adopted and identified by the legislation is nationality.

Entry onto national territory

According to law, foreigners who wish to enter Morocco must have valid documents in the form of a passport or its equivalent, as well as a visa specifying the purpose of the entry. Those who attempt to enter without any documents are eligible for sanctions that could extend to imprisonment. As with entry, the law regulates exit from Morocco. No person is allowed to leave Morocco without authorization. According to Art. 4(2), the national authorities have discretionary power to authorize the entry of a foreigner or not. This principle applies in particular to all individuals who do not satisfy the necessary requirements or represent a risk for national security. In case of refusal of entry the migrant can be detained in identified areas such as ports or airports.

6.2.1.2. Legal consequences of irregularity

Coercive measures

The third chapter listed several coercive measures to guarantee the effective implementation of the provisions listed in Law 02/03 with a specific emphasis on expulsion.
Article 25 stipulates that

> Expulsion may be pronounced by the administration if the presence of a foreigner on the Moroccan territory constitutes a serious threat to public order. It is pronounced against the foreigner by a decision of the General Director of the National Police and notified to the foreigner by an officer of the police or gendarmerie, with a grace period to leave the territory. It may be executed *ex officio* by the administration.[626]

626 Art. 28: "*La décision prononçant l'expulsion d'un étranger peut être exécutée d'office par l'administration. Il en est de même de la décision de reconduite à la frontière, qui n'a pas été*

Article 26 enumerates however a long list of foreign persons who cannot be subject to expulsion measures.[627] All these provisions are, however, overridden by those of Article 27, which provides for expulsion when it constitutes a "pressing necessity for public security".

Sanctions regime

A relevant part of this instrument is devoted to restricting and fighting the migratory phenomenon through the imposition of specific

---

contestée devant le Président du Tribunal Administratif ou son délègue en sa qualité de juge des référés, dans le délai prévu à l'article 23 de la présente loi, ou qui n'a pas fait l'objet d'une annulation en première instance ou en appel, dans les conditions fixées au même article". ("The decision to expel a foreigner may be executed automatically by the administration. It is the same with the decision to send someone back to the border, if the case is not contested by the president of the administrative tribunal or his delegate in the capacity as summary judge within the time limit specified in Art. 23 of the present law, and which has not been annulled in the first instance or upon appeal under terms specified in the same article."– Translation provided by the author).

627 Art. 26: " *1) l'étranger qui justifie par tous moyens qu'il réside au Maroc habituellement depuis qu'il a atteint au plus l'âge de six ans; 2) l'étranger qui justifie par tous moyens qu'il réside au Maroc habituellement depuis plus de quinze ans; 3) l'étranger qui réside régulièrement sur le territoire marocain depuis dix ans, sauf s'il a été étudiant pendant toute cette période; 4) l'étranger, marie depuis au moins un an, avec un con joint marocain; 5) l'étranger qui est père ou mère d'un enfant résidant au Maroc, qui a acquis la nationalité marocaine par le bienfait de la loi, en application des dispositions de l'art. 9 du dahir n. 1-58-250 du 21 safar 1378 (6 septembre 1958) précité, a condition qu'il exerce effectivement la tutelle légale a l'égard de cet enfant et qu'il subvienne a ses besoins; 6) l'étranger résidant régulièrement au Maroc sous couvert de l'un des titres de séjour prévus par la loi ou les conventions internationales, qui n'a pas été condamne définitivement a une peine au moins égale a un an d'emprisonnement sans sursis; 7) la femme étrangère enceinte; 8) l' étranger mineur*" ("1) foreigners who have been regularly resident in Morocco since their sixth birthdays; 2) foreigners who have been resident in Morocco for more than 15 years; 3) migrants who have been resident in Morocco for at least 10 years; 4) migrants who have been married for at least 4 years to a Morrocan citizen; 5) parents of a child resident in Morocco and who has obtained Moroccan citizenship; 6) migrants regularly staying who have not been sentenced to at least one year of imprisonment; 7) pregnant women migrants; 8) child migrants"– Translation provided by the author).

penalties, which are among the main measures and mechanisms identified by the government of Morocco for this purpose. To this end, Morocco adopted a peculiar approach of contrasting not only irregular entry onto its territory but also irregular exits from its territory.[628] Complementary to its normative design is the need to punish all actors involved in the process. A clear distinction is made between the provisions that apply to all migrants (Title 1, chapter 8) and the provisions that apply only in the case of irregular migration (Title 2).

The provisions established in the first Title list several infractions to punish:

- foreigners who enter in Morocco without respecting the national rules (i.e. the need to have a passport and possibly a visa) or who stay after the expiration of his or her residence permit (Art. 42 applies a sanction of 2000 to 20000 DH and/or term of imprisonment of one to six months);
- foreigners who stay without any title, such as a permit of stay or residence (Art. 43, penalty of 5000 to 30000 DH and/or term of imprisonment of one month to one year);
- foreigners who submitted to an order to removal, and then enter in an illegal way, can be subjected to imprisonment from six months to two years (Art. 45(1)).

A specific number of penalties apply to carriers if they collaborate in the irregular entry of migrants (Art. 37) and carriers have the specific obligation to carry those foreigners back (Art. 37(2). As mentioned above, in case the local authority refuses the entry of a foreigner, all fees are paid by the carrier (Art. 37(3)) and severe penalties have been adopted to this end (e.g. Art. 48 provides a sanction of 5000 to 10,000 DH for each passenger). This provision cannot be applied in the following cases: 1) foreigners who submit an application for the recognition of refugee status; 2) carriers who prove that at the moment of departure the foreigners had the necessary documents; 3)

628 *See* Cholewinski & Touzenis, *supra* note 542, at 18. *See* Rbii, *supra* note 580, at 41.

carriers who were unable to verify the documents (Art. 48(4)). In all these exceptions the burden of proof lies with the carrier.

In addition, a specific provision, Art. 50 address irregular migration. This article applies to illegal emigration from Morocco and provides for fines of 3000 to 10,000 DH, imprisonment for a term of one to six months or both of these sanctions against any person who illegally leaves over Morocco's land, sea, or air borders, notwithstanding the relevant provisions of the penal code. The act includes a regime of severe fines and imprisonment for migrants for irregular entry and stay, and for any persons facilitating illegal entry or exit. Even more severe are the penalties in the case of collaboration with these crimes. Article 51 establishes imprisonment of two to five years and/or a fine of 50,000 to 500,000 DH.

*** *** ***

Based on the information available and the jurisprudence issued on the application of this instrument, it is too early to see its concrete impact, although some preliminary conclusions are possible, taking as a starting point the active debate, at a national and international level, raised by its adoption, with regard to the treatment of irregular migrants.[629]

The above analysis demonstrated that several areas need improvement so irregular migrants and refugees have their rights respected.[630] There exists a binding international legal framework to ensure the rights of migrants in irregular situation, nevertheless there needs to be a legal framework that not only works on an international level but also on the national level.[631] International instruments of international human rights law provide a strong normative framework but much more needs to be done to empower migrants in ir-

629 For instance the FIDH in several occasions informed the government of Morocco of the need to put in place the procedural guarantees listed in the migration law, particular at Art. 11 and 16. FIDH, *Espagne–Maroc: situation des immigrants et demandeurs d'asile, non a la répression comme politique migratoire*, 2003; see also Boubakri, *supra* note 516, at 104.

630 ABDELKRIM BELGUENDOUZ, ENJEUX MIGRATOIRES MAGHREB–EUROPE–AFRIQUE–UN REGARD DU SUD (Konrad Adenauer Stiftung, 2006).

631 *See* Rbii, *supra* note 580, at 60.

regular situation to denounce violations that occur and claim their rights. In particular, in order for Morocco to act in accordance with its international obligations, the government must give irregular migrants access to social rights, among which are the right to healthcare and to adequate living conditions.[632] There is an urgent need to enhance capacity to increment national legislative provisions in order to implement and properly interpret the provisions of the International Migrant Worker Convention. There must be greater effort to promote respect for legal standards and rights of migrants, irrespective of their status. There must be adequate dissemination of information about migrants' rights to make national authorities aware of those rights.

Second, there is a need to guarantee a minimal judicial control to avoid absolute discretion over deportation orders.

For instance, art. 29(2) of Law 02/03 states that a pregnant woman migrant cannot be returned.[633] It is clear that this provision explicitly implements the content of the Convention against Women and the Convention Against Torture, but, as will be described in the next chapter, the gap in implementation is an urgent challenge for the national authorities. On the issue of arbitrary and collective expulsions, the HRC in 2004 also urged the government of Morocco to provide adequate safeguards to migrants who are particularly vulnerable to abuse.[634] In addition the HRC specifically informed the gov-

632 *See* de Guchteneire & Pecoud, *supra* note 604, at 264. Also the implementing regulation (B.O. No. 5836-21 I 1431, adopted 6 May 2010) did not address this issue.

633 Art. 29 (2): "*Aucune femme étrangère enceinte et aucun mineur étranger ne peuvent être éloignes. De mémé, aucun étranger ne peut être éloigne a destination d'un pays s'il établit que sa vie ou sa liberté y sont menacées ou qu'il y est expose a des traitements inhumains, cruels ou dégradants*". ("No pregnant woman or child migrant may be removed. Also, no foreigner may be removed to a country where he would risk his life or liberty or if he would be subject to inhuman or cruel treatments".– Translation by the author).

634 HRC, *Considered the fifth periodic report of Morocco,* ¶178–188, U.N. Doc. CCPR/C/MAR/2004/5 (Apr. 15, 2004).

ernment of Morocco of the need to protect irregular migrants against the risk of being subjected to torture or ill treatment if removed.[635]

The Human Rights Committee, examining the fifth periodic report presented by Morocco on the implementation of the International Covenant on Civil and Political Rights, raised several questions concerning the adoption of Law 02/03 and its compatibility with the provisions of the Covenant.[636] The experts on the Human Rights Committee specifically voiced a concern about the current situation of migrants, particularly those in irregular situation, asking what might be the legal status of migrants in general, including irregular migrants, granted by the new provision.[637] However, no further measures have been formulated by the government. In this light, the content of the national provision envisages a potential conflict with international treaties, and it is relevant to consider which rules will ultimately be followed, according to the predominant jurisprudence.

What is of extreme importance is that at the domestic level, courts have started to deal with a number of cases about the entry of irregular migrants. For example, they have been faced with a number of cases addressing the issue of respecting legal guarantees in cases of deportation under Law 02/03. Although these provisions are being imple-

635 "No expulsion of aliens without judicial guarantees (Art. 13): 20) Please indicate the remedies available, in conformity with article 13 of the Covenant, to persons who face the risk of being forced to leave Morocco on the grounds that they present a threat to the security of the State or to public order, or on grounds of terrorism (¶178–188)". HCR, *List of issues to be taken up in connection with the consideration of the fifth periodic report of Morocco*, U.N. Doc. CCPR/C/MAR/2004/5 (Aug. 13, 2004). HRC, *Summary Record of the 2236th meeting–Consideration of Reports submitted by States parties under Article 40 of the Covenant–Fifth periodic report of Morocco,* 10, U.N. Doc. CCPR/C/SR.2236 (1 Nov. 1 2004).

636 *See* HRC *supra* note 635, at 25; Elisa Fornalé, *Protection of migrants in irregular situation and EU border control, in* SHAPING THE NORMATIVE CONTOURS OF THE EUROPEAN UNION: A MIGRATION-BORDER FRAMEWORK 134 (CIDOB Monograph, 2010).

637 HRC, *Compte rendu analytique (partiel) de la 2237e séance (publique),* U.N. Doc. CCPR/C/SR.2237 (Jan. 31, 2005).

mented only with discontinuity, the law does have some impact indirectly.

The 2003 legal provision cannot be considered an instrument that suitably balances the need to protect basic human rights of migrants alongside the introduction of specific measures to control the migratory flow, as solicited by the growing pressure on the Moroccan government.[638] By putting the accent on penalties for migrants who do not follow the rules of entry and residence, the new law seems to neglect the rights of these migrants.[639]

638 This instrument was described by some Moroccan legal scholars as "emergency legislation".

639 As stated by Prof. Khachani "*Si l'élaboration de ce projet de loi présente incontestablement une avancée sur le plan de la culture juridique au Maroc, il n'en demeure pas moins que le contenu de ce texte soulève de sérieuses interrogations. Ce projet de loi semble répondre, au moins en partie, a des pressions extérieures s'inscrit dans une conjoncture internationale et régionale qui privilégie la dimension sécuritaire au détriment de celle des droits humains*" ("If this legislative instrument represents an innovation within the legal culture in Morocco, its content raises several concerns. In fact, this draft seems to respond, at least partially, to external influence which promote a securitarian approach instead of the respect of human rights"–Translation provided by the author). Mohamed Khachani, *Les nouveaux défis de la question migratoire au Maroc*, ILO, Geneva, 2010, at 43.

7. Specific issues concerning Morocco practices and human rights violations against irregular migrants

The existence of the aforementioned legal standards–embodied in specific conventions and national provisions–is not sufficient to prevent an escalation of abuse, discrimination, and exploitation corresponding with the increase in irregular migration. In fact, specific challenges to ensure the enjoyment of rights at the national level remain unsolved.[640]

In recent years, human rights concerns have been raised by different international and national organizations[641] about the particularly vulnerable situation of migrants in irregular situation and allegations of human rights violations against them.[642] After the "fatal border incidents" that occurred near the border fences of Ceuta and Melilla in 2005, irregular migration appeared more evident and more information became available on the current situation.[643] The Special

640 Note that data recently presented by AMERM during a symposium held in Geneva on 27–28 May 2010 listed some of the problems illegal and irregular migrants most often encountered during the trip: 80% thirst, 79% hunger, 64% diseases that have arisen during the trip, 43% theft, 44% aggression, 15.5% sexual harassment, 11% rape, 52% arrest by police, 43% refusal of the police authorities, 35% death during the trip, 30% accidents.

641 *See* for example, Friends and Families of the Victims of Clandestine Immigration (AFVIC) and the Moroccan Association of Human Rights (AMDH), GADEM, the International Organization for Migration and the High Commissioner for Refugee.

642 FIDH, *Statement submitted to the Universal Periodic Review*, 2008.

643 Between August and October 2005, fifteen migrants were killed and hundreds injured in the attempt to cross the borders of the Spanish villages of Ceuta and Melilla. This episode is one of the worst acts documented, where the Moroccan security forces were deployed against irregular migrants destroying their camps, aggravating the repression, and carrying out savage acts of

Rapporteur on the human rights of migrants expressed deep concern at the reports of deaths of migrants of sub-Saharan origin on the border between the Spanish enclaves and Morocco.[644]

Those events have raised a particular attention on the difficulties that the government was facing at administrative and practical level to address this growing phenomenon, as stated by the Advisory Council on Human Rights (*Conseil Consultatif des droits de l'homme,* CCDH)[645] in the report published on those dramatic events.[646]

---

violence against them. MSF, *Violence et immigration, deux ans plus tard, Rapport sur l'immigration d'origine subsaharienne en situation irrégulière au Maroc et dans les zones frontalières*, MSF, 2008; Migreurop, *Le livre noir de Ceuta et Melilla*, June 2006. *See* Amnesty Int'l, *supra* note 78.

644 *See* SRHRM, *supra* note 528, at 14–15.

645 The Advisory Council for Human Rights was established by a Royal Decree, issued on 8 May 1990, and represents one of the major developments in the protection of human rights. This institution was subsequently amended in 2001 to ensure higher compliance with international standards. "*Dans le cadre d'une monarchie constitutionnelle, démocratique et sociale, fortement attachée aux droits de l'homme tels qu'ils sont universellement reconnus; demeurant, déterminée à consolider et promouvoir les acquis démocratiques dans leurs expressions culturelles et leur traduction dans la réalité […]. Eu regard, en outre, a nos engagements internationaux en faveur de la protection, la préservation et la promotion des droits de l'homme, engagements considères, chacun, comme référent normatif en la matière […] Pur que le Royaume du Maroc demeure au cœur de la dynamique de son ère, toujours fidèle a ses engagements internationaux dans le domaine des droits de l'homme*". (Within a constitutional, democratic and social monarchy, strongly linked to universally recognized human rights, engaged in the promotion and recognition of democratic foundations in their concrete translations […] Moreover bearing in mind its international commitments to the promotion and protection of human rights, commitments considered as binding references in legal matters […] To allow the Kingdom of Morocco to stay involved in the dynamics of the era, always faithful to its international commitments in the framework of the protection of human rights.– Translation provided by the author). MOHAMED SAADI, LE DIFFICILE CHEMIN DES DROITS DE L'HOMME AU MAROC 19 (Harmattan, 2009).

646 "*Le Conseil Consultatif des droits de l'homme n'a, à aucun moment, douté de la complexité du sujet ni de ses ramifications multiples. De par sa nature, la question est multifactorielle. Elle se situe aussi bien au niveau national qu'international, au niveau politique autant qu'au niveau social. Elle pose des exigences de droit au même titre que des nécessités humanitaires. Le*

7.1. Right to life

The incidents that occurred on the border with the Spanish enclaves of Ceuta and Melilla have sadly highlighted how the vulnerability of the migrants in irregular situation makes them susceptible to even the most extreme violation that can be envisaged, that of the right to life.[647] Not only do the authorities not seem to be able to protect the lives of migrants that try to cross the border, but at the same time the increase in the number of border checks seems to worsen the risks that migrants meet.[648]

In fact, news of the events between August and September 2005 document how much danger migrants' lives are in. Moroccan police shot at migrants trying to cross the border, wounding most of those present and killing fifteen. Testimonies from Doctors Without Borders (MSF) collected between 2005 and 2007 showed that of the 7533 medical consultations conducted, 1077 were linked to violence attributable to acts of the Moroccan police force.[649] Injuries documented include various forms of trauma caused by falls at the time of the crossing of the borders and various injuries during flight, pursuit, detention, and removal.

---

problème dépasse, par se embranchements, les seules capacités du Maroc à y répondre". (The Advisory Council of Human Rights has not at any time doubted the complexity of the subject or its many ramifications. By its nature, the question is multifaceted. It is as much national as international, as much political as social. It imposes requirements of law and at the same time humanitarian necessities. The problem exceeds, by its bifurcations, the only capabilities of Morocco to respond to them.–Translation provided by the author). CCDH, *Etablissement des faits relatifs aux événements de l'immigration illégale. Evénements de Ceuta et Melilla durant l'automne 2005*, CCDH, March 2007.

647 European Commission, *Technical Mission to Morocco, Visit to Ceuta and Melilla on Illegal Migration*, 7th October to 11th October 2005.

648 *See* GADEM, *supra* note 513, at 29.

649 *See* MSF, *supra* note 643, at 9.

7.2. *Socio-economic rights*

7.2.1. *Right to health*

The lack of access to basic services and medical care for migrants in irregular situation arises first from the absence of any explicit legislative provision. As came out from the analysis, the recent law does not step in here and seems to reserve access to medical care only for legal migrants.

Although Morocco, as mentioned above, is bound by international human rights instruments, migrants who live in irregular status in Morocco also are subjected to human rights violations that affect their security, living conditions, work, and residence, and they are also exposed to multiple forms of discrimination based on race and religion.[650]

On 30 September 2010 MSF raised concerns "over the medical condition of migrants after mass expulsions by the Moroccan police", revealing that between 600 and 700 migrants were arrested between August and September 2010 and deported from Morocco into the desert at the border with Algeria.[651] These migrants were left at the border without any food or water. Martin Jorge, MSF chief in Morocco, remarked,

> Our team has witnessed the direct impact of these mass raids and expulsions on the medical condition and mental health of the migrants [...] We provided medical support to a woman who had given birth to her child just six days before. She was arrested by the police forces and spent five days in a police cell with her newborn child. Then she was taken back to the border. She has managed to come back to Oujda, but is now suffering from acute gastrointestinal syndrome.

650 GADEM, *Foreigners in Morocco: a legal overview*, 1 MAROC COSMOPOLITE, 20–21 (2012).

651 "MSF raises concern over the medical condition of migrants after mass expulsions by the Moroccan police", MSF Press Release, 30 September 2010.

Women are forced to give birth under egregious hygienic conditions and without any medical attention whatsoever. Unfortunately, this case is confirmed to be only one part of a trend developing in Morocco, denounced repeatedly by the organizations that work in this sector. First MSF, in a report published in 2009, focused attention on the fact that the medical care in the towns of Rabat, Oujda, and Casablanca is provided only by their own staff, and that throughout 2008 they carried out more than 4000 medical interventions.

Connected to this are the poor working conditions in which migrants find themselves, often inducing them to assume risk-taking behaviours, such as prostitution and forced labour through human trafficking networks. This necessarily involves the rise of new medical issues such as the spread of sexually transmitted diseases.[652] In addition, the situation seems to be particularly acute when Moroccan police officers initiate collective expulsions, when migrants are literally abandoned on the border between Morocco and Algeria, without food and water.[653]

652 MSF, *International Report, Morocco 2008*, Doctor Without Borders, August 2009, at 34. It referred *ex multis* to a recent case reported by the collective DRARI, which showed how the situation concerning migrants is further deteriorating. On 16 February 2010 a Liberian woman gave birth to a baby in Tangier. The day after, the child was having breathing problems so she went back to the hospital. No one attended her and the day after, when she returned to the hospital, the child died. The hospital staff called the police because the couple was irregular; the husband was held in prison, and the wife was also arrested. The couple was permanently expelled from Morocco, along with their first child.

653 MSF in a Press Release, 30 September 2010, "*MSF raises concern over the medical condition of migrants after mass expulsions by the Moroccan Police*". MSF has reported that around 600 to 700 migrants were arrested between August and September 2010 and brought to the border between Morocco and Algeria. They are often at risk of being attacked by groups of bandits who patrol this area or from traffickers. The few who escape and get back to town have lost all their food, money, and personal belongings. Martin Jorge, an MSF officer in Morocco, declared "Our team has witnessed the direct impact of these mass raids and expulsions on the medical condition and mental health of the migrants [...] We provided medical support to a woman who had given birth to her

There are several cases documented by MSF of injured migrants being deprived of medical care during sudden removals by Moroccan police or during their arrest and subsequent detention to check their legal status. [654]

7.2.2. Housing

In 2007, the town of Rabat launched a campaign to prohibit real estate intermediaries from renting or leasing any property to migrants of African origin that decided to settle in Rabat.

In a press release, widely circulated,[655] it was expressly ordered that the intermediaries abstain from every conducting such business. The press release claimed that migrants only wanted to settle for the purpose of performing acts of proselytism and converting the citizens and resident in the area to Christianity.

In addition the fanciful news was spread that migrants were being recruited by fundamentalist groups and converted to Islam with dangerous intent; furthermore it was believed that some migrants devoted themselves to the illicit drug trade by exploiting their marginal position to skip normal state controls, and lastly the female population was suspected of practicing prostitution. For all these alleged reasons public authorities issued the ban.[656]

---

child just six days before. She was arrested by the police forces and spent five days in a police cell with her newborn child. Then she was taken back to the border. She has managed to come back to Oujda, but is now suffering from acute gastrointestinal syndrome".

654 In particular MSF documents the detention of a woman, eight months pregnant, who was arrested in Rabat and after the control sent back to Oujda at 5 am in the morning. The police ordered her to return to her own country of origin, to give birth, and leave the border by herself. She was found by MSF workers, who helped her for the delivery, and a few days later she was transferred to Rabat. *See* MSF, *supra* note 652, at 18.

655 6 February 2007, Newspaper Al Nahar Al Maghribia, No. 835.

656 *See* GADEM, *supra* note 520, at 12.

Such propaganda seems to be still widespread, in spite of the concern expressed by various international bodies and non-governmental organizations, including MSF, which last 30 September railed against Moroccan military forces breaking into camps and destroying tents and houses between 19 August and 10 September 2010, in various towns of Morocco, including Oujda, Tangier, Rabat, and Casablanca.[657]

7.2.3. Right to work

Access to the labour market is another serious concern. As stressed by the Special Rapporteur, the irregularity of the migrants' status in Moroccan territory and the high unemployment rate in Morocco prevents them from accessing the labour market.[658]

As mentioned above, most of the sub-Saharan migrants in transit to Morocco seem to fulfil the requirements for benefiting from the provisions of the Convention on Migrant Workers, and therefore for receiving from the protection that Morocco, as a transit country, is expressly obligated to grant them. In practice, their situation prevents them from connecting with their statutory rights. In fact, as is well documented, many migrants are employed in informal and unregulated positions, thereby lacking any form of legal protection and subject to expulsions by national authorities, as well as being vulnerable to abusive behaviour from their employers.

In this regard, it is significant that Ministry of Labour officers reported that Morocco does not seem to respect the rights of migrant workers in irregular situation in it application of existing national labour law, but they do not identify anyone and do not try to provide suitable protection.[659]

657 *See* MSF, *supra* note 642, at 10.

658 *See* SRHRM, *supra* note 528, ¶54.

659 *See* Cholewinski & Touzenis, *supra* note 542, at 27.

7.2.4. Discriminatory practices

Another problem that has been repeatedly described in the past few years is the spread of discriminatory and racist attitudes towards sub-Saharan migrants, attributable not only to their legal status, but also to other factors such as skin colour, language, and religion.[660]

This situation is also influenced by historical factors, such as the dynamics that have oriented the relationship between Morocco and other sub-Saharan countries (master–slave) or moreover due to discriminatory attitudes often going unpunished.[661]

The problem is aggravated by the national press, which paints a negative picture of irregular migrants, referring to them as criminals and thieves. Such language consequently leads to a range of discriminatory practices that appear to the eyes of the average citizen more or less justified, for example with respect to accommodation: the rent payments demanded from a foreigner are always much higher than average.

CERD, during the session held in August 2010, expressed strong concerns in relation to discrimination against towards sub-Saharan migrants.[662]

Attention has been directed to the absence of specific national legislation on the subject and to the lack of appeal process, which could present a powerful and relevant instrument for the protection of migrants.[663]

660 *See* GADEM, *supra* note 551, at 20.

661 *See* GADEM, *supra* note 520, at 22.

662 *See* CERD, *supra* note 589, ¶9.

663 G.A., *Report of the Working Group on the Universal Periodic Review, Morocco*, U.N. Doc. A/HRC/21/3 (Jul. 6, 2012).

7.3. Procedural rights and the appeal to the Judicial Authority

As shown above, Law No. 02/03 introduces a number of procedural guarantees including the possibility to appeal to judge, which may occur at the judge's discretion or upon an individual appeal to an administrative court.

To understand the role of administrative justices in this context, it is important to introduce and outline the national mechanisms established to allow foreigners access to basic tools for legal protection of their rights, and to explain the operation of those instruments.

The most important measure, stemming from Article 20 of Law No. 02/03, is the ability appeal to an administrative authority to contest the decisions made by the court. Article 23 provides that the appeal should be introduced within forty-eight hours, a deadline that may be hard to meet, considering the extreme conditions which foreigners are in.[664] The same article also provides a very short deadline for the appeal; in fact, the judge must make a decision within four days. In any case it is expressly provided that the judge ask for the intervention of an interpreter, in order to help conduct the proceedings fairly.

The concerned is also allowed access to his or her case file. The hearing is public and the applicant must be assisted by a lawyer, even if he or she requires that one be appointed by the court.[665]

In the meantime, the police may only detain foreigners in facilities not belonging to prison authorities (which are expressly identified as such) for the duration of the proceedings.

664 *See* Rbii, *supra* note 580, at 57.

665 Different criticism has been raised by NGOs concerning the practical application of this provision. Specifically it appears that the procedure for the appeal to the administrative authority is not respected. *See* GADEM, *supra* note 551, at 23–24.

It is important to emphasize that expulsion measures cannot be taken as long as the 48 hours have not elapsed or judge has not ruled on the case (Art. 24).[666] In the meantime the foreigner benefits from various rights since the moment in which he is notified of deportation:

- Request of legal assistance;
- Informing the consulate of his or her own country, or a personal contact;
- Right to appeal.

The judge will accept or reject the appeal and consequently confirm or annul the expulsion. Of course, the public authorities are still responsible for implementing the court ruling and, in the event of annulment, the migrant must be immediately released and automatically becomes eligible for a temporary residence permit until his or her migration situation can become better defined.[667]

The decision adopted by the court of first instance can be subsequently appealed before the Supreme Court within a month from the date of notification, although this appeal does not suspend the expulsion, so it will be carried out anyway. In fact Art. 28 provides:

> *la décision prononçant l'expulsion d'un étranger peut être exécutée d'office par l'administration. Il en est de même de la décision de reconduite a la frontière, qui n'a pas été contestée devant le Président du Tribunal Administratif ou son délégué en sa qualité de juge des référés, dans le délai prévu a l'article 23 de la présente loi, ou qui n'a pas fait l'objet d'une annulation en première instance ou en appel, dans les conditions fixées au même article.*[668]

666 Also in reference to the practical application of this rule, several concerns were raised, especially looking to the documented phenomenon of collective expulsions. For a full analysis *see* GADEM, *supra* note 518.

667 *See* Rbii, *supra* note 580, at 57.

668 (The decision to expel a foreigner may be carried out officially by the administration. It is the same for a decision to escort the foreigner to the border if the decision has not been contested in the Administrative Court or its delegate, as provided for in Art. 23 of this law, or if it has not been annulled in the court of first instance, under the conditions of in the same Article–Translation provided by the author).

The foreigner has also the opportunity to submit, together with the application, a petition to defer implementation of the decision; if the petition is accepted deportation may be delayed until the whole process, including all appeals, is completed. This takes into consideration that the consequences of a deportation order are, in most cases, irreparable and irreversible.[669] Unfortunately, the jurisprudence in such cases is not unanimous even contradictory and displays the weaknesses of the process.[670]

7.3.1. Collective expulsion

The absence of legal clarity on collective expulsion has facilitated a number of human rights violations. When people are intercepted by national authorities they are often immediately unlawfully expelled across the border closest to Algerian territory.[671] In several cases they are not given the opportunity to obtain legal advice nor are they given access to an interpreter, despite those rights being guaranteed

669 Art. 33: "*L'étranger qui a fait l'objet d'une mesure administrative de reconduite à la frontière et qui saisit le président du tribunal administratif, en sa qualité de juge de référés, peut assortir son recours d'un demande de sursis à l'exécution*". (The foreigner who was ordered by an administrative measure to leave the border, and who applies to the President of the Administrative Court, in its quality of summary judge, together with its appeal can enclose a request for the suspension of the execution– Translation provided by the author).

670 By way of example we cite the following decisions: C.S.A. sentence No. 787, 30 July 1998, *Policemen vs. Zahra Moutarif*, REMALD, No. 34, Sept.–Oct. 2000, 170–171; C.S.A. sentence No. 608, 20 May 1999, *Policemen vs. Ahmed Chaouki*, REMALD, No. 41, Nov.–Dec. 2001, 121–122; T.A., Casablanca, 13 July 1994, *Building Society Sidi Yahya vs. Oujda Chief City Council Sidi Ziyane*, REMALD, No. 9, Oct.–Dec. 1994, 70–75; T.A. Casablanca, O.R. No. 24, 26 July 1994, *Mohamed Takouti and others vs. Moroccan Gov.*, REMALD, No. 0 Oct.–Dec. 1994, 78–79; T.A. Marrakesh, 10 January 1995, *Brahim Amrai vs. Marrakesh Chief City Council Menara*, REMALD, No. 12, July–Sept. 1995, 134–136. *See* Rbii, *supra* note 580.

671 They have to walk across the border into Algeria to reach the nearest Algerian village, which is around 30 km away.

by Moroccan law.[672] In particular they were not informed that they were going to be expelled and no one, as reported by Amnesty International, had recourse to their rights appeal the decision before an administrative court, to examine the elements on which the decision was taken, to be assisted by a lawyer, or to contact the consulate of their country of origin.[673]

During the collective expulsions from Morocco to the desert it was not only irregular migrants that were arrested, however; there were also people who had made asylum claims at the UNHCR office in Rabat. Even if they produced a UNHCR document confirming that they had initiated the refugee status procedure, some officers said that they did not have instructions from competent authorities to give them any special protection or handling. The SRHRM expressed his concerns about the mass expulsions stating that "collective deportations in these conditions endanger the right to life."[674] Collective expulsions are prohibited by the provisions of Articles 22 and 23 of the UN Migrant Workers Convention, which as noted above Morocco has ratified, and according to the definition of migrant worker adopted in the Convention; those provisions apply to these circumstances. The issue was raised by a communication sent by the SRHRM[675] to the government of Morocco; the government replied that it excluded the application of the Migrant Workers Con-

672 Art. 23 and art. 24 of Law No. 02–03 concerning the entry and residence of foreigners in the Kingdom of Morocco, and Irregular Emigration and Immigration.

673 *See* Amnesty Int'l, *supra* note 78.

674 UN Press release, *Rights expert expresses deep concern over situation of migrants in Morocco and Spanish enclaves, urges to end to collective deportations*, 12 October 2005.

675 According to information received, since October 2005 mass expulsions of migrants and asylum seekers have been taking place. About 800 individuals have been left at the Algerian border without water and food. Most of the migrants deported are from sub-Saharan regions. On 3 October 2005, around 240 migrants were deported to Mauritania. More than 1000 migrants have been found by humanitarian organizations in need of urgent medical assistance. The possibility to visit the individuals detained in the military facilities of Guleimin is restrained to international organizations.

vention by arguing that the Convention applies only to migrant workers and members of their families irregularly present on the national territory. Instead, the persons deported were irregular migrants trying to cross the border into Europe.[676]

More cases of mass expulsions of illegal migrants are among the violations have been documented since then.[677] According to CIMADE's report published in 2004 following an investigation conducted of sub-Saharan migrants staying at Oujda camps, it revealed that more than half had been expelled to the border at least once. Some were also rejected up to seven times.[678]

As an example, it is necessary to pay attention to what Amnesty International stated in a 2008 report: "Hundreds of people suspected to be irregular migrants, including refugees and asylum seekers, were arrested and collectively expelled." The report even notes the murder of two Senegalese in the night between 30 and 31 July 2007.[679]

These operations do not seem to stop despite the concern expressed by various international bodies and non-governmental organizations, including MSF, that report on the mass expulsions over the border with Algeria, call on Morocco to respect the dignity and the integrity of migrants, and to avoid placing them in a situation of vulnerability and insecurity.[680]

676 SRHRM, *Report of the Special Rapporteur on the human rights of migrants, Jorge Bustamante, Summary of cases transmitted to Governments and replies received,* U.N. Doc. E/CN.4/2006/73/Add.1 (Mar. 23, 2006).

677 *See* SRHRM, *supra* note 528, ¶47–52.

678 *See* CIMADE, *supra* note at 536, at 34.

679 (Translation provided by the author). Amnesty Int'l, *The state of the world's human rights*, Amnesty International Report 2008, Amnesty International Publications, 2008, at 215.

680 Press release, *MSF exprime son inquiétude sur l'état de santé des migrants suite aux expulsions en masse menées par la police marocaines,* 30 September 2010.

7.4. Categories of particularly vulnerable migrants

7.4.1. Migrant women and sex crimes

A report published by Doctors Without Borders in March 2010, entitled "*Violence sexuelle et migration*" discussed another growing phenomenon: violence against migrant women in irregular status.[681] The report addressed a highly sensitive issue that is not always properly considered,[682] turning attention to the fact that migrant women during their journeys are particularly vulnerable to abuse and sexual violence. The paradox, plain to see on the basis of testimonies, is that many of them are fleeing from situations of generalized violence (for example involuntary marriage and domestic violence) and along the migratory route and even after their arrival in Morocco, they can be further abused and attacked. Their condition is not easily documented, as most refuse to denounce it openly. It is complex to seize the full extent of the phenomenon, and to try to put proper mechanisms of protection in place. In fact, their status as irregular generally blocks any type of complaint for such violations. On the basis of data provided by MSF between May 2009 and January 2010, one third of the women assisted by MSF in Rabat and Casablanca admitted to suffering one or two episodes of sexual violation.[683] "*Le Gouvernement du Maroc doit améliorer la prise en charge des migrantes subsahariennes victimes*

681 MSF, *Violence sexuelle et migration–La réalité cachée des femmes sub-sahariennes arrêtées au Maroc sur la route de l'Europe*, MSF, March 2010.

682 The phenomenon of sexual violence was highlighted in the report published by MSF, reporting that since 2005 in several episodes of violence happened to women and children, it seems that 43.3% of the cases followed up concerned rapes. It appeared hard to determine the profile of these aggressors; MSF supposed that in many cases they were Nigerians gangs patrolling Morocco-Algeria's borders. *See* MSF, *supra* note 681, at 16.

683 *See* MSF, *supra* note 681, at 5. The interviewed women are mainly from the Democratic Republic of Congo, from areas where here are armed conflicts, and from Nigeria.

de violences sexuelles sur son territoire",[684] declared Alfonso Verdu, MSF's chief operation officer in Morocco, "*Mais les pays de l'Union européenne doivent également être conscients des graves conséquences résultant des politiques de migration et d'asile de plus en plus restrictives sur la santé et la sécurité des migrants et en particulier sur les personnes les plus vulnérables que sont les femmes et les jeunes filles*".[685]

In addition, on this topic major research conclusions were recently published by the High Commissioner for Refugees, which emphasized the issue of violence suffered by migrant women during their migratory journey, analysing four country case studies, including Morocco, through the collection of nineteen testimonies of women.[686] In the report, *La violence sexuelle et Trans-migrants subsahariens au Maroc: un partenariat participatif pour la prévention*, the analysis gives an introductory description of different acts of violence, distinguishing among: *sexual violence:* rape, sexual torture, forced prostitution, sexual harassment (such as being forced to dance naked in front of the police); *psychological violence:* threat, imprisonment, insults; *physical violence:* beating with sticks, throwing of boiling water on the body; and *traditional practices* such as sexual mutilation.[687]

684 (The Moroccan Government must improve protection of sub-Saharan migrant victims of sexual violence within its territory–Translation provided by the author).

685 (But the European Union countries must be aware of the serious consequences resulting from migration and asylum policies that are more and more restrictive in relation to health and safety of migrants and in particular of the most vulnerable people, such as women and teenagers.–Translation provided by the author).

686 Smaïn Laacher, *Les violences faites aux femmes pendant leur voyage clandestin: Algérie, France, Espagne, Maroc*, UNHCR, April 2010. *See* also Jane Freedman & Jamal Bahija, *Violence à l'égard des femmes migrantes et réfugiées dans la région Euro-méditerranéenne*, Réseau Euro-méditerranéen des droits de l'homme, December 2008. *La violence sexuelle et Trans-migrants subsahariens au Maroc: un partenariat participatif pour la prévention.* Information letter 1 February 2009. Gand, Liège, Rabat. Under the editorship of Ines Keygnaert, Abdssamad Dialmy, and Altay Manço.

687 *See* Laacher, *supra* note 686.

It must be emphasized that especially in transit countries there are different types of abuses, occurring in private and/or in public places, suffered by a single individual, or collective aggression. According to the MSF report, acts of violence are committed also by the public officials such as the police,[688] at the borders, in urban area, or, in the desert.[689]

. Violence against women is committed with extreme cruelty, , and in many cases are committed publicly. A witness documents:

> *Un matin, à 6 h, en décembre 2006, j'avais 16 ans et je me suis fait arrêter par la police au Maroc. Ils m'ont emmenée sur une grande place avec plein d'autres Noirs, des hommes et des femmes. Après on nous a amenés à Oujda. On a marché pendant toute une nuit. Les policiers ont divisé le groupe pour la marche. Je pleurais beaucoup. Toutes les femmes ont été violées, dans une tente, par les 18 policiers marocains. Ils ont aussi violé les hommes, devant tout le monde. On est resté pendant 2 jours. Je n'ai pas mangé ni bu, je n'ai fait que dormir (Femme nigériane, Maroc).*[690]

One of the most worrying aspects is that facing the suffered violence and harassment, migrant women live in the silence and the darkness, feeling unable to report the crimes against them because of the deficiency of suitable tools to provide and ensure minimal legal protection.

688 MSF documented several cases of violence carried out by the Moroccan military forces. *See* MSF, *supra* note 681, at 19.

689 MSF Report, *Violence et immigration. Rapport sur l'immigration d'origine subsaharienne en situation irrégulière au Maroc,* MSF, September 2005. This report highlights the issue of irregular sub-Saharan immigration in Morocco, focusing mainly on the year 2005. The work of foreign organizations was very tightly controlled, almost impossible for example in Algeria, and it had in particular a monitoring role, able to collect the testimonies of assisted migrants.

690 (One morning, at 6 am, in December 2006, I was 16 and apprehended by the police in Morocco. I was taken in a big square together with other blacks, men and women. After that I was taken to Oujda. We walked all night long. The cops divided the group for the march. I cried a lot. All the women were raped in a tent by 18 Moroccans policemen. They also abused men in front of all the others. We stayed two days. I did not eat, nor drink, I slept – Translation provided by the author). *See* MSF, *supra* note 689, at 43.

One interesting note that deserves to be analysed is how and if violence and mistreatment along the way can be independently taken under consideration to grant the refugee status or not.. As it was pointed out by an officer of the UN High Commissioner for Refugees in Rabat that, within certain limits, women who are victims of violence may be eligible to invoke humanitarian protection because such violence hinders the return to their own countries of origin:

> *La violence pendant le parcours n'est pas fondamentale pendant l'entretien avec le HCR. Ça peut permettre de décider si on doit donner des soins médicaux ou psychologiques. On fait attention de voir s'il y a un risque de trafic. Du point de vue de l'éligibilité, les violences hors du pays d'origine ne sont pas prises en compte. On ne peut pas vérifier ce qui s'est passé en cours de route. Le récit sur le trajet n'est parfois pas assez documenté. On sort un peu de la définition du réfugié. La question est: est-ce que quelqu'un peut rentrer chez lui ou pas? Les violences sur la route ne l'empêche pas de rentrer chez lui [...] par contre, peut-être que si une personne a une histoire particulièrement horrible et traumatisante et que dans son pays il n'y a ni soins ni structures pour l'aider, alors peut-être, il faudrait se poser la question (Officier de protection, HCR, Rabat).*[691]

7.4.2. Victims of smuggling and human trafficking

Another issue that particularly involves migrants in irregular situation and especially women and children is the spread of smuggling and

691 ("The violence that occurs during the trip is not an significant issue during the interview with the UNHCR. This is relevant only to allow them to decide if medical or psychological support is necessary or not. It is noted if there is a risk of the person being a victim of trafficking. Regarding eligibility, the violence that occurred outside the countries of origin is not taken into consideration. It is not easy to monitor what happens during the trip, as it is often not well documented. This can be understood from the definition of 'refugee'. The point is: can an individual return to his country of origin or not? The violence that occurs during the trip does not stop them returning home [...] however, at the same time, if a person has a particularly awful and traumatic background and if his or her own country lacks treatment facilities, then perhaps, it would be necessary to ask the question."–Protection officer at UNHCR–Translation provided by the author), *see* Laacher, *supra* note 686, at 4.

human trafficking. Specifically, human trafficking has become a problem of international significance, as documented by a recent study published by the United Nations High Commissioner for Refugees, together with the International Organization for Migration and the Ministry of Justice in Morocco.[692]

The report noted how, from a political point of view,[693] the Moroccan Government was made aware of this phenomenon. From available data, the extent of the phenomenon is not very great, but hides several risks. In particular, irregular migrants, due to the vulnerability of their condition, are more easily drawn into the nets of exploitation and trafficking in human beings.

Currently what emerges is the considerable difficulty that exists in the identification of specific cases of human trafficking, because of the lack of specific domestic rules. In fact, the absence within the Moroccan legislative framework of the criminalization of human trafficking makes it difficult to identify its victims. In addition, this also deprives government of the power to act for the protection of the victims and to punish this crime.

Among the documented cases of trafficking, there is the recruitment of young Nigerian women (mainly from the city of Benin) that pass through Morocco to reach Europe through a network of women who manage the passage. Unfortunately at present it is difficult to establish the magnitude of this flow, also because victims are often kidnapped from their homes and they meet doctors in secret if they have health problems. Frequently during the imprisonment they suffer a different kind of violence that could be described as torture.[694]

Another recently documented case by IOM is one of Philippines migrant workers trafficked to carry out domestic work in Morocco.[695] They are women between 20 and 40 years old who decided to leave

692 *See* IOM, *supra* note 55.

693 In particular the Council of Ministers joined Palermo Protocol on 7 May, 2009.

694 *See* IOM, *supra* note 55, at 34 and 41.

695 *Id.* at 20, 22 and 37.

their home country, mainly for economic reasons. They are easily recruited because they do not need visas to enter Morocco, and once in Moroccan territory, their passports are confiscated and they are employed in Moroccan houses to do housekeeping. Working conditions agreed before departures are not respected and generally they do not receive any salary. Once the 90 days of legal staying on Moroccan territory had expired, they are in an irregular situation. Thus, these women are clearly in a vulnerable condition, devoid of a contract of employment, without the opportunity to apply for any form of legal protection from Moroccan authorities, and lacking of any knowledge of the Moroccan dialect.

Together with these documented cases of trafficking, the IOM report has turned the attention also to the latent risk of possible trafficking of minors, in particular of children born during transit. Moroccan law expressly provides that for the registration of birth of a child it is necessary to show a certificate issued by a doctor, or a woman who has witnessed the birth, or by the local authority.[696] Many migrants, for fear of being arrested, when requested by the registry office do not make such a declaration and prefer not to declare the birth, believing this declaration mostly unnecessary. Consequently, there have been a number of cases of child abduction, documented by NGOs that provide assistance to migrants. Service Aid to Migrants (SAM) is one such NGO and has documented the disappearance of three new-born babies.[697]

This emergency will require the introduction at the national level of specific tools to contrast it, while Morocco appears to lack the necessary legal framework. In the specific cases it emerges, as an imminent need, the introduction of specific protection measures for victims of trafficking so that are not prosecuted. Legal instruments must exist to provide punctual protection, such as to issue a residence permit on humanitarian grounds, as well as those that specifi-

696 IOM, supra note 55, at 38. Article 17, Decree No. 2-99-665 9 October 2002, in application of Law No. 37-99 concerning the status, B.O. No. 5054, 7 November 2007, 1198.

697 See IOM, supra note 55, at 39.

cally provide for criminal sanctions to those responsible for human trafficking or to anyone party to the crime.

7.4.3. Asylum seekers–refugees–migrants in irregular situation

A large group of foreigners live in Morocco, asylum seekers or refugees, who, given the above-noted absence of a suitable legislative instrument at the national level tend to converge with and to be assimilated to the general phenomenon of migrants in an irregular situation.

As CERD recently confirmed: "*Le Comité recommande à l'Etat partie d'établir un cadre juridique et institutionnel visant à clarifier les procédures d'asile et à garantir la protection des droits des réfugiés et des demandeurs d'asile, notamment en ce qui concerne l'accès à l'emploi et l'accès au logement, ainsi que leur protection contre la discrimination raciale*".[698]

This precarious situation leaves room for the occurrence of abuses and violations committed by police responsible for controlling the entry and stay of irregular migrants.[699]

The sweeping casuistry, documented by various non-governmental organizations operating in this sector, which supports the thesis that in the absence of an appropriate legal tool for refugees, even if they possess a document issued by the Office of the High Commissioner for Refugees, do not benefit from any protection and especially are treated as illegal migrants in irregular situation.[700]

698 (The Committee recommends the state party to establish a legal and institutional framework that seeks to clarify asylum procedures and to ensure the protection of the refugees and asylum seekers rights, concerning for example access to employment, accommodation, and protection against racial discrimination.– Translation provided by the author). *See* CERD, *supra* note 589, ¶13.

699 *See* Cholewinski & Touzenis, *supra* note 542, at 27.

700 *See* CIMADE, *supra* note 536; FIDH, *Espagne–Maroc: situation des immigrants et demandeurs d'asile, non a la répression comme politique migratoire*, 2003.

An example is the arrest of five refugees by police in Rabat on 3 July 2009,[701] with serious violations coming out in the reports drawn up by the police themselves. [702] In the first place there is a total lack of respect for the basic right of defence. Secondly there is the absence of suitable interpretation, supported by the drawing up of five identical proceedings coercively arranged by a police officer.

This is in plain contrast to both international commitments and the agreement explicitly signed between the Kingdom of Morocco and the High Commissioner for Refugees. These agreements dictate that refugees are not ever to be treated as migrants in irregular status, a condition still not met as police records show a strong discrepancy between the content of the international agreements and their realistic application.[703] It is not significant that in the minutes drawn up by the police, every defendant came out and declared: "I confirm I live in Morocco in an illegal situation, as all the other African immigrants". It is hard to believe that such declarations were spontaneous and they may foster an extremely dangerous and widespread belief that associates the African migrant with the clandestine one.[704]

Between 2 and 4 July the five refugees who were arrested were detained at the police station and escorted to a prison in Salé, await-

701 The detailed description and transcription of the minutes written by the police is in the Annex.

702 It is important to remember that the arrest of these five refugees can be considered as part of a problem that reached its apex during the month of July 2009, but certainly there had been signs of it since 2006. The fights that occurred in July were preceded by various demonstrations held in front of High Commissioner for Refugees premises in June. The clash itself took place on 2 July, between refugees and the military forces and there were forty wounded, five of whom were taken to the hospital and one in very serious condition. Between 2 and 4 July the five refugees who were arrested were detained by the Police and escorted then to Salé s prison to await the decision of their case. The trial was conducted at the Court of First Instance in Rabat and among the charges appeared "irregular stay", in accordance with art. 40 of Law 02-03.

703 *See* Li Rosi & Ryan, *supra* note 546, at 15.

704 GADEM, *Note informative sur le procès de cinq refugiés*, July 2009.

ing the end of the trial. The trial was held at the Rabat Court of First Instance and among the charges appeared "irregular stay", in accordance with Art. 40 of Law No. 02/03.

A verdict was adopted on 26 July 2009,, overturned the finding of irregular residence for refugees recognized by the High Commission for Refugees in Rabat.[705]

The mobilization that has reached its peak on 2 July has seen since 2006 increasing turmoil, as the refugees bore several requests. First was the introduction of a suitable procedure to obtain recognition of their status by the Moroccan authorities, and then the need to establishfinancial assistance services into place.[706]

705 *Available at* <www.abc.es/20090727/internacional-africa/carcel-para-cinco-refugiados-200907271912.html> (last visited Jun. 20, 2012).

706 There were several protest sit-ins, on among other dates: 20 June 2006, 24 July 2006, 19 January 2007, 18 May 2007, 12 February 2008 and 18 June 2004. They are considered key dates in this tenaciously claim pursued by refugees in Moroccan territory.

Conclusion

This work has shown how the phenomenon of irregular migration faces the exercise of national authority in the implementation of international law, in particular the implementation of human rights law.

The exploration of different legal systems and standards in place allowed the assessment of existing normative gaps concerning the protection of migrants in irregular situation and additionally the identification of where there is unnecessary overlap. In the case of irregular migration, the fact that distinctions cannot be made among other groups of migrants, as the so-called mixed migratory flows, raises significant challenges at the practical level. The result is that international legal standards have not always had a strong impact on prevention of and protection from violence and abuse. As a consequence, the governance of migration cannot be influenced by a sovereign and securitarian logic disconnected from a human-rights based approach.

The analysis in chapter 1 sought to affirm that the existing normative framework lacks an established and consistent legal definition of "irregular migrant", limited by the exercise of sovereign authority. Such fluidity facilitates the destabilization of the condition of migrants, exposing them to, and in a certain way "justifying", the absence of binding obligations for states. In particular, a number of implications exist for the use of inappropriate and negative terms such as "illegal" or "clandestine" that implicitly support the vision of a strong interrelationship between irregular migration and criminal activity. Instead this work invokes the need to opt for more neutral terminology to avoid any potential abuse or violation. The problem of the "illegal" categorization is its relation to the application of international standards to migrants. It is self-evident that in our legal system the legal status of an individual affects his or her enjoyment of rights, and it is difficult to see how an individual might have access to any measures of protection if officially he or she does not exist.

The first section focused on a number of issues raised by the interconnection between human rights and the protection of irregular migrants. First, it investigated the way in which existing international standards, both general and specific, involve a hard core of rights and obligations, though their full implementation is subject to limitations and the absence of meaningful national mechanisms. The High Commissioner for Human Rights clearly stated that the mere affirmation of a right does not replace its fulfilment:

> Border security and immigration controls cannot, and as a matter of international law do not, trump the obligations of the State to respect the internationally guaranteed rights of all persons, to protect those rights against abuses, and to fulfil the rights necessary for them to enjoy a life of dignity and security.[707]

Chapters two and three were devoted to demonstrating, first from a general perspective and later from a more sectorial perspective, how the appearance of irregular migration was gradually dealt by international law, with direct advantages and disadvantages, as the analysis made clear. In particular, the recent entry into force of the International Convention on the Human Rights of Migrants and Members of Their Families captures this ambivalent perspective. On one side, this international instrument is invoked to contain important provisions to the benefit of irregular migrants, following its innovative approach. On the other side, the explicit differentiation made by this Convention in the illustration of rights, especially maintaining a distinction between regular and irregular migrants, seems to confirm their vulnerable situation, and, as argued by some scholars, their inferiority due to this arbitrary category.

This is exacerbated by the limited protection ensured by international human rights instruments, which, despite their universal mission, do not always appear capable of responding to the challenges raised by real cases and the binding power of these instruments seems to fade in the face of irregular migration.

707 *See* GMG, *supra* note 15, at 43.

Chapter four outlined the relevant progress made in this context, particularly in the efforts deployed by several judicial authorities, who allowed the identification of minimum standards in the enjoyment of civil, economic, and social rights of irregular migrants. In particular, the work of these bodies has been to progressively reconcile the discretion of national states in regulating migratory flows and the need to identify the fundamental rights granted to irregular migrants. This responsibility is increasing the role of jurisprudence, even if the evidence from so few cases does not allow the establishment of a solid and coherent practice for the full application of human rights to migrants.

In light of the results of the second section, even if the limited availability of information impedes a comprehensive analysis of the current legal context concerning migration, the case study of Morocco further elaborates the concepts illustrated in the previous chapters. Obligations of member states to provide minimum standards to the migrants under their jurisdiction of may be limited by the prerogatives of national sovereignty. As highlighted by Prof. Foblets, there are tensions between the exercise and enforcement of national security prerogatives (e.g. the regulation of the entry and stay of migrants) and claims of individuals' interests.[708] The Morocco case is a concrete illustration of the difficulties and limitations facing international human rights standards with regard to irregular migrants.

Chapter five highlighted how the stay of irregular migrants in national territory is in general the result of a very complex legal framework concerning the entry and stay of foreigners, including economic migrants, and how the boundaries between irregular migrants and asylum seekers are in many cases unclear.

Chapters six and seven tried to complement the analysis on the international standards ratified by Morocco with the country's national legal background. Although Morocco is a party to the main relevant international human rights agreements, this does not guarantee the effectiveness of rights provided by these instruments. In par-

708 *See* Foblets, *supra* note 37, at 146–149.

ticular Morocco was among the first states to ratify the International Convention on the Protection of Migrant Workers and Member of Their Families and the Refugees Conventions, yet it has not yet adopted national measures to implement them. A wide discrepancy between its international obligations and the measures taken at national level seems to persist, in particular the recognition and safeguarding of economic and social rights. This discrepancy is more marked in regard to the implementation of the ICRMW.

Indeed, at national level the elaboration and adoption of Law 02/03 regulating the entry and the stay of migrants is a significant step made by the government of Morocco to articulate and improve the domestic legal framework, even though this instrument, when translated into practise, seems to fall short of expectations. The tool aims at stopping irregular immigration instead of protecting irregular migrants from abuse and rights violations. At the same time, the analysis shows that in relation to these issues the government of Morocco appears in some way to be taken hostage by external pressures imposed to conduct a restrictive migration policy. In addition, available information on the situation of vulnerable groups, such as migrant women and victims of traffic and smuggling, is limited, and this makes it difficult to assess a comprehensive picture of the way into which their rights are actually implemented.

The study demonstrated the persistence, over time, of a deep imbalance between the exercise of national authority in the field of migration and the legitimization of individual rights and interests.

Annex: Selection of testimonies and articles published between 2004 and 2010 related toviolence and abuses against irregular migrants in Morocco[709]

Year 2010

2010: Amnesty International Annual Report 2010 [710]

Migrants' rights

Authorities kept arresting and expelling foreign citizens suspected of being irregular migrants, often without taking into consideration their individual protection needs or allowing them to appeal their expulsions. As reported, some of them were attacked and mistreated during or after their arrest or during their expulsion, and it was reported that some of them had been unloaded at the border of Algeria or Mauritania without enough food and water.

A 29-year-old migrant from Cameroon died on 1 January after being shot by security officials, part of a group of about 50 migrants trying to reach the fence between Morocco and the Spanish enclave of Melilla. Fourteen other members of that group were arrested, beaten, and finally released at the border with Algeria, nearby Oujda town. No investigations into these episodes were done.

Refugees and asylum seekers

Even though Morocco is party to the 1951 Refugee Convention and the related 1967 Protocol, authorities have not given residence

709 All translations are my own unless otherwise noted.

710 *Available at* <www.amnesty.it/Rapporto-Annuale-2010/Marocco-Sahara-occidentale-9d3fb2> (last visited Jun. 20, 2012).

permits or other necessary documents to recognized refugees by UNHCR. On 15 June a group of refugees organized a sit-in in front of UNHCR's office in Rabat to complain and ask to be resettled in other countries. Two weeks later there were clashes between the police and the refugees when the latter refused to go away. Five refugees were arrested, judged guilty of violent behaviour, sentenced to one month imprisonment, and sanctioned. They were acquitted of the indictment of remaining in the country irregularly. They were reportedly beaten during the arrest.

2010: In Morocco the organization Migreurop reports the readmission agreements set out by EU

Press release of the network of associations on going to meet in Bouznika[711]

Migreurop will hold a meeting of its board of directors 5–7 March in Bouznika in Morocco. The location is geographically strategic, being at the gates of Europe and considering that Morocco's engagement with the European Union has long focused on migration issue. The European Union and Morocco will meet next Monday, 8 March in Granada, Spain, to discuss the negotiation of a free trade agreement rather than human rights issues and democracy. Since 2003 the official negotiations have been reopened on a putative EU–Morocco readmission agreement, which until this moment has not materialized.

Migreurop wants to warn about the danger in signing such an agreement during this coming summit. In a campaign that started at the beginning of 2008, denouncing the conclusion of such an agreement, Migreurop asks that transparent procedures be put in place.

Readmission agreements, whatever form they assume, have as a direct consequence the "industrialization" of expulsion because it facilitates expulsions and allows only a *fortiori* control of the violation

711 *Available at* <terreerrance.wordpress.com/2010/03/page/2/> (last visited Jul. 20, 2012).

of human rights of these migrants to be exerted: very often, as it is known, potential asylum seekers are sent back, while other rejected persons are sent to third countries different from those of origin.

The European Union and Morocco are carrying on a kind of "*do ut des*" where the exchange currency is migrants: the Union orchestrates development aid in exchange for the readmission of partner country nationals, but also of those who are not nations of the country, into the territory of the partner country from time to time; on the other hand, the third countries are seeking facilities in granting visas, in concluding economic agreements and the like, to the detriment of the rights of migrants.

Franco Frattini, former European Commissioner, pointed out in 2006 that "the good end of the negotiations depends a lot on the 'levers' that are used, or better to say from the 'carrots' of which the Commission has to obtain the cooperation of third countries involved."

The "carrot" for Morocco today is in the promise of creation of a free trade area with the EU, as well as in a series of massive investments in the Moroccan market. The "stick" would be silence on human rights violations: even if the European Union pretends to worry about the human rights situation in Morocco, it continues to negotiate the signing of a readmission agreement for irregular migrants to a country which, it is better to remember, "does not yet recognize officially refugees arrived in recent years within its territory, neither provides them any assistance."

Migreurop denounces the opacity and the exclusion of the civil society in the negotiations of the EU agreement with Morocco.

2010: Morocco, the migratory thorn in the side of Mediterranean Europe [712]

Amnesty Report

Yet even in the face of the many stories of misery and violence told by Amnesty International, Doctors Without Borders, and independent media, the rulers of Madrid and Rabat for years continue to smile at each other and hug each other, making the mutual blackmail the means for achieving each their own national targets. "Morocco expresses confidence to Spain that the thorny issue of immigration will be dealt with openly and within the framework of Spanish-Moroccan friendship," said the former Prime Minister Driss Jettou in April 2005, welcoming Mrs Maria Teresa Fernandez de la Vega, former first vice-president of the Zapatero's government, in an official visit to Rabat. "We know that it is a difficult process and that there are human tragedies, but we are convinced of the generosity of the Spanish people and in the way in which the Spanish government seeks to address this sensitive and difficult issue [...]. The two parties must make more efforts and mobilize the most important resources to continue on this way."

This is the path that was laid out for many years: do more and do better against illegal immigration. That means putting into practice agreements on whose basis, in connection with loans, investments, special lanes for export, and military supplies, the Moroccan government undertakes to oppose migratory flows vigorously, and even to allow European military units to patrol the coast. For a long time and with different actors, the same play has been staged in France, Italy, and Greece. Africa is close and the pressure from immigration increases from year to year. Since 2005 the European Union agency Frontex has been in operation with the purpose of "promoting a pan-European model of Integrated Border Security". That means cooperation among the members of the European Union with regard

712 *Available at* <www.terranews.it/news/2010/03/marocco-la-spina-migratoria-delleuropa-mediterranea> (last visited Jun. 20, 2012).

to border control, exchange of information, harmonization of deportation policies, and cooperation with countries of origin and transit.

An ancient southern proverb says: "share the wealth and become impoverished". Today the apparent goal of every policymaker is to prevent armies of migrants from invading the continent, and every European government, left or right, it is nothing more than a worker engaged responsibly to build the bulwarks of "fortress Europe". In Spain, Zapatero seems to have won a battle against illegal immigration. Yet the war continues and has deep roots. At the moment Morocco agrees to do the dirty work, stopping and expelling without many compliments those who pass the border illegally. If over time the flows increase, as is predicted to happen, different solutions will be needed that act on the causes of the phenomenon. Such ideas, at this time, seems not be possible to be proposed.

2010: Violence suffered by women migrants in an irregular situation, Doctors Without Borders[713]

The case of O.A., a 26-year-old Congolese woman who left her country because of a political conflict and suffered violence at the hands of a group of men dressed as soldiers. In Mauritania, since she had no documents, a driver proposed to carry her hidden under the seat of the car. During the route, the vehicle stopped in the middle of the desert, the driver and his friend have started talking, and afterward the driver approached her and beat her. He fondled her and grabbed her chest as an insult. Then his friend raped her. She screamed but there was no one around, they were in the middle of the desert. When they finished they fled. O.A. was able to reach Morocco thanks to the help of another driver. The passage on the border between Morocco and Algeria, Oujda and Morocco is the example of the extreme danger of the journey. On the basis of testimonies gathered from Doctors Without Borders, 63 per cent of the women surveyed have suffered violence or aggression of a sexual

713 *See* MSF, *supra* note 679, at 6.

nature during the way. In spite of the borders still being blocked, the Moroccan security forces moved away migrants toward this area. The expulsions occur generally at night, increasing the risk of aggression.

T.D., a 19-year-old woman, was stopped by the police while she was going to the market in Oujda and was conducted to the Police Station where there were 28 other sub-Saharan migrants. The entire group was deported in the middle of the desert, the same evening. While she was walking together with three men and two other women, a group of Moroccans bandits had attacked them. Every woman was raped by three bandits, one after the other, according to T.D.

A.A., a girl of 14 years, was alone in her country after the death of her mother and the departure of her father, who fled due to political persecution. A friend of the family came to take her; took a plane up to Casablanca and then to Paris. Once they arrived at the airport were sent back to Morocco. Upon arrival in Casablanca, A.A. was separated from the woman who was escorting her and traced back to Oujda by the Police. That same night she was taken to the border with 15 other irregular migrants of various nationalities. She was a minor and the only female of the group. Four policemen with dogs took them to the middle of the desert, and two more policemen took A.A. apart from the others. According to her testimony, she was asked to take off her clothes and since she refused, they undressed her and after raping her they led her back to the other migrants.

Year 2009

July 2009: Arrest of 5 asylum seekers[714]

3rd July, 2009=10:00 am Testimony of S.D., Ivorian, gathered from the official of the Judicial Police (translation from Arabic–GADEM).

S.D. does not know how to read and write in Arabic.

714 GADEM, Note informative sur le procès de cinq réfugiés, July 2009.

At the end of 2008, I left my country to reach Europe due to the serious economic problems that Ivory Coast suffers. Together with my citizens we crossed the African desert on foot and we arrived at the border. After making contact with a person on the spot, who helped us in exchange for 100 Euro, we crossed the border into Morocco. After entering in Morocco, I remained, like the rest of the illegal immigrants, in a forest in the north of the country, to prepare to enter Morocco and to wait the moment to enter Europe. In order to move freely, I wrote to the High Commissioner for Refugees of the UN and I obtained an identity document from this institution, knowing that I do not belong to any political or military party against the government, but it is a trick invented by illegal migrants to live and stay in the country. I confirm that I live in an illegal manner in the country, as all the other African migrants and I don't have any document.

Question/Answer: "I know myself to be in the country in an irregular manner, I confirm that I have fought the military forces and that I refuse to stick to their orders. After I was armed with a wood stick, I beat someone to the arm."

Question/Answer: "In fact I got the stick and I beat civilians, I assure you that the people who were arrested with me have committed the same offenses."

After the translation done by A.C., police officer, the declarations were signed. S.D. was in jail from 2nd July 2009 at 13:00 till 4th July 2009 at 14:00. Authorities were informed.

The same minutes were drawn up for N.S., Ivorian at 11:00; D.S., Ivorian, at 13:00; M.K., Ivorian, at 16:00; and M.D., Congolese, at 17:00.

2009: Melilla: migrants killed by the Moroccan police. Amnesty calls for survey [715]

ROME, 9 January 2009–A week after the murder of a migrant by auxiliary forces of the Moroccan army that patrol the border of the Spanish enclave of Melilla, Amnesty International has officially asked to Rabat to open an investigation to shed light on what happened.

715 *Available at* <fortresseurope.blogspot.com/2006/01/melilla-migrante-ucciso-dalla-polizia.html> (last visited Jun. 20, 2012).

On New Year's Eve, a group of about fifty sub-Saharan migrants attempted to skip the double fencing that runs six meters high along the border of Melilla. To stop them, Moroccan military forces fired a series of shots. One of the migrants was seriously wounded and died soon thereafter at hospital El Hassani, in Nador. This is a young Cameroonian, 29 years old, known as Alino. Fourteen other men were arrested and arbitrarily deported to Algerian border, near Oujda.

Alino is not the first sub-Saharan migrant killed by Moroccan auxiliary forces. Between 2005 and 2006, at least 15 migrants were killed by gunfire along the border of Ceuta and Melilla. The last murder there was news of dates back to 24 December, 2006. On 31 July, 2007 two migrants were killed in the western Sahara, close by El Ayun, while boarding to the Canary Islands–not to mention the dinghy sunk at the dawn of 28 April, 2008 by agents of the Moroccan royal navy, off the coast of Al-Hoceima, on the route to Spain. This accident cost the lives of at least 28 migrants.

Year 2008

2008: Sub-Saharan migrants: a human ping-pong between Morocco and Algeria[716]

In several cities, including Rabat, Nador, Laayoune, Tetouna, Fès, and Oujda, police have arrested several sub-Saharan Africans in their houses, in the markets, in the streets. It is genuinely hunting; denounce the associations that defend migrants in transit in Morocco.

After arrest these migrants were transferred to the town of Oujda, the village in the eastern region where the majority of the sub-Saharans are. From there they are directed to the entry/exit point on the Morocco-Algeria border. Once removed from Morocco to Alge-

716 *Available at* <www.lereporter.ma/article.php3?id_article=5927> (last visited Jun. 20, 2012).

ria, these migrants are driven to the Algerian authorities, sometimes impelled with gunfire. They return automatically to Oujda and at that point it begins a true human "ping-pong" between Algeria and Morocco.

"After the arrest of a huge number of sub-Saharan migrants", explains one of the members of ABCDS (an association that helps migrants), "that evening the police removed them to the Algerian border, although it has been closed for years, in violation of the Moroccan law that prohibits the collective expulsions and requires case examinations of the persons deported, on a case by case basis."

According to the current association statistics, the number of migrants who find themselves in the neighbourhood of Oujda is between 900 and 1000 people. Added to this are 500 other sub-Saharan removed in during this time period.

Migrants are forced to cross a dangerous "no man's land". This border area is a desert without water, food, or accommodation.

The thermal variations to which they are subjected are between 6 degrees in winter to 43 degrees in summer. This area is characterised by the traffic of people and goods, as for the presence of criminal gangs that do not hesitate to attack the migrants.

2008: IOM report on trafficking in Morocco[717]

Precious, victim of trafficking for sexual exploitation in Europe: Precious and her daughter were buried today April 30, 2008 in Morocco with 11 other corpses. Precious was the victim of trafficking. She had left Benin to travel to Europe, but, like other women, was forced into prostitution during the way. Once arrived in Morocco, she escaped in the forest with her partner, in the meantime her daughter was born. She wanted to try to propose request for asylum and exit from the network of prostitution. Unfortunately, she was rescued from the network but failed to survive.

717 MSF, *Violence et immigration, deux ans plus tard, Rapport sur l'immigration d'origine subsaharienne en situation irrégulière au Maroc et dans les zones frontalières,* MSF, 2008.

Stella, victim of exploitation of domestic work in Morocco: Stella, 23-year-old-Filipino, searched for job opportunities. The employment agency promised her a contract of employment for 400 dollars per month. Once she arrived in Morocco her passport was confiscated and was forced to work 10 hours a day and without being able to escape. She decided to leave, but the employer for giving back the passport asked for 3,550 dollars, the cost he had paid for her contract.

2008: Amnesty International Report [718]

Refugees, asylum seekers, and migrants

Thousands of people suspected of being irregular migrants, including refugees and asylum seekers, were arrested and subjected to collective expulsion. In most cases, their rights under Moroccan law to appeal against the decision to repatriate them or to examine the motivations for the sentence were not respected. Often they are dropped at the border with Algeria without sufficient food or water.

On the night between 30 and 31 July, two Senegalese migrants, Aboubakr Sedjou and Siradjo Kébé, were killed and other three wounded by the police near Laayoune in Western Sahara. They were among the 30 migrants who were trying, according to the authorities, to reach the coast to migrate to the Canary Islands, and had refused to stop at calls to halt. The authorities stated that they would open an investigation on killings, but the results were not disclosed.

In March, the National Advisory Council on Human Rights has published a report on deaths of migrants at the border with Ceuta and Melilla in 2005. The report recommended to the authorities to make a greater commitment to comply with their international human rights duties, but abstained from recommending an investigation on deaths.

718 *Available at* <http://www.amnesty.it/flex/cm/pages/ServeBLOB.php/L/IT/IDPagina/841> (last visited Jun. 20, 2012).

Year 2007

2007: Killed in shootings in Laayoune, abused and massive deporting to Oujda[719]

Two years after the tragic events of September–October 2005, where 11 people were killed by gunfire just because they tried to cross the border between Ceuta and Melilla, two people died the night of 30–31 July, 2007 attack by the Moroccan armed forces as they were about to take to the sea in south Morocco. Two other persons were seriously injured.

A few days before the Moroccan police started the large-scale expulsion of persons of sub-Saharan origin and this new operation led to the arrest of 450 people.

Oujda has become, in the past few years, a large detention centre under the open sky for migrants and asylum seekers, who come from all regions of Morocco, are loaded onto police vans and escorted to the towns on the border; among these persons were identified six women and two children in an incident two months ago.

2007: Massive arrests of migrants in Morocco [720]

Rabat, Friday October 26, 2007

On the morning of Friday, 26 October, 2007, between 4 am and 6 am the Moroccan police carried out two major arrests of sub-Saharan migrants and asylum seekers, one in Rabat and another in Oujda. According to information gathered by civil society organizations, at least 100 people were arrested and taken away by the Moroccan police. Among those arrested, there were refugees and asylum seekers.

719 *Available at* <http://www.migreurop.org/rubrique210.html> (last visited Jun. 20, 2012).

720 *Available at* <http://www.meltingpot.org/articolo11382.html> (last visited Jun. 20, 2012).

Following a consultation with the UNHCR, the refugees and asylum seekers were released by the Moroccan authorities. All the other people were transferred by bus to Oujda, from where they were to be sent to the Algerian border, as has already happened in the previous raids.

We, civil society organizations and human rights defenders.

We express our concern about the risks of such arresting operations and massive *refoulement* of migrants and asylum seekers in Morocco.

We denounce the manner in which such operations are carried out;

We stress that these arrests were made in an arbitrary manner.

We remember Morocco's obligations, which, according to article 3 of UN Convention Against Torture, prohibits expelling any person to a country where he or she is likely to be subjected to bad treatments and we believe that *refoulement* of migrants and asylum seekers to the Algerian border, in the conditions in which occurred, constitutes a violation of this principle.

We are asking Moroccan authorities to make public the list of people arrested and its immediate release.

We emphasize the existing bond between the intensification of Moroccan policy on the management of migratory flows and border control and the increasing pressure on Morocco from the EU in the field of cooperation in fight against illegal immigration directed towards the borders of Europe.

We regret that the policy currently pursued in the framework of the cooperation between the EU and Morocco does not include the protection of migrants' rights among the priorities of action and we denounce human rights violations committed in the name of the control of European borders.

We are asking the revision of the chapter "Migration and Asylum" in the action plan EU–MOROCCO, adopted in the framework of the European Neighbourhood Policy (ENP) and we insist that the security approach is not the appropriate response to the migration phenomenon.

We remember the commitments of all the partners involved with Euro-Mediterranean cooperation in the field of human rights, including those of the migrants, and lastly, we emphasize on the fact that every migrant person, including irregular ones, benefits from fundamental rights that it is imperative to respect.

2007: Refugee–ghosts in the ghettos of Rabat[721]

From the Manifesto of 21 June, 2007

Hundreds of sub-Saharans have obtained refugee status in Morocco. But they remain in a state of illegality, because the UNHCR is not recognized. Trapped in a country that does not want them, they curse the effects of the externalization of the European borders.

"We are called refugees, but ours is a suspended life. We are stuck here, without rights and with the risk of being expelled at any time." Sitting on the big bed that occupies half of the room she shares with her partner Roger, the young Congolese Marie-Claire has an afflicted appearance. For about a year she has lived in Hay Nahda, a popular suburb of Rabat. Arriving after a long journey full of hazards in which she crossed large part of the continent, she was finally granted refugee status by the office of the United Nations High Commission for Refugees (UNHCR) in Morocco. But the sheet that serves as a document is equivalent to waste paper. "If the Moroccan gendarmes stop us, they tear it up and have no compunction about deporting us to Algeria." Marie-Claire was rejected twice at the border of Oujda-Maghnia, in the northeast of the country as a result of one of those police operations that the Cherifian Kingdom organizes from time to time to give the impression that it wants to combat illegal immigration on its territory. "I showed them the document from the UNHCR, but they laughed. I have been pushed across the

721 *Available at* <http://www.meltingpot.org/articolo10762.html> (last visited Jun. 20, 2012).

border. Here, we were captured by Algerian policemen. I was abused and I have been sent back."

There are about 450 sub-Saharan refugees officially recognized in Morocco, and more than 1200 asylum seekers waiting for their cases to be examined. But their situation is completely Kafkaesque: the UNHCR office is not officially recognized by the government of Rabat, and therefore the documents it issues are not recognized. Asylum seekers and refugees do not have any right to work, nor receive any legal assistance and health care. So, they live exactly the same life of illegal immigrants, among informal jobs and the terror of falling victims of raids and being deported to the Algerian border.

Locked in slums

At Hay Nahda, as in the nearby Takadoum–a huge slum where the houses are crowded in tight and smelly alleys–asylum seekers are trying to give a meaning to their existence. Most of them are Congolese and Ivorians, fled from situations of danger and war. "Their dossiers were carefully examined," says Johannes Van der Klaauw, chief of the UNHCR office in Rabat. "Their reasons are absolutely genuine, they are people in need of international protection." The official admits that this is not an easy situation for refugees in Morocco. "Our problem is that we do not have a budget that enables us to give assistance to all those who have obtained refugee status. We do what we can and we try to help those in greatest difficulty." Relations with Rabat, which absolutely does not want to hear about refugees on its own territory, are tense enough.

UNHCR lives in a long-lasting juxtaposition to the authorities, trying to exert pressure when there are situations of abuse: "Last January we were able to trace about 70 refugees rejected at the border to Rabat," sighs Van der Klaauw. He adds: "What we do is just a little, but this is better than nothing. On the other hand, if today we closed, what we could tell to those with whom we followed up and for whom we constitute a reference point?"

But many of the refugees do not agree with this assessment. They think the High Commissioner for Refugees is nothing but the visible face of a policy whose main objective is to prevent them from asking for asylum in Europe. "What does UNHCR do in Morocco? Nothing!" exclaims Fiston Massamba, a young Congolese, 28 years old, living in Rabat for two years. "Then it is better to close." Massamba is a prominent member of the new political class grown from the struggles of sub-Saharan refugees in Rabat. Secretary of the Sub-Saharan Migrants Council in Morocco, seems to have clear ideas. "The truth of the matter is that UNHCR is an integral part of the mechanism of externalization of the frontier established by the European Union recently. In the name of an illusory 'responsibility sharing', the reception of refugees is left to countries that do not have the infrastructure, nor the necessary legal instruments." Migrants accuse UNHCR of being an integral part of the security mechanism put in place by the European Union and remitted to Morocco–which received 67 million Euros from Brussels for the strengthening of border controls–to play the role of gendarme on the south shore, "betraying its African brothers".

Troubles for the UNHCR

Gathered in various associations and at the same time in consortium with the most combative organizations of Morocco's vibrant civil society, sub-Saharan refugees are determined to see recognition for their rights, even at the cost of creating trouble for the UNHCR. In May last year, they demonstrated for a week in front of UNHCR offices, asking for more assistance, and considering the impossibility to settlement in Morocco, the possibility to be resettled in third countries. But the resettlement is a distant prospect. "This can only be done for a few cases. The Western states are not very well disposed to it. They believe that it can generate an effect called en chain," clarified Van der Klaauw, suggesting that the accusations made by the representatives of the refugees are not totally bizarre.

More and more angry with UNHCR, Massamba and his Council of Sub-Saharan Migrants announced new initiatives to protest, "even spectacular ones". Meanwhile, in the darkness of their miserable rooms in Hay Nahda and Takadoum, Marie-Claire and the other hundreds of refugees, ghosts, begin to lose heart and to revise their hopes to obtain a better future downward.

Year 2006

2006: Access to medical care–Doctors Without Borders[722]

S. is a 27-year-old man that left Ivory Coast in February 2005 to reach Europe in about a month. Unfortunately, he is still in Morocco where he lives between Nador and Berkane. He tried four times to enter into Melilla by jumping the barrier, but the Spanish authorities have always rejected him, and the Moroccan police beat him before escorting him to the border with Algeria. He has tried to swim across, but also in this case he was arrested and sent back to Morocco. In 2006 his health condition got worse. Unfortunately he had no access to medical care and MSF brought him to the hospital and since that time is taking care of him. Begging is the only way for him to have food. S. is blocked in Morocco: does not have any money to pay for the journey to Europe and cannot return to his country, where the situation that forced him to leave remains unchanged.

2006: "We are lost in the desert"[723]

Dozens of sub-Saharan migrants rejected from Morocco have been locked in Western Sahara for six months, waiting for someone to take an interest in their destiny and carry them home.

722 MSF, Violence et immigration, deux ans plus tard, Rapport sur l'immigration d'origine subsaharienne en situation irrégulière au Maroc et dans les zones frontalières, 2008.

723 *Available at* <http://www.meltingpot.org/articolo7595.html> (last visited Jun. 20, 2012).

"Do something for us. We are still stuck in the middle of the desert!" The voice of Moussa reaches nervously and blinkingly through the satellite phone. Behind him, you can hear the shouts of his companions in misfortune, 44 other sub-Saharan immigrants suspended for nearly six months in the sands of Bir Lahlou, an outpost lost in the midst of the Western Sahara. Deported in October last year by the Moroccan police after the assaults to the fencing of Ceuta and Melilla and abandoned in a desert full of mines, rescued by members of the *Polisario Front*–the organization that fights for the independence of this former Spanish colony–are still there, counting the days under a burning sun. They have no contact with the world: communication with those who write is made possible only by the availability of a rare stranger equipped with satellite telephone. And the rest of the world doesn't care about them. They survive thanks to the assistance of the *Polisario Front*, which provides them with a little flour, oil, and water; the little that refugees can afford, which on its own side is dependent on international aid.

These castaways suspended in a sea of sand and despair do not enjoy any assistance; only a small *Polisario* dispensary offers them minimal care ("Many are sick; they have fever," states Moussa). But, above all, they cannot take any more: almost all already shouldered a long and exhausting journey in order to be able to embrace the European dream; then they spent months hidden in Morocco awaiting the good opportunity; now they are stuck in a present with no help on the horizon. "We want only to return home. Please help us!" cried Ghanaian Rashid on the phone, here after three years in Morocco and two failed attempts to jump Melilla's fences. "We are suffering too much, we no longer know what to do." At the time of the facts, we all hoped for a rapid solution to the crisis. The story appeared widely in the media. Several journalists, mostly Spanish, had arrived at the bottom of the desert to meet the damned of Bir Lahlou; some NGOs were involved in their case, and even a delegation of the Minurso, the UN peacekeepers deployed in the area to monitor a cease-fire, came to dispense reassurance and good words. Then, off the cameras, silence fell. "Since November, no one come any more. Minurso members are no longer seen. We continue to live here, cut off from the world", Moussa keeps complaining.

Their tragedy is that they are in the midst of a sort of no man's land of indeterminate contours. The eastern area of Western Sahara is under the authority of the *Polisario Front*, which does not have the means nor the forces to provide for their repatriation. Minurso, for its part, "has no mandate to deal with such cases," as spokesman for the mission Enrico Magnani repeats over the telephone. He adds: "The Polisario Front must ask UN to intervene." No one takes the initiative and, in this ping-pong of responsibility, 45 sub-Saharans are abandoned to themselves.

Their case is not really news for Western Sahara: in the past two years various groups of immigrants–mostly Asian–were found lost in the middle of the desert and were rescued by *Polisario Front* members. Even that time, several months went by before someone, in this case the International Organization for Migration (IOM), cared for them and looked after their repatriation. But the Africans of Bir Lahlou appear even more forgotten: IOM office in Rabat was not aware of their situation. Once informed, the chief ensured that the organization–in particular the office in–would be responsible for their situation. They, for the moment, wait for only one thing: that someone will pull out them and allow them to return to the world.

Year 2005

2005: Spain/Morocco–you don't die only at the borders…

In this article, Andrea Accardi of Doctors Without Borders presents to us the report on violence on the border between Morocco and Spain published on 29 September by the organization.

For the fifth consecutive time in the last week, at dawn on 6 October, approximately 1,000 sub-Saharan immigrants armed with rudimentary wooden stairs attempted to climb over the double fence separating the Spanish town of Melilla from Moroccan territory.

The attempt was nonetheless stopped by the Spanish and Moroccan security forces that used suppression resources and a helicopter.

Last Thursday controls of the two borders were strengthened sending 480 soldiers of the army from the Spanish government and 1,600 officials from a part of the Moroccan government, since during a mass attempt to climb over the fence, five immigrants died, killed by gun shots. In this case, however, no one is yet being held responsible. But you don't die only at the border.

Last week the Moroccan authorities have intensified the massive deportations. On the night of 5 October 1,000 sub-Saharan immigrants have been abandoned in the Sahara desert where there is only sand, neither a town nor water nor food. Already 14 people have died, according to the activists of *Indymedia Estrecho*.

A few hours after a trip to Melilla by the vice president of Spain, Maria Teresa Fernandez de la Vega, she will also go today to the other Spanish enclave of Ceuta, to reassure the mayor-presidents of the two Spanish towns, who accuse the government of not doing enough to protect the "safety" of the two enclaves.

However, at exactly this time in Spain, images showing agents of the Guardia Civil punching and kicking an immigrant immobilized on the ground in the frontier zone of Melilla, taken from the broadcaster *Telecinco* and broadcast last Tuesday, opened a discussion.

The declarations of the Guardia Civil that define the episode as an "isolated and exceptional case" are denied by MSF report published on 29 September that denounces the escalation of violence in the application of the measures for the control of immigration at the border between Morocco and Spain, through testimonials and medical reports of immigrants examined.

2005: Increase of the xenophobic attitude? [724]

Under the title *Arrestation de plus de 264 clandestins dans la provinces de Nador* the Arabic newspaper *Al Ahdath Al Maghribia* announced in its issue of 16 January, 2005 the organization of two stop operations in the forest of Gourougou, with the participation of 1200 members of the security force, of which 350 were policemen.

Remember that the same newspaper on 12 January, 2005 had talked about the problem by invoking the absence of cooperation with Algeria, reminding that the arrangement of flights to Nigeria "was carried out with respect for the dignity of migrants and Moroccan law."

2005: "Algeria seeks to deny its African roots", interview with Mehdi Lahlou, 16 October 2005 [725]

You have published several reports on the issue of sub-Saharan migration: since when does it start your interest?

Since 1998 I have made a survey of residents in Europe. There were an increasing number of migrants coming from sub-Saharan Africa, with a dominance of Congolese and Nigerians. In 1999, I wrote on the thematic of support of the United Nations Fund, then in 2000 through the ILO I did a survey on migration in the main Moroccan towns.

Did you lower your arms in the face of the European Commission refusal to launch a comprehensive study on the issue?

Since 1999 I thought only on the phenomenon of the increased size and from an academic point of view it was necessary to follow especially the draft law that was adopted in 2002 on the issue of migration. When Morocco presented its draft law on irregular migration, relationships between Rabat and Madrid certainly improved,

724 *Available at* <http://www.ahdath.info> (last visited Jun. 20, 2012).

725 *Available at* <http://www.lematin.ma/mailing/article.asp?an=&id=natio&ida=53293> (last visited Jun. 20, 2012).

although Madrid continued to play a dual role in the region by signing a strategic partnership agreement with Algeria and closing its eyes on the migration approach.

Where precisely are the candidates from?

The different surveys conducted have shown that they depart from Congo, then pass though Cameroon, Nigeria, then Niger and Algeria. Another way is from the west coast toward Algeria, Morocco, Ghana or Ivory Coast and than Burkina Faso and Mali. But migrants pass especially through Mali.

2005: Europe deceives Morocco[726]

According to Abdelkarim Belguendouz, Morocco should not succumb to the pressure of the European Union concerning the phenomenon of illegal migration of sub-Saharans. Moroccan authorities are trying to recognize that it is due to colonial memories in Africa. Catching sub-Saharans is the sore point that pushes the European Union toward Morocco. Europe wants Morocco to take the role of policeman or auxiliary, but Morocco brings the sub-Saharans going to Algeria. This is not repatriation, as much as it is human ping-pong.

2005: Morocco between two fires[727]

The Maghreb is located between two fires: a Europe that seeks to emerge and an Africa, in contradiction to the world, that knocks on its doors. Maghreb countries have taken the role of alternates for repression, amplifying in the eyes of African migrants the violations against their fellows. This meets the demands of Europe, which obliges them to readmit, in addition to their national migrants, also

726 *Available at* <http://www.aujourdhui.ma/couverture-details40419.html> (last visited Jun. 20, 2012).

727 *Available at* <www.lemonde.fr/web/article/0,1-0,36-704363,0.html> (last visited Jun. 20, 2012).

those that have passed through their territory. The strengthening of the repressive function on the part of the Maghreb countries in the moment on which democracy hinges, risks favouring the instability and the migration of its own citizens. This policy seeks to empty the state itself of its own substance. The externalization of the migration issue through Europe is increasing tensions among the Maghreb countries, but also between the latter and the Sahel countries.

If the tragedy that is played out is not the responsibility of the Maghreb countries, they contribute to make it worse. Maghreb regimes that kill migrants and drive them toward the desert are the same that killed young people in Morocco, Algeria, Tunisia, and Libya. Maghreb regimes see in this role of supplementing repression a means of exchange with the European countries.

2005: Immigrants who have been victims of violence at the border between Morocco and Spain

Doctors Without Borders (MSF) complains, in a report published today, of an escalation of the violence in applying the measures for the control of immigration at the border between Morocco and Spain.[728]

Madrid/Rabat/Rome, 29 September, 2005–Doctors Without Borders (MSF) complains, in a report published today, of an escalation of violence in applying the measures for the control of immigration at the border between Morocco and Spain.

Since 2003 MSF has worked in Morocco in a project on immigration. After 27 months of activity, thanks to the collection of detailed medical data and testimonies, the organization found that approximately 25% of examinations done between April 2003 and August 2005 are not linked to pathologies correlated to the precarious living conditions in which the foreigners live, but to direct or indirect acts of violence.

728 *Available at* <www.medicisenzafrontiere.it/msfinforma/comunicati_stampa.asp?id=778> (last visited Jun. 20, 2012).

According to the statements made by foreigners examined by MSF, 44% of the incidents of violence are attributable to the Moroccan police, 17% to gangs, 18% to Spanish forces, 12% to groups related to human trafficking, 2% to disputes between immigrants and the remaining 7% to accident. Patients showed various types of wounds: severe trauma, caused by falls from the barriers that separate the two countries, or from an attempt to escape from the Moroccan security forces; firearm wounds; wounds caused by sticks or from attacks by dogs. There have also been registered cases of deaths.

MSF expresses its dismay when faced with such facts and underlines how the practice of violence and degrading treatment increases the suffering and the exclusion of people who, in search of better living conditions, are exposing themselves to risks for the survival, and often inhumane conditions.

Through its clinical activity and humanitarian aid, in collaboration with Moroccans health services, MSF is working to improve the living conditions of this population extremely vulnerable. Currently MSF activities are focused in north Morocco, in the regions of Tangier, Nador, and Oujda.

Year 2004

2004: Agreement on Repatriation of Sub-Saharan[729]

Morocco has carried out in Laayoune a first repatriation of illegal sub-Saharan immigrants stopped in Spain. The Moroccan Commission of bilateral cooperation has rejected the contested agreement that provides for the reception of all illegal immigrants by Morocco that travelled through its territory in the past twelve years.

729 *Available at* <www.lagazettedumaroc.com/articles.php?id_artl=4181&n=357&sr=811&r=2> (last visited Jun. 20, 2012).

On the other hand, more than 600 sub-Saharans might be ready to be repatriated to Morocco. This may not raise any particular issues.

This occurred last May, on 27 February 2004. The Moroccan authorities have accepted, for the first time, the repatriation of 30 sub-Saharan illegal immigrants arrested a few days before by the Spanish police on the island of Fuerteventura in the Canary Islands.

These candidates came from different English-speaking and French-speaking African countries and were trying to reach Europe through south of Morocco. Once arrested on Spanish territory, were not subject to the repatriation procedures, but were board on a charter that led them in Laayoune where they should be repatriated under Moroccan oversight, to their origin country. The agreement signed in 1992 applies to citizens of all third countries.

History of the most serious events occurring with regard to migrants, years 2005–2007[730]

30.09.2005	MSF accuses the Moroccan military forces of causing 62 per cent of the wounds inflicted on migrants and MSF notes that a quarter of the rescued people were attacked by the Moroccan police.
04.10.2005	Attempt to get into Melilla (135 wounded).
07.10.2005	Six sub-Saharans die under Moroccan police gunfire, while 400 illegal migrants were trying to cross the border at Melilla.
08.10.2005	Morocco abandons hundreds of migrants in the desert; MSF identifies 500 at the border with Algeria, in a desperate situation, that are hungry and without water.
12.10.2005	MSF asks to treat sub-Saharan migrants located on the southern border, approximately 1,000 people.
05.12.2005	600 irregular migrants transferred to the south of Algeria to proceed to their forced repatriation.
19.12.2005	30 sub-Saharan migrants die in the sinking of a boat from Mauritania to Canary Islands.
12.01.2006	At Nador an irregular migrant, previously wounded by the Moroccan police, dies.
21.02.2006	570 irregular migrants from sub-Saharan Africa are returned to the border with Algeria.
06.03.2006	45 people died during the sinking of two boats on the way to Canary Islands.
09.03.2006	Between 1200 and 1300 die, according to Mauritania Red Cross, in an attempt to reach the Canary Islands.
03.07.2006	Two irregular immigrants die trying to cross the border with the town of Melilla.

730 MSF, *Violence et immigration, deux ans plus tard, Rapport sur l'immigration d'origine subsaharienne en situation irrégulière au Maroc et dans les zones frontalières*, MSF, 2008.

07.07.2006	The Moroccan military killed some migrants who were trying to cross the border in Melilla.
02.08.2006	28 corpses are discovered in El Aioun while trying to reach the Canary Islands.
23.12.2006	500 irregular migrants and asylum seekers are rejected at the border with Algeria.
28.12.2006	It is estimated that about 6000 sub-Saharan migrants die at sea while trying to reach the Canary Islands.
26.07.2007	200 illegal immigrants are arrested by the Moroccan police in Oujda, among whom 70 are returned directly to the frontier.
31.07.2007	Two died and two are seriously injured during the failed attempt of 37 illegal migrants to escape from Morocco.
26.10.2007	More than 100 illegal migrants and asylum seekers were arrested between 4am and 6am in Rabat and directly send to the border with Algeria.

Bibliography

Books

ABI-SAAB GEORGE, COUR GÉNÉRAL DE DROIT INTERNATIONAL PUBLIC, Recueil des cours, Hague Academy of International Law, The Hague (1987).

ALEINIKOFF T. ALEXANDER & CHETAIL VINCENT (EDS.), MIGRATION AND INTERNATIONAL LEGAL NORMS, Asser Press, The Hague (2003).

ALSTON PHILIP (ED.), LABOUR RIGHTS AS HUMAN RIGHTS, Oxford University Press, Oxford (2005).

AMARELLE CESLA & NGUYEN MINH SON (EDS.), MIGRATIONS ET ECONOMIE- L'ACCES DES ETRANGERS A LA VIE ECONOMIQUE: LES NORMES ET LEUR APPLICATION, Stämpfli Editions SA, Bern (2010).

AMARELLE CESLA & NGUYEN MINH SON (EDS.), LE PRINCIPE DE NON-REFOULEMENT–FONDEMENTS ET ENJEUX PRATIQUES, Stämpfli Editions SA, Bern (2010).

ARENDT HANNAH, LE ORIGINI DEL TOTALITARISMO, Einaudi Editore Torino (2009).

ASBJØRN EIDE, GUDMUNDUR ALFREDSSON, MELANDER GORAN, REHOF LARS ADAM & ALLAN ROSAS (EDS.), THE UNIVERSAL DECLARATION OF HUMAN RIGHTS: A COMMENTARY, Scandinavian University Press, Oslo (1992).

BALDACCINI ANNALIESE, GUILD ELSPETH & TONER HELEN (EDS.), WHOSE FREEDOM, SECURITY AND JUSTICE? EU IMMIGRATION AND ASYLUM LAW AND POLICY, Hart Publishing, Oxford (2007).

BASRI DRISS, ROUSSET MICHEL & VEDEL GEORGES (EDS), REVISION DE LA CONSTITUTION MAROCAINE (1992), ANALYSE ET COMMENTARIES, Rabat (1992).

BELGUENDOUZ ABDELKRIM, ENJEUX MIGRATOIRES MAGHREB–EUROPE-AFRIQUE- UN REGARD DU SUD, Konrad Adenauer Stiftung (2006).

BELGUENDOUZ ABDELKRIM, POLITIQUE MIGRATOIRES IN MAROC, D'hier à l'horizon, Salé (2007).

BETTS ALEXANDER (ED.), GLOBAL MIGRATION GOVERNANCE, Oxford University Press, Oxford (2011).

BRAND A. LAURIE, CITIZENS ABROAD: EMIGRATION AND THE STATE IN THE MIDDLE EAST AND NORTH AFRICA, Cambridge University Press, Cambridge (2005).

BOGUSZ BARBARA, CHOLEWINSKI RYSZARD, CYGAN ADAM AND SZYSZCZACK ERIKA (EDS.), IRREGULAR MIGRATION AND HUMAN RIGHTS: THEORETICAL, EUROPEAN AND INTERNATIONAL PERSPECTIVES, Martinus Nijhoff Publishers, The Hague (2004).

BUSTAMANTE A. JORGE, MIGRACION INTERNATIONAL Y DERECHOS HUMANOS, Universidad Nacional Autonoma de Mexico, Mexico (2002).

CANCADO TRINIDADE ANTONIO AUGUSTO, INTERNATIONAL LAW FOR HUMANKIND: TOWARDS A NEW *JURIS GENTIUM* – GENERAL COURSE ON PUBLIC INTERNATIONAL LAW, PART I, Recueil des Cours, Hague Academy of International Law, The Hague (2005).

CARLIER JEAN-YVES, DROIT D'ASILE ET DES RÉFUGIÉS. DE LA PROTECTION AUX DROITS, Recueil des Cours, Hague Academy of International Law,The Hague (2007).

CARLIER JEAN-YVES (ED.), L'ETRANGER FACE AU DROIT, Louvain, Bruylant (2010).

CHAHDI OUAZZANI, LA PRATIQUE MAROCAINE DU DROIT DES TRAITES, ESSAI SUR LE DROIT CONVENTIONNEL MAROCAIN, L.g.d.j., Paris (1982).

CHETAIL VINCENT (ED.), MONDIALISATION, MIGRATION ET DROITS DE L'HOMME: LE DROIT INTERNATIONAL EN QUESTION, Vol. I, Bruylant, Bruxelles (2007).

CHOLEWINSKI RYSZARD, MIGRANT WORKERS IN INTERNATIONAL HUMAN RIGHTS LAW, Clarendon Press Oxford, Oxford (1997).

CHOLEWINSKI RYSZARD, RICHARD PERROUCHOUD & EUAN MACDONALD (EDS.), COMPENDIUM OF INTERNATIONAL MIGRATION LAW INSTRUMENTS, Asser Press, The Hague (2007).

CHOLEWINSKI RYSZARD, RICHARD PERROUCHOUD & EUAN MACDONALD (EDS.), INTERNATIONAL MIGRATION LAW, DEVELOPING PARADIGMS AND KEY CHALLENGE, Asser Press, The Hague (2007).

COLEMAN NILS, EUROPEAN READMISSION POLICY–THIRD COUNTRY INTERESTS AND REFUGEES RIGHTS, Martinus Nijhoff Publishers, London (2009).

COOMANS FONS & MENNO T. KAMMINGA (EDS.), EXTRATERRITORIAL APPLICATION OF HUMAN RIGHTS TREATIES, Intersentia, Antwerp/Oxford (2004).

CORNELISSE GALINA, IMMIGRATION DETENTION AND HUMAN RIGHTS, Martinus Nijoff Publishers, London (2010).

DAUVERGNE CATHERINE, JURISPRUDENCE FOR AN INTERCONNECTED GLOBE, Ashgate Press, Burlington (2003).

DAUVERGNE CATHERINE, MAKING PEOPLE ILLEGAL: WHAT GLOBALISATION MEANS FOR MIGRATION AND LAW, Cambridge University Press, Cambridge (2008).

DOEBBLER F. CURTIS, THE PRINCIPLE OF NON-DISCRIMINATION IN

INTERNATIONAL LAW, CDP Publishing, Washington (2007).
DUVELL FRANK (ED.), ILLEGAL IMMIGRATION IN EUROPE, BEYOND CONTROL, Palgrave, New York (2005).
GHOSH BIMAL, MANAGING MIGRATION, TIME FOR A NEW INTERNATIONAL REGIME?, Oxford University press, Oxford (2000).
GHOSH BIMAL, ELUSIVE PROTECTION, UNCERTAIN LAND: MIGRANTS' ACCESS TO HUMAN RIGHTS, IOM, Geneva (2003).
GHOSH BIMAL, HUMAN RIGHTS AND MIGRATION–THE MISSING LINK, SIM Special No. 31, Utrecht (2008).
GOMEZ ISA FELIPE & DE FEYTER KOEN (EDS.), INTERNATIONAL HUMAN RIGHTS LAW IN A GLOBAL CONTEXT, Duesto University Press, Bilbao (2009).
GONDEK MICHAL, THE REACH OF HUMAN RIGHTS IN A GLOBALIZING WORLD, Intersentia, Antwerp/Oxford (2009).
GUILD ELSPETH, SECURITY AND MIGRATION IN THE 21 CENTURY, Polity Press, Cambridge (2009).
GUILLON MICHELLE, LEGOUX LUC & MA MUNG EMMANUEL (EDS.), L'ASILE POLITIQUE ENTRE DEUX CHAISES: DROITS DE L'HOMME ET GESTION DES FLUX MIGRATOIRES, Harmattan, Paris (2003).
LAHLOU MEHDI (ED.), MIGRATION, DROITS DE L'HOMME ET DEVELOPPMENT, Friedrich Ebert Stiftung, Rabat (2008).
LILLICH B. RICHARD, THE HUMAN RIGHTS OF ALIENS IN CONTEMPORARY INTERNATIONAL LAW, Manchester University Press, Manchester (1984).
MARTIN L. PHILIP, BORDERING ON CONTROL: COMBATING IRREGULAR MIGRATION IN NORTH AMERICA AND EUROPE, International Organisation for Migration, Geneva (2003).
MCMURRAY A. DAVID, IN AND OUT OF MOROCCO: SMUGGLING AND MIGRATION IN A FRONTIER BOOMTOWN, University of Minnesota Press, Minneapolis (2001).
NYBERG SORENSEN NINNA (ED.), MEDITERRANEAN TRANSIT MIGRATION, Danish Institute for International Studies (DIIS), Copenhagen (2006).
NOWAK MANFRED, U.N. COVENANT ON CIVIL AND POLITICAL RIGHTS: CCPR COMMENTARY, Arlington Publisher (1993).
NUALA MOLE, LE DROIT D'ASILE ET LA CONVENTION EUROPEENNE DES DROITS DE L'HOMME, Council of Europe Publishing, Areaburg (2008).
OLESCHAK REKHA, THE INTERNATIONAL LAW OF DEVELOPMENT-INDUCED DISPLACEMENT, Niedermann Druck, St. Gallen (2009).
PAPADOPOULOU-KOURKOULA ASPASIA, TRANSIT MIGRATION, THE MISSING LINK BETWEEN EMIGRATION AND SETTLEMENT, Palgrave, New York (2008).
PEERS STEVE, EU JUSTICE AND HOME AFFAIRS LAW, Oxford University Press, Oxford (2011).
PLENDER RICHARD, INTERNATIONAL MIGRATION LAW, Martinus Nijoff

Publishers, Dordrechtt (1988).
RYAN BERNARD & MITSILEGAS VALSAMIS (EDS.), EXTRATERRITORIAL CONTROL LEGAL CHALLENGES, Martinus Nijoff Publishers, London (2010).
SAADI MOHAMED, LE DIFFICILE CHEMIN DES DROITS DE L'HOMME AU MAROC, Harmattan, Paris (2009).
SAROLEA SYLVIE, DROITS DE L'HOMME ET MIGRATIONS: DE LA PROTECTION DU MIGRANT AUX DROITS DE LA PERSONNE MIGRANTE, Bruylant, Bruxelles (2006).
SASSEN SASKIA, PERDIENDO EL CONTROL? LA SOBERANIA EN LA ERA DE LA GLOBALIZACION, Editions Bellaterra, Barcelona (2001).
SOCIÉTÉ FRANÇAISE POUR LE DROIT INTERNATIONAL, L'ÉTAT SOUVERAIN A' L'AUBE DU XXI SIÈCLE, COLLOQUE DU MANS, Pedone, Paris (1994).
SOCIÉTÉ FRANÇAISE POUR LE DROIT INTERNATIONAL, PROTECTION DROITS DE L'HOMME, COLLOQUE DU STRASBOURG, Pedone, Paris (1998).
SOCIÉTÉ FRANÇAISE POUR LE DROIT INTERNATIONAL, RESPONSABILITÉ DES ETATS, COLLOQUE DU MANS, Pedone, Paris(1999).
SOCIÉTÉ FRANÇAISE POUR LE DROIT INTERNATIONAL, LE SUJET EN DROIT INTERNATIONAL, COLLOQUE DU GENÈVE, Pedone, Paris (2005).
TIBURCIO CARMEN, THE HUMAN RIGHTS OF ALIENS UNDER INTERNATIONAL AND COMPARATIVE LAW, Martin Nijhoff Publishers, The Hague (2001).
TORPEY JHON, THE INVENTION OF THE PASSPORT: SURVEILLANCE, CITIZENSHIP AND THE STATE, Cambridge University Press, Cambridge (2000).
WATTERS CHARLES, REFUGEE CHILDREN: TOWARDS THE NEXT HORIZON, Routledge, London (2008).
WEISSBRODT DAVID, THE HUMAN RIGHTS OF NON-CITIZENS, Oxford University Press, Oxford (2008).
YOU PAUL, LE PREAMBULE DES TRAITES INTERNATIONAUX, Thèse de Fribourg, Fribourg (1941).

Articles

Abdelmalek Sayad, *Etat, Nation et Immigration: l'ordre national a l'épreuve de l'immigration*, PEUPLES MEDITERRANEENS 191 (1984).
Abdelmalek Sayad, *Immigration et pensée d'Etat*, 7 ACTES DE LA RECHERCHE EN SCIENCES SOCIALES 129 (1999).

Abell Nazare Albuquerque, *The Compatibility of Readmission Agreements with the 1951 Convention relating to the Status of Refugees*, 11(1) INTERNATIONAL JOURNAL OF REFUGEE LAW 60 (1999).

Abi Saab George, *Humanité et communauté internationale dans la dialectique du droit international*, *in* Mélanges en honneur du professeur René-Jean Dupuy, Pedone, Paris (1991), 1–12.

Adepoju Aderanti, *Undocumented migration in Africa: trends and policies, Geneva: Intergovernamental Committee for Migration*, Expert paper No. 6, paper presented to the Sixth Seminar on Adaptation and Integration of Immigrants: Undocumented Migrants or Migrants in Irregular Situation, CDR LAW/MIG/17 B (1983).

Adepoju Aderanti, *The challenge of Labour Migration Flow between West Africa and Maghreb*, International Migration Papers, ILO, Geneva (2006).

Aderghal Mohamed & Berriane Mohamed, *Country Report: Morocco*, African Perspective Programme on human mobility, MacArthur Foundation (2008).

Alami M'chichi Houria, *Les migrations maghrébines en Europe et la question de droits de l'homme*, 43 REVUE MAROCAINE DE DROIT ET D'ECONOMIE DU DEVELOPPEMENT 117 (2000).

Awad Ibrahim, *Keynote speech, Meeting of Experts and Policy makers on Irregular Migration into and through Southern and Eastern Mediterranean Countries*, European University Institute, Florence (January 2009).

Awad Ibrahim, *International Labour Migration: Evolution of the multilateral policy framework*, *in* CHRISTIANE KUPTSCH (ED.), THE INTERNATIONALIZATION OF LABOUR MARKETS, ILO, Geneva (2010).

Baldwin Edwards Martin, *"Between a rock and a hard place": North Africa as a region of emigration, immigration and transit migration*, 33 REVIEW OF AFRICAN POLITICAL ECONOMY 311 (2010).

Barbou des Places Ségolène, *Les étrangers "saisis" par le droit: enjeux de l'édification des catégories juridiques de migrants*, 22 (128) MIGRATIONS SOCIETE 35 (2010).

Bartel Barry & Nafziger James A.R., *The Migrant Workers Convention: its place in human rights law*, 4 INTERNATIONAL MIGRATION REVIEW 771 (1991).

Barros Lucile, Lahlou Mehdi, Escoffier Claire, Pumares Pablo & Ruspini Paolo, *L'immigration irrégulière subsaharienne à travers et vers le Maroc,* Cahiers de Migrations Internationales, No. 54 F, ILO, Geneva (2002).

Belguendouz Abdelkrim, *Le Maroc et la migration irrégulière: une analyse sociopolitique,* CARIM 2009/07 (2009).

Bensaad Ali, *L'irrégularité de l'immigration en Mauritanie: une appréhension nouvelle, conséquence d'enjeux migratoires externes*, CARIM 2008/76 (2008).

Berg Laurie, *At the border and between the cracks: the precarious position of irregular migrant workers under international human rights law*, 8 MELBOURNE JOURNAL OF INTERNATIONAL LAW 1 (2007).

Betts Alexander, *Towards a Mediterranean solution? Implications for the Region of Origin*, 18 INTERNATIONAL JOURNAL OF REFUGEE LAW 652 (2006).

Betts Alexander, *Towards a "Soft Law" Framework for the Protection of Vulnerable Irregular Migrants*, 22 INTERNATIONAL JOURNAL OF REFUGEE LAW 209 (2010).

Bilgili Ozge & Weyel Silja, *Migration in Morocco: History, Current Trends and Future Prospects*, Paper Series: Migration and Development Country Profile, Maastricht Graduate School of Governance (Dec. 2009).

Billet Carole, *EC Readmission Agreements: a prime instrument of the external dimension of the EU's fight against irregular migration. An Assessment after ten years of practice*, 12 EUROPEAN JOURNAL OF MIGRATION AND LAW 45 (2010).

Bohning Roger, *The ILO and the new UN Convention on migrant workers: the past and the future*, 4 INTERNATIONAL MIGRATION REVIEW 698 (1991).

Bosniak S. Linda, *Human rights, State sovereignty and the protection of undocumented migrant under the international migrant workers Conventions*, 4 INTERNATIONAL MIGRATION REVIEW 737 (1991).

Boubakri Hassen, *Le Maghreb et les migrations en transit: le piège?*, 107 MIGRATION SOCIETE: REVUE BIMESTRIELLE 104 (2006).

Boudahrain Abdellah, *The new International Convention: a Moroccan perspective*, 4 INTERNATIONAL MIGRATION REVIEW 866 (1991).

Boustamante B. Jorge, *Immigrants vulnerability as subjects of human rights*, 36 INTERNATIONAL MIGRATION REVIEW 333 (2002).

Boutellet Paquet Daphné, *Passing the buck: a critical analysis of the readmission policy implemented by the European Union and Its member states*, 359 EUROPEAN JOURNAL OF MIGRATION AND LAW 5 (2003).

Cancado Trindade Antonio Augusto, *Le déracinement et la protection des migrants dans le droit International de droits de l'homme*, 74 REV. TRIM. DR. H. 289 (2008).

Carling Jorgen, *Unauthorized Migration from Africa to Spain*, 45 INTERNATIONAL MIGRATION 4 (2007).

Carrera Sergio & Merlino Massimo, *Undocumented Immigrants and Rights in the EU*, CEPS (Dec. 2009).

Cassese Antonio, *International protection of the right to leave and to return* in STUDI IN ONORE DI MANLIO UDINA (1975), 219–229.

Cassarino Jean-Pierre, *Informalizing readmission agreements in the EU Neighbourhood*, 179 THE INTERNATIONAL SPECTATOR 2 (2007).

Cassarino Jean-Pierre, *Readmission Policy in the European Union*, Directorate General for Internal Policies, Policy Department C: Citizens' Rights and Constitutional Affairs, Civil Liberties, Justice and Home Affairs, Brussels, European Parliament (Sep. 2010).

Castles Stephen, *The Factors that Make and Unmake Migration Policies*, 38(3) INTERNATIONAL MIGRATION REVIEW 852 (2004).

Chadi Ouazzani, *L'article 31 de la Constitution de 1972 et le droit des traités*, 1 REVUE

MAROCAINE DE DROIT ET D'ECONOMIE DU DEVELOPPEMENT 87 (1982).

Chetail Vincent, *Le Comité des Nations Unies contre la torture et l'éloignements des étrangers: dix ans de jurisprudence (1994–2004)*, 1 REVUE SUISSE DE DROIT INTERNATIONAL ET DROIT EUROPEEN 63 (2006).

Chetail Vincent, *Le droit d'avoir droit en droit international public: réflexion sur la subjectivité international de l'individu, in* MARIE-CLAIRE CALOZ-TSCHOPP (ED.), LIRE HANNAH ARENDT AUJOURD'HUI: POUVOIR, GUERRE, PENSEE, JUGEMENT POLITIQUE, l'Harmattan, Paris (2008).

Chetail Vincent & Giacca Gilles, *Who Cares? The Right to Health of Migrants* (2009), *in* MARY ROBINSON & ANDREW CLAPHAM (EDS.), REALIZING THE RIGHT TO HEALTH, Vol. 3, Swiss Human Rights Book, Zurich (2009).

Cholewinski Ryszard & Kristina Touzenis, *Irregular Migration into and through Southern and Eastern Mediterranean Countries: Legal Perspectives*, CARIM Analytic and Synthetic Notes 2009/01, CARIM-AS 2009/01 (2009).

Cholewinski Ryszard, *The need for effective individual legal protection in immigration matters*, 7 EUROPEAN JOURNAL OF MIGRATION AND LAW 262 (2005).

Cholewinski Ryszard, *International Labour Law and the Protection of Migrant Workers: revitalizing the agenda in the era of globalization, in* JOHN D.R. CRAIG & S. MICHAEL LYNK (EDS.), GLOBALIZATION AND THE FUTURE OF LABOUR LAW, Cambridge University Press, Cambridge (2006).

Claret Andreu & Valcarel Dario, *Immigration africaine. L'Europe cherche des solutions*, 10 AFKAR: REVUE TRIMESTRIELLE POUR LE DIALOGUE ENTRE LE MAGHREB, L'ESPAGNE ET L'EUROPE (2006).

Cleveland H. Sarah, *Legal status and rights of undocumented migrants*, 2 AMERICAN JOURNAL OF INTERNATIONAL LAW 460 (2005).

Collyer Michael, *L'immigration clandestine en Méditerranée en 2006*, ANNUAIRE DE LA MEDITERRANEE 288 (2007).

Collyer Michael & de Haas Hein, *Developing Dynamic Categorisations of Transit Migration*, POPULATION, SPACE AND PLACE (forthcoming 2012).

Collyer Michael, Frank Duvell & de Haas Hein, *Critical Approaches to Transit Migration*, POPULATION, SPACE AND PLACE (forthcoming 2012).

Courbage Youssef, *Changements et perspectives de la population dans le sud de la Méditerranée*, ANNUAIRE DE LA MEDITERRANEE 40 (2007).

Crépeau Francois, *Right and access to healthcare for undocumented children: addressing the gap between international conventions and disparate implementations in North America and Europe*, 70(2) SOCIAL SCIENCE AND MEDICINE(Jan. 2010).

Dauvergne Catherine, *Beyond justice the consequences of liberalism for immigration law*, CANADIAN JOURNAL OF LAW AND JURISPRUDENCE 323 (1997).

Dauvergne Catherine, *Challenges to sovereignty: migration laws for the 21 century*, Working Paper No. 92, Evaluation and Policy Analysis Unit, UNHCR (July 2003).

De Guchteneire Paul & Pecoud Antoine, *Migration, Human Rights and the United*

Nations: an investigation into the obstacles to the UN Convention on Migrant Workers' Rights, 24 WINDSOR Y. B. ACCESS JUST. 241 (2006).

De Guchteneire Paul & Pecoud Antoine, *International Migration, Border Controls and Human Rights: Assessing the relevance of a right to mobility*, 21 JOURNAL OF BORDELANDS STUDIES 69 (2006).

De Guchteneire Paul & Pecoud Antoine, *The International Convention on the human rights protection of migrants workers and member of their families, in* DE GUCHTENEIRE PAUL, PECOUD ANTOINE & CHOLEWINSKI RYSZARD (EDS.), MIGRATION AND HUMAN RIGHTS, Cambridge University Press, Cambridge (2009), 1–4.

De Varennes François, *Strangers in Foreign Lands–Diversity, Vulnerability and the Rights of Migrants*, UNESCO–MOST Working Paper No. 9, Paris (2003).

Di Bartolomeo Anna, Fakhoury Tamirace & Perrin Delphine, *Morocco*, CARIM–Migration Profile, RSCAS (2009).

Dijon Xavier, *Les masques du droit en Afrique- Une lecture européenne des sources de la norme*, 4 REVUE DE DROIT INTERNATIONAL ET DE DROIT COMPARE 1 (2009).

Douzinas Costas, *Six Theses on the end(s) of Human Rights*, 11 FINNISH YEARBOOK OF INTERNATIONAL LAW 201 (2000).

Dowd Rebecca, *Trapped in transit: the plight and human rights of stranded migrants*, UNHCR, Research Paper No. 156 (2008).

Dris Cherif, *La question migratoire dans les relations euro-méditerranéennes*, 1266 HOMMES ET MIGRATIONS 140 (2008).

Duplessis Isabelle, *Soft Law et droit international du travail: Rôle, impact et avenir de la législation du travail*, EDUCATION OUVRIERE (2006).

Düvell Frank, *Illegal immigration in Europe: patterns, causes and consequences*, COMPAS (2006).

Düvell Frank, *Crossing the Fringes of Europe: Transit Migration in the EU's Neighbourhood*, COMPAS WP-06-33 (2008).

Düvell Frank, *The Pathways in and out of Irregular Migration in the EU: A Comparative Analysis, Special Issue*, 13 EUROPEAN JOURNAL OF MIGRATION LAW 275 (2011).

Elmadmad Khadija, *Migration irrégulière et migration illégale, l'exemple des migrants subsahariens au Maroc*, CARIM Notes d'analyse et de synthèse (2008).

Ennaji Moha, *Migration, Development and Gender in Morocco*, MIGRATION AND DIVERSITE CULTURELLE 85 (2007).

Fargues Philippe, *Afrique du Nord et Moyen-Orient: des migrations en quête d'une politique*, 4 POLITIQUE ETRANGERE 1017 (2006).

Fargues Philippe, *Irregularity as normality among immigrants South and East of the Mediterranean*, CARIM AS No. 02 (2009).

Fauchille Paul, *The rights of emigration and immigration*, 3 INTERNATIONAL LABOUR REVIEW 317 (1924).

Fornalé Elisa, *Protection of migrants in irregular situation and EU border control, in* SHAPING THE NORMATIVE CONTOURS OF THE EUROPEAN UNION: A MIGRATION-BORDER FRAMEWORK, CIDOB Monograph, Barcelona, (2010).

Freedman Jane & Bahija Jamal, *Violence à l'égard des femmes migrantes et réfugiées dans la région Euro-méditerranéenne*, Réseau Euro-méditerranéen des droits de l'homme (Dec. 2008).

Gaja Giorgio, *Expulsion of Aliens: some old and new issues in International Law*, in CURSOS EUROMEDITERRANEOS BANCAJA DE DERECHO INTERNATIONAL, Centro International Bancaja para la Paz y el Desarollo, Castello, Volume III (1999).

Gil-Bazo Maria-Teresa, *The Practice of Mediterranean States in the context of the European Union's Justice and Home Affairs External Dimension. The Safe Third Country Concept Revisited*, 18 INTERNATIONAL JOURNAL OF REFUGEE LAW 571 (2006).

Ghosh Bimal, *Migrants' access to human rights: a road strewn with stones*, ICHRP Working Paper (2003).

Goodwin-Gill G. S., *International Law and Human Rights: trends concerning International migrants and refugees*, 23 INTERNATIONAL MIGRATION REVIEW 526 (1990).

Grant Stephanie, *International Migration and Human rights,* Report prepared for the GCIM, Geneva (2005).

Grant Stephanie, *The recognition of migrants' rights within the UN human rights system: the first 60 years, in* MARIE-BENEDICTE DEMBOUR & TOBIAS KELLY (EDS.), ARE HUMAN RIGHTS FOR MIGRANTS? CRITICAL REFLECTIONS ON THE STATUS OF IRREGULAR MIGRANTS IN EUROPE AND THE UNITED STATES, Routledge, Oxon (2011), 25–47.

Guimezanes Nicole, *La lutte contre l'immigration clandestine dans l'Union Européenne et les Etats membres,* 326 REGARD SUR L'ACTUALITÉ 86 (2006).

Hailbronner Kay, *Readmission Agreements and the obligations on States under Public International Law to Readmit their Own and Foreign Nationals*, 57 ZEITSCHRIFT FÜR AUSLÄNDISCHES ÖFFENTLICHES RECHT UND VÖLKERRECHT 1 (1997).

Heikki S. Mattila, *Protection of Migrants' Human Rights: Principles and Practise*, 38 INTERNATIONAL MIGRATION 53 (2000).

Held David, *Law of States, Law of Peoples: three models of sovereignty,* 8 LEGAL THEORY 1 (2002).

Hennebel Ludovic, *L'humanisation du droit international des droits de l'homme–Commentaire sur l'Avis Consultatif No. 18 de la Cour Interaméricaine relatif au droits des migrantes,* 59 REV. TRIM. DR. H. 747 (2004).

Higgings Rosalyn, *The right in International law of an individual to enter, stay in and leave a country*, 49 INTERNATIONAL AFFAIRS (1973).

Hune Ahirley, *Migrant women in the context of the International Convention on the protection of the rights of all migrants workers and members of their families*, 4 INTERNATIONAL MIGRATION REVIEW 800 (1991).

Humes Schulz Stacy, *Limiting sovereign immunity in the age of human rights*, 21 HARV. HUM. RTS. J. 105 (2008).
Huysmans Jef, *The European Union and the securitization of Migration,* 5 JOURNAL OF COMMON MARKET STUDIES 777 (2000).
Jayasuriya Kanishka, *Globalization, law and transformation of sovereignty: the emergence of global regulatory governance* 6 INDIANA JOURNAL OF GLOBAL LEGAL STUDIES 425 (1999).
Kalin Walter & Schrepfer Ninna, *Protecting People Crossing Borders in the Context of Climate Change Normative Gaps and Possible Approaches,* UNHCR, Legal and Protection Policy Research Series, Geneva (2012).
Khachani Mohamed, *Les nouveaux défis de la question migratoire au Maroc*, ILO, Geneva (2010).
Khachani Mohamed, *Maroc, Migration, marché du travail et développement*, ILO, Geneva (2010).
Khachani Mohamed, *La question migratoire au Maroc: données récentes*, CARIM Notes d'analyse et de synthèse 2001/11, Robert Schuman Center for Advanced Studies, Florence (2011).
Kitamura Yasuzo, *Recent development in Japanese Immigration Policy and the United Nations Convention on Migrant Workers*, 27 UBC L. Rev. 113 (1993).
Klerk Yvonne, *Working paper on article 2(2) and article 3 of the International Covenant on Economic, Social and Cultural Rights*, 9 HRQ 250 (1987).
Kojanec Giovanni, *The UN Convention and the European instruments for the protection of the migrants*, 4 INTERNATIONAL MIGRATION REVIEW 818 (1991).
Kruse Imke, *EU readmission policy and its effects on transit countries–the case of Albania*, 8 EUROPEAN JOURNAL OF MIGRATION AND LAW 115 (2006).
Kubal Agnieszka, *Conceptualizing semi-legality in migration research,* IMI Working Paper No. 58 (2012).
Laacher Smaïn, *Les violences faites aux femmes pendant leur voyage clandestin: Algérie, France, Espagne, Maroc*, UNHCR (Apr. 2010).
Lacroix Thomas, *Contrôle et instrumentalisation de la société civile maghrébine: dans la coopération Euro-méditerranéenne le cas du Maroc et de la Tunisie*, L'ANNÉE DU MAGHREB 115 (2004).
Lahlou Mehdi, *Migrations transméditerranéennes et stratégies euro-africaines,* ANNUAIRE DE LA MÉDITERRANÉE 48 (2007).
Lahlou Mehdi, *Undocumented Migration. Counting the Uncountable. Data and Trends accross Europe. Country report Morocco,* Report for the research project CLANDESTINO (2008).
De Larramendi Miguel Hernando & Bravo Fernando, *La frontière hispano-marocaine à l'épreuve de l'immigration subsaharienne*, I L'ANNÉE DU MAGHREB 153 (2004).
Lesser Taryn, *The role of United Nations Special procedures in protecting the human rights of migrants*, 4 REFUGEE SURVEY QUARTERLY 139 (2010).

Li Rosi Angela & Ryan Alanna, *Refugee protection and international migration: a review of UNHCR's role and activities in Morocco*, UNHCR (Mar. 2010).

Lönnroth Juhani, *The International Convention on the Rights of All Migrant Workers and Members of Their Families in the context of international migration policies: An analysis of ten years of negotiations*, 4 INTERNATIONAL MIGRATION REVIEW 710 (1991).

Lyon Beth, *The unsigned United Nations migrant worker rights convention: an overlooked opportunity to change the "brown collar" migration paradigm*, 42 INTERNATIONAL LAW AND POLITICS 389 (2010).

Lyotard Jean Fracois, *The other's right, in* STEPHEN SHUTE & SUSAN HULEY (EDS.), ON HUMAN RIGHTS, THE OXFORD AMNESTY LECTURES, Oxford University Press, New York (1993).

Lutterbeck Derek, *Policing migration in the Mediterranean*, 1 MEDITERRANEAN POLITICS 52 (2006).

Magliveras Konstantinos, *Protecting the rights of migrant workers in the Euro-Mediterranean partnership*, 3 MEDITERRANEAN POLITICS 488 (2004).

Maiani Francesco, *Le droit communautaire et l'éloignement des ressortissants de pays tiers–vers des procédures de retour communes ?, in* ALBERTO ACHERMANN, MARIA CARONI, ASTRID EPINEY, WALTER KÄLIN, MINHN SON NGUYEN & PETER ÜBERSAX (EDS.) JAHRBUCH FÜR MIGRATIONSRECHT 2006/2007, Stämpfli, Bern (2007), 69–96.

Maroufi Abdellatif, *L'immigration dans la politique de partenariat euro-marocain*, 2 REVUE MAROCAINE D'ÉTUDES INTERNATIONALES 46 (1999).

Martin Susan, *The legal and normative framework of international migration*, Global Commission on International Migration (2005).

McDougall Myres, Lasswell Harold & Lung-Chu Chen, *The Protection of Aliens From Discrimination and World Public Order: Responsibility of States Conjoined with Human Rights*, 3 AJIL 432 (1976).

Mendelson Margot, *The legal protection of Identities: a narrative analysis of conversations with battered undocumented women*, 19 BERKLEY WOMEN'S LAW JOURNAL 139 (2004).

Mghari Mohamed, *L'immigration subsaharienne au Maroc*, CARIM notes d'analyse et de synthèse 2007/77, Robert Schuman Centre for Advanced Studies, Florence (2008).

Minkkinen Panu, *The Ethos of sovereignty: a critical appraisal*, 8 HUMAN RIGHTS REVIEW 33 (2007).

Morgan Edward, *Aliens and Process Rights: the open and shut case of legal sovereignty*, 7 WIS. INT'L L. J. 107 (1988).

Morice Alain, *Ni immigrés ni clandestins: au Maroc et ailleurs, vocabulaire du "transit" dans l'impasse*, Immigration, transit et rétention: le Maghreb à l'épreuve des circulations transsahariennes (2–4 Novembre 2006).

Moureeon Jacques, *Les pactes internationaux relatives aux droits de l'homme*, A.F.D.I.,

Tomo XIII (1967).

Mrabet El Arbi, *Elargissement de l'Union Européenne et politique marocaine relative à la migration internationale irrégulière*, LE PARTENARIAT EURO-MEDITERRANEEN A L'HEURE DU CINQUIEME ELARGISSEMENT DE L'UNION EUROPEENNE, 408 (2005).

Mrabet El Arbi, *Readmission Agreements. The case of Morocco*, 5 EUROPEAN JOURNAL OF MIGRATION AND LAW 379 (2003).

Nafiziger James, *The general admission of aliens under International law*, 77 AM. J. INT'L L. 804 (1983).

Noll Gregor, *Readmission Agreements, in* MATTHEW GIBNEY & HANSEN RANDALL (EDS.), IMMIGRATION AND ASYLUM: FROM 1900 TO PRESENT, ABC–CLIO, Oxford (2005).

Noll Gregor, *Introduction–The law of undocumented Migration*, 12 EUROPEAN JOURNAL OF MIGRATION AND LAW 143 (2010).

Noll Gregor, *Why Human Rights Fail to protect Undocumented Migrants*, 12 EUROPEAN JOURNAL OF MIGRATION AND LAW 241 (2010).

Olwan Mohamed, *Irregular Migration in Jordan–A Policy of No Policy*, CARIM Analytic and Synthetic Notes 2008/60, 2008 (2008).

Panizzon Marion, *Migration and Trade: Prospects for Bilateralism in the face of skill-selective Mobility Laws*, 11(2) MELBOURNE JOURNAL OF INTERNATIONAL LAW 96 (2011).

Panizzon Marion, *Readmission Agreements of EU Member States: a case for EU Subsidiarity or Dualism*, 31(4) RFQ (forthcoming 2012).

Papadopoulou Aspasia, *Exploring the asylum-migration nexus: case study of transit migrants in Europe*, 23 GLOBAL MIGRATION PERSPECTIVE 1 (2005).

Pasqualucci Jo, *Advisory Practice of the Inter-American Court of Human Rights: contributing to the Evolution of International Human Rights Law*, 38 STAN. J. INT'L L. 241 (2002).

Perrin Delphine, *La nouvelle politique juridique de l'Europe en matière de contrôle et de limitation des migrations*, 137 L'ANNEE DU MAGHREB 117 (2004).

Perrin Delphine, *Le Maghreb sous influence: le nouveau cadre juridique de migrations transsahariennes*, 185 MAGHREB-MACHREK (2005).

Perrin Delphine, *Sémantique et faux-semblants juridiques de la problématique migratoire au Maghreb*, 123 MIGRATIONS SOCIETE 19 (2009).

Perruchoud Richard, *Droit International et migration*, 24 (4) RSQ 81 (2005).

Poutignat Philippe, *Transit, etc.*, 13 CAHIERS DE L'URMIS (2011).

Rbii Hamid, *Le juge marocain face aux Conventions internationales des droits de l' Homme liant le Maroc: méconnaissance ou reconnaissance?*, paper presented at the International Conference *La protections de droits de l'Homme entre la législation interne et le droit international*, 21 e 22 January 2002, Marrakesh, published in REMALD (2001).

Rbii Hamid, *Droits de l'homme et souveraineté: réflexions sur le cas du Maroc*, REMALD,

Série Thème Actuels 37 (2002).
Rbii Hamid, *L'obligation des décisions de l'administration*, REMALD, Série Thème Actuels 43 (2003).
Rbii Hamid, *La loi 02/03 relative à l'entrée et au séjour des étrangers au Maroc, à l'émigration et l'immigration irrégulières: contrôles des flux migratoires et droits des étrangers*, 17 LA GAZETTE DU PALAIS: REVUE TRIMESTRIELLE D'ETUDES ET DE DOCUMENTATION JURIDIQUES 29 (2007).
Rodriguez Pizarro Gabriela, *The role of the United Nations Special Rapporteur on the Human Rights of Migrants*, 38 INTERNATIONAL MIGRATION 73 (2000).
Sadiqi Fatima, *Migration-Related Institutions and Policies in Morocco*, Analytic and Synthetic Notes 2004/05, RSCAS, 2004.
Satterthwaite L. Margaret, *Crossing borders, claiming rights: using human rights law to empower women migrant workers*, 8 YALE HUM. RTS. & DEV. L. J. 1 (2005).
Smith Rebecca, *Prosecute, Prevent, Protect: migrant labor, forced labor, and human rights*, *in* JAMES A. GROSS AND LANCE COMPA (EDS.), HUMAN RIGHTS IN LABOR AND EMPLOYMENT RELATIONS, (2010).
Schundlmayr Thomas, *Sovereignty, Legal Regimes and International Migration*, 41 INTERNATIONAL MIGRATION 109 (2003).
Suy Eric, *Le préambule*, *in* EMILE YAKPO & TAHAR BOUMEDRA (EDS.), LIBER AMICORUM JUDGE MOHAMMED BEDJAOUI, Kluwer Law International, The Hague/London/Boston (1999).
Van der Klaauw Johannes, *Refugee rights in times of mixed migration: evolving status and protection needs*, 28 REFUGEE SURVEY QUARTERLY 59 (2009).
Valluy Jerome, *Les logiques de stigmatisation, de mise a l'écart et d'enfermement des étranger-de zone de non-droit*, 57 CULTURES ET CONFLITS 5 (2005).
Verschueren Herwig, *European (Internal) Migration Law as an instrument for defining the boundaries of national solidarity system*, 9 EUROPEAN JOURNAL OF MIGRATION AND LAW 346 (2007).
Vogel Dita, Triandafyllidou Anna & Duvell Franck, *Introduction*, 49(5) INTERNATIONAL MIGRATION 48 (2011).
Weiner Mairon, *Ethics, National Sovereignty and the Control of Immigration*, 30 INTERNATIONAL MIGRATION REVIEW 171 (1996).
Weinert S. Matthew, *Bridging the human rights-sovereignty divide: theoretical foundations of a democratic sovereignty*, HUMAN RIGHTS REVIEW 5 (2007).
Wickramasekara Piyasiri, *Protection of Migrant Workers in an Era of Globalization: the role of International Instruments, in* ROBERT BLAINPAIN (ED.), COMPARATIVE LABOUR LAW AND INDUSTRIAL RELATIONS IN INDUSTRIALIZED MARKET ECONOMIES, Kluwer Law International BV, The Netherlands (2010), 245–284.
Wickramasekara Piyasiri, *Globalisation, International Labour Migration and the rights of Migrant Workers*, 29 THIRD WORLD QUARTERLY 1247 (2008).

Wickramasekara Piyasiri, *Irregular Employment of Migrants: an ILO Perspective*, *in* MAREK KUPISZEWSKI & MATTILA HEIKKI (EDS.), ADDRESSING THE IRREGULAR EMPLOYMENT OF IMMIGRANTS IN THE EUROPEAN UNION: BETWEEN SANCTIONS AND RIGHTS, Geneva, 2008, 297–313.

You Paul, *L'interprétation des traités et le rôle du préambule des traités dans cette interprétation,* REVUE DE DROIT INTERNATIONAL, DE SCIENCES DIPLOMATIQUES ET POLITIQUES, Tome XX (1942).

United Nations documents

ECOSOC, Resolution 1706 (LIII) (Jul. 28, 1972).

GA, Measures to improve the situation of migrant workers, G.A. Res. 3224 (XXIX), 29th session, Geneva (1974).

Halima Warzazi, Exploitation of labour through illicit clandestine trafficking, U.N. Doc. E/CN.4/Sub.2/351 (Jun. 1, 1974).

GA, Exploitation of labour trough illicit and clandestine trafficking, G.A. Res. 2920 (XXVII) (Nov. 15, 1975).

GA, Measures to ensure the human rights and dignity of all migrant workers, G.A. Res. 3449 (XXX) (Dec. 9, 1975).

GA, Measures to improve the situation and ensure the human rights and dignity of all migrant workers, U.N. Doc. A/RES/33/163 (Dec. 20, 1978).

Sub-Commission on Prevention of Discrimination and Protection of Minorities, International Provisions the Human Rights of Non-Citizens, Study prepared by the Baroness Elles, U.N. Doc. E/CN.4/Sub.2/392/Rev.1 (1980).

HRC, General Comment No. 7: Article 7 (Prohibition of Torture or Cruel, Inhuman or Degrading Treatment or Punishment), U.N. Doc. HRI/GEN/1/Rev.6 (May 30, 1982).

U.N. GAOR, Report of the Open-ended Working Group on the Elaboration of an International Convention on the Protection of the Rights of All Migrant Workers and Their Families, U.N. Doc. A/C.3/37/1 (1982).

U.N. GAOR, Report of the Open-ended Working Group on the Elaboration of an International Convention on the Protection of the Rights of All Migrant Workers and Their Families, U.N. Doc. A/C.3/37/7 (Nov. 1, 1982).

U.N. GAOR, Report of the Open-ended Working Group on the Elaboration of an International Convention on the Protection of the Rights of All Migrant Workers and Their Families, U.N. Doc. A/C.3/38/1 (Jun. 16, 1983).

U.N. GAOR, Report of the Open-ended Working Group on the Elaboration of an

International Convention on the Protection of the Rights of All Migrant Workers and Their Families, U.N. Doc. A/C.3/38/5 (Oct. 11, 1983).
ICM, International regulations on Illegal Migration, U.N. Doc. MC/SAI/VI/5, (1983).
OHCHR, Effects of undocumented migration for individual concerned, U.N. Doc. MC/SAI/VI/7, ICM (1983).
U.N. GAOR, Report of the Open-ended Working Group on the Elaboration of an International Convention on the Protection of the Rights of All Migrant Workers and Their Families, U.N. Doc. A/C.3/39/1 (Jun. 14, 1984).
U.N. GAOR, Report of the Open-ended Working Group on the Elaboration of an International Convention on the Protection of the Rights of All Migrant Workers and Their Families, U.N. Doc. A/C.3/39/4 (Oct. 11, 1984).
U.N. GAOR, Report of the Open-ended Working Group on the Elaboration of an International Convention on the Protection of the Rights of All Migrant Workers and Their Families, U.N. Doc. A/C.3/40/1 (Jun. 20, 1985).
U.N. GAOR, Report of the Open-ended Working Group on the Elaboration of an International Convention on the Protection of the Rights of All Migrant Workers and Their Families, U.N. Doc. A/C.3/40/6 (Oct. 15, 1985).
GA, Declaration on the Human Rights of Individuals who are not Nationals of the Country in which They Live, U.N. Doc. A/RES/47/144 (Dec. 13, 1985).
HRC, General Comment No. 15: The position of aliens under the Covenant, U.N. Doc. HRI/GEN/1/Rev. 6 (Apr. 11, 1986).
U.N. GAOR, Report of the Open-ended Working Group on the Elaboration of an International Convention on the Protection of the Rights of All Migrant Workers and Their Families, U.N. Doc. A/C.3/41/3 (Oct. 10, 1986).
U.N. GAOR, Report of the Open-ended Working Group on the Elaboration of an International Convention on the Protection of the Rights of All Migrant Workers and Their Families, U.N. Doc. A/C.3/42/1 (Jun. 21, 1987).
U.N. GAOR, Report of the Open-ended Working Group on the Elaboration of an International Convention on the Protection of the Rights of All Migrant Workers and Their Families, U.N. Doc. A/C.3/42/6 (Oct. 9, 1987).
U.N. GAOR, Report of the Open-ended Working Group on the Elaboration of an International Convention on the Protection of the Rights of All Migrant Workers and Their Families, U.N. Doc. A/C.3/43/1 (Jun. 20, 1988).
U.N. GAOR, Report of the Open-ended Working Group on the Elaboration of an International Convention on the Protection of the Rights of All Migrant Workers and Their Families, U.N. Doc. A/C.3/43/7 (Oct. 17, 1988).
U.N. GAOR, Report of the Open-ended Working Group on the Elaboration of an International Convention on the Protection of the Rights of All Migrant Workers and Their Families, U.N. Doc. A/C.3/44/1 (Jun. 19, 1989).
U.N. GAOR, Report of the Open-ended Working Group on the Elaboration of an

International Convention on the Protection of the Rights of All Migrant Workers and Their Families, U.N. Doc. A/C.3/44/4 (Oct. 17, 1989).

CESCR, General Comment No. 3: The nature of States parties' obligations (Fifth session, 1990), U.N. Doc. E/1991/23, (1990).

HRC, U.N. Doc. Res. 1990/68 (Mar. 7, 1990).

U.N. GAOR, Report of the Open-ended Working Group on the Elaboration of an International Convention on the Protection of the Rights of All Migrant Workers and Their Families, U.N. Doc. A/C.3/45/1 (Jun. 21, 1990).

HRC, Consideration of Reports submitted by States parties under Article 40 of the Covenant–Second periodic report of Morocco, U.N. Doc. CCPR/C/SR.1032 (Nov. 12, 1990).

CESCR, General Comment No. 4: The right to adequate housing, U.N. Doc. E/1992/23, (1991).

CERD, General Recommendation No. 11: Non-citizens, U.N. Doc. A/48/18 at 112 (Mar. 19, 1993).

CERD, General Recommendation No. 14: Definition of racial discrimination (Forty-second session, 1993), U.N. Doc. A/48/18 (Mar. 22, 1993).

CEDAW, General Recommendation No. 19: Violence against women (Eleventh session, 1992), U.N. Doc. A/47/38 (1993).

HRC, General Comment No. 20: Article 7 (Forty-Fourth Session, 1992), U.N. Doc. HRI/GEN/1/Rev.1 (1994).

CRC, Concluding observations of the Committee on the Rights of the Child, Norway, U.N. Doc. CRC/C/15/ add.23 (Apr. 25, 1994).

ECOSOC Commission on Human Rights, 51th Session, U.N. Doc. E/CN.4/1995/SR.21 (Feb. 17, 1995).

Commission on Human Rights, The rights of migrant workers, Human Rights fact Sheet, No. 24, Geneva UNOCHR (1996).

OHCHR, Freedom of Movement, Working paper on the right to freedom of movement and related issues prepared by Mr. Volodymyr Boutkevitch in implementation of Decision 1996/109 of the Sub-Commission, U.N. Doc. E/CN.4/Sub.2/1997/22 (Jul. 29, 1997).

CEDAW, Report of the CEDAW, Official Records–Fifty-second Session, Supplement No. 38, U.N. Doc. A/52/38/Rev.1 (Aug. 12, 1997).

CESCR, General Comment No. 7: Forced evictions, and the right to adequate housing (Sixteenth session, 1997), U.N. Doc. E/1998/22 (1997).

CHR, 54th Session, Report of the working group of intergovernmental experts on the human rights of Migrants, Measures to improve the situation and ensure the Human Rights and Dignity of all Migrant Workers, U.N. Doc. E/CN.4/1998/76 (Mar. 10, 1998).

CERD, Conclusions and recommendations of the Committee on the Elimination of Racial Discrimination, Ukraine, U.N. Doc. CERD/C/304/Add.48 (1998).

CHR, Working paper of Jorge A. Bustamante, Chairman/Rapporteur of the Working Group of intergovernmental experts on the human rights of migrants, U.N. Doc. E/CN.4/AC.46/1998/5 (Oct. 8, 1998).
WGAD, Report of the Working Group on Arbitrary Detention: addendum: report on the visit of the Working Group to the United Kingdom on the issue of immigrants and asylum seekers, U.N. Doc. E/CN.4/1999/63 (Dec. 18, 1998).
HRC, Concluding Observations of the Human Rights Committee: Morocco, U.N. Doc. CCPR/C/79/Add.113 (Nov. 1, 1999).
WGAD, Deliberation No. 5: Situation regarding immigrants and asylum-seekers, U.N. Doc. E/CN.4/2000/4 (Dec. 28, 1999).
CESCR, General Comment No. 13: The right to education (Twenty-first session, 1999), U.N. Doc. E/C.12/1999/10 (1999).
CERD, Concluding observations of the Committee on the Elimination of Racial Discrimination, Azerbaijan, U.N. Doc. A/54/18 (1999).
HRC, Conclusions and recommendations of the Special Rapporteur on the sale of children, child prostitution and child pornography, U.N. Doc. E/CN.4/1999/71 (1999).
SRHRM, Report of the Special Rapporteur on Human rights of migrants, Ms. Gabriela Rodriquez Pizarro, U.N. Doc. E/CN.4/2000/82 (Jan. 6, 2000).
GA, Protection of Migrants, G.A. Res. 54/166, U.N. Doc. A/RES/54/166 (Feb. 24, 2000).
CESCR, General Comment No. 14: The right to the highest attainable standard of health, U.N. Doc. E/C.12/2000/4 (Aug. 11, 2000).
GA, UN Millennium Declaration, U.N. Doc. Res. 55/2 (Sep. 8, 2000).
SRHRM, Migrant Worker-Report of the Special Rapporteur on the human rights of migrants, Ms Gabriela Pizarro, U.N. Doc. E/CN.4/2001/83 (Jan. 9, 2001).
CRC, Concluding Observations of the Committee on the Rights of the Child for the Dominican Republic's Initial Report, U.N. Doc. CRC/C/15/Add.150 (Feb. 21, 2001).
GA, Protection of Migrants, G.A. Res. 55/92, U.N. Doc. A/RES/55/92 (Feb. 26, 2001).
CERD, Conclusions and Recommendations of the Committee on the Elimination of Racial Discrimination, China, U.N. Doc. A/56/18 (2001).
CERD, Conclusions and recommendations of the Committee on the Elimination of Racial Discrimination, Azerbaijan, U.N. Doc. CERD/C/304/Add.75 (2001).
CERD, Concluding observations of the Committee on the Elimination of Racial Discrimination, Sudan, U.N. Doc. CERD/C/304/add.116 (2001).
CESCR, Conclusions and recommendations of the Committee on Economic, Social and Cultural Rights, France, U.N. Doc. E/C.12/1/Add.72 (2001).
SRHRM, Report prepared by Ms. Gabriela Rodríguez Pizarro, Special Rapporteur

in pursuance of resolution 2001/52, U.N. Doc. E/CN. 4/2002/94 (Feb. 18, 2002).
CERD, Conclusions and recommendations of the Committee on the Elimination of Racial Discrimination, Costa Rica, U.N. Doc. CERD/C/60/CO/3 (2002).
CERD, Conclusions and recommendations of the Committee on the Elimination of Racial Discrimination, Canada, U.N. Doc. A/57/18 (2002).
CERD, Report of the UN Committee on the Elimination of Racial Discrimination, Sixtieth Session (4–22 March 2002) and Sixty-first Session (5–23 August 2002), Estonia, U.N. Doc. A/57/18 (2002).
SRHRM, Report of the Special Rapporteur on the human rights of migrant workers, Ms. Gabriela Rodriquez Pizarro, Ecuador, U.N. Doc. E/CN.4/2002/94/Add.1 (Feb. 18, 2002).
GA, Protection of Migrants, U.N. Doc. A/RES/56/170 (Feb. 28, 2002).
CHR, U.N. Doc. Res. 2002/50 (Apr. 23, 2002).
CERD, Conclusions and recommendations of the Committee on the Elimination of Racial Discrimination, Canada, U.N. Doc. A/57/18 (2002).
SRHRM, Report submitted by Ms. Gabriela Rodríquez Pizarro, Special Rapporteur on human rights of migrants, Mexico, U.N. Doc. E/CN.4/2003/85/Add.2 (30 October, 2002).
SRHRM, Report of the Special Rapporteur on human rights of migrants, Ms. Gabriela Rodríguez Pizarro, submitted pursuant to Commission on Human Rights resolution 2002/62, U.N. Doc. E/CN.4/2003/85 (Dec. 30, 2002).
HRC, Human Rights Committee, General Comment No. 18: Non-discrimination (Thirty-seventh session, 1989), Compilation of General Comments and General Recommendations Adopted by Human Rights Treaty Bodies, U.N. Doc. HRI/GEN/1/Rev.6 at 146 (2003).
GA, Protection of Migrants, U.N. Doc. A/RES/57/218 (Feb. 23, 2003).
HRC, Elimination of violence against women, U.N. Doc. E/CN.4/RES/2003/45 (Apr. 23, 2003).
GA, Mr David Weissebrodt, Final report on the rights of non-citizens, U.N. Doc. EC/CN.4/Sub. 2/2003/23 (May 26, 2003).
WGAD, Report of the Working Group on Arbitrary Detention, U.N. Doc. E/CN.4/2004/3 (Dec. 15, 2003).
CERD, General Recommendation XXX: Discrimination against Non-citizens (Sixty-fourth session, 2004), U.N. Doc. CERD/C/64/Misc.11/rev. 3 (2004).
SRHRM, Report submitted by Ms. Gabriela Rodriquez Pizarro, Special Rapporteur on the human rights of migrants, Morocco, U.N. Doc. E/CN. 4/2004/76/Add.3 (Jan. 15, 2004).
SRHRM, Specific Groups and Individuals: Migrant Workers: Report submitted by Jorge Bustamante, Special Rapporteur on the human rights of migrants, Spain, U.N. Doc. E/CN.4/2004/76/Add.2 (Jan. 14, 2004).

SRHRM, Report of the Special Rapporteur on the human rights of migrants, Ms. Gabriela Rodriquez Pizarro, U.N. Doc. E/CN. 4/2004/76/Add.1 (Feb. 16, 2004).
GA, Protection of Migrants, U.N. Doc. A/RES/58/190 (Mar. 22, 2004).
HRC, Considered the fifth periodic report of Morocco, U.N. Doc. CCPR/C/MAR/2004/5 (Apr. 15, 2004).
HCR, List of issues to be taken up in connection with the consideration of the fifth periodic report of Morocco, CCPR/C/MAR/2004/5 (Aug. 13, 2004).
HRC, Summary Record of the 2236th meeting–Consideration of Reports submitted by States parties under Article 40 of the Covenant–Fifth periodic report of Morocco, U.N. Doc. CCPR/C/SR.2236 (Nov. 1, 2004).
CERD, General Recommendation XXX: Discrimination against Non-citizens (Sixty-fourth session, 2004), U.N. Doc. CERD/C/64/Misc.11/rev. 3 (2004).
SRHRM, Report submitted by Jorge Bustamante, Special Rapporteur on the human rights of migrants, Italy, U.N. Doc E/CN.4/2005/85/Add.3 (Nov. 15, 2004).
WGAD, Report of the Working Group on Arbitrary Detention, U.N. Doc. E/CN.4/2005/6 (Dec. 1, 2004).
HRC, Consideration of Reports of submitted by States parties under Article 40 of the Covenant–Concluding observations of the Human Rights Committee, U.N. Doc. CCPR/CO/82/MAR (Dec. 1, 2004).
SRHRM, Report of the Special Rapporteur on human rights of migrants, Jorge Bustamante, U.N. Doc. E/CN.4/2005 (Dec. 27, 2004).
HRC, Compte rendu analytique (partiel) de la 2237e séance (publique), U.N. Doc. CCPR/C/SR.2237 (Jan. 31, 2005).
CMW, Working Paper, U.N. Doc. CMW/C/2/L.1 (Mar. 25, 2005).
HRC, Consideration of reports submitted by Morocco, U.N. Doc. CCPR/C/SR.2235 (Jan. 31, 2005).
SRHRM, Report of the Special Rapporteur on the human rights of migrant workers, Ms. Gabriela Rodriquez Pizarro, Addendum–Communications sent to Governments and replies received, U.N. Doc. E/CN.4/2005/85/Add.1 (Feb. 4, 2005).
HRC, Comments by the Government of Morocco to concluding observations, U.N. Doc. CCPR/CO/82/MAR/Add.1 (Feb. 28, 2005).
GA, Protection of Migrants, U.N. Doc. A/RES/59/194 (Mar. 18, 2005).
CHR, Human rights of migrants, Human Rights Resolution 2005/47, U.N. Doc. E/CN/RES/2005/47 (Apr. 20, 2005).
CRC, General Comment No. 6: Treatment of unaccompanied and separated children outside their country of origin, U.N. Doc. CRC/GC/2005/6 (Sep. 1, 2005).

WGAD, Report of the Working Group on Arbitrary Detention, U.N. Doc. E/CN.4/2006/7 (Dec. 12, 2005).
GA, Note by the Secretary-General transmitting the interim report of the Special Rapporteur of the Commission on Human Rights on the human rights of migrants, U.N. Doc. A/60/357 (Sep. 30, 2005).
SRHRM, Report of the Special Rapporteur on the human rights of migrant workers, Ms. Jorge Bustamante, Addendum–Communications sent to Governments and replies received, U.N. Doc. E/CN.4/2006/73 (Dec. 30, 2005).
GA, Protection of Migrants, UN. Doc. A/RES/60/169 (Mar. 7, 2006).
SRHRM, Report of the Special Rapporteur on the human rights of migrants, Jorge Bustamante, Summary of cases transmitted to Governments and replies received, U.N. Doc. E/CN. 4/2006/73/Add.1 (Mar. 27, 2006).
SRHRM, Report submitted by Jorge Bustamante, Special Rapporteur on the human rights of migrants, Burkina Faso, U.N. Doc. E/CN.4/2006/73/Add.1 (Jan. 3, 2006).
SRHRM, Report of the Special Rapporteur on the human rights of migrants, Jorge Bustamante, Summary of cases transmitted to Governments and replies received, UN Doc. E/CN.4/2006/73/Add.1 (Mar. 23, 2006).
International Law Commission, Expulsion of aliens: Memorandum by the Secretariat, U.N. Doc. A/CN.4/565 (August, 2006).
GA, Summary of the High-level Dialogue on International Migration and Development: Note of the President of the General Assembly, New York, 61st Session, U.N. Doc. A/61/515 (Oct. 16, 2006).
GA, Report of the Special Rapporteur on the right of everyone to the enjoyment of the highest attainable standard of physical and mental health (Mr. Paul Hunt), Sweden, U.N. Doc. A/HRC/4/28/ Add.2 (2007).
SRHRM, Report of the Special Rapporteur on the human rights of migrants, Jorge Bustamante, U.N. Doc. A/HCR/4/24 (Feb. 14, 2007).
GA, Protection of Migrants, U.N. Doc. A/RES/61/165 (Feb. 27, 2007).
CMW, Concluding observations of the Committee on the Protection of the Rights of All Migrant Workers and Members of Their Families, Egypt, U.N. Doc. CMW/C/EGY/CO/1 (May 25, 2007).
HRC, Human Rights Council Special Rapporteur on contemporary forms of slavery, U.N. Doc. Res. 6/14 (Sep. 28, 2007).
CMW, Concluding observations of the Committee on the Protection of the Rights of All Migrant Workers and Members of Their Families, Ecuador, U.N. Doc. CMW/C/ECU/CO/1 (Dec. 5, 2007).
ECOSOC, Committee on Economic, Social and Cultural Rights, General Comment 19, The right to social security (art. 9) (Thirty-ninth session, 2007), U.N. Doc. E/C.12/GC/19 (2008).

CEDAW, Concluding observations, Morocco, U.N. Doc. CEDAW/C/MAR/CO/4 (2008).
GA, Report of the Special Rapporteur on adequate housing as a component of the right to an adequate standard of living, Miloon Kothari, Spain, U.N. Doc. A/HRC/7/16/Add.2 (Feb. 7, 2008).
SRHRM, Report of the Special Rapporteur on the human rights of migrants, Jorge Bustamante, U.N. Doc. A/BRC/7/12 (Feb. 25, 2008).
GA, Protection of Migrants, U.N. Doc. A/RES/62/156 (Mar. 7, 2008).
SRHRM, Report of the Special Rapporteur on the human rights of migrants, Jorge Bustamante, United States, U.N. Doc. A/HRC/7/12/Add.2 (Mar. 5, 2008).
HRC, Report submitted by the Government of Morocco, on the basis of para. 15(A), Annex to the resolution No. 5/1, U.N. Doc. A/HRC/WG.6/2/MAR/1 (Mar. 11, 2008).
CERD, Consideration of Reports submitted by states parties under article 9 of the convention, Concluding observations of the Committee on the Elimination of Racial Discrimination, United States of America, U.N. Doc. CERD/C/USA/CO/6 (May 8, 2008).
CMW, Concluding observations of the Committee on the Protection of the Rights of All Migrant Workers and Member of Their Families, Syria, U.N. Doc. CMW/C/SYR/CO/1 (May 2, 2008).
HRC, Human Rights Council: Mandate of the Special Rapporteur on the Human Rights of Migrants, U.N. Doc. A/HRC/RES/8/10 (Jun. 18, 2008).
HRC, Protection of Migrants, U.N. Doc. Res. 9/5 (Sep. 24, 2008).
CEDAW, General Recommendation No. 26 on Women Migrant Workers, U.N. Doc. CEDAW/C/2009/WP.1/R (Dec. 5, 2008).
WGAD, Report of the Working Group on Arbitrary Detention, U.N. Doc. A/HRC/10/21 (Feb. 16, 2009).
SRHRM, Report of the Special Rapporteur on the human rights of migrants, Jorge Bustamante, Guatemala, U.N. Doc. A/HRC/11/7/Add.3 (Mar. 18, 2009).
SRHRM, Report of the Special Rapporteur on the human rights of migrants, Jorge Bustamante, Mexico, U.N. Doc. A/HRC/11/7/Add.2 (Mar. 24, 2009).
SRHRM, Report of the Special Rapporteur on the human rights of migrants, Jorge Bustamante, U.N. Doc. A/HRC/11/7 (May 14, 2009).
CMW, Consideration of reports submitted by states parties under article 74 of the convention, Concluding observations of the Committee on the Protection of the Rights of All Migrant Workers and Members of Their Families, Azerbaijan, U.N. Doc. CMW/C/AZE/CO/1 (May 19, 2009).
SRHRM, Report of the Special Rapporteur on the human rights of migrants, Jorge Bustamante, Summary of cases transmitted to Governments and replies received, U.N. Doc. A/HRC/11/7/Add.1 (May 20, 2009).

CMW, Consideration of reports submitted by states parties under article 74 of the convention, Concluding observations of the Committee on the Protection of the Rights of All Migrant Workers and Members of Their Families, Colombia, U.N. Doc. CMW/C/COL/CO/1 (May 22, 2009).

WGAD, Report of the Working Group on Arbitrary Detention, Malta, U.N. Doc. A/HRC/13/30/Add.2 (Jan. 18, 2010).

GA, Report of the Special Rapporteur on adequate housing as a component of the right to an adequate standard of living, and on the right to non-discrimination in this context, Raquel Rolnik, United States of America, U.N. Doc. A/HRC/13/20/Add.4 (Feb. 12, 2010).

SRHRM, Report submitted by the Special Rapporteur on the human rights of migrants, Jorge A. Bustamante, Addendum, Communications sent to Governments and replies received, U.N. Doc. A/HRC/14/30/Add.1 (May 25, 2010).

SRHRM Report submitted by the Special Rapporteur on the human rights of migrants, Jorge A. Bustamante, U.N. Doc. A/HRC/14/30 (Apr. 16, 2010).

CMW, Concluding observations of the Committee on the Protection of the Rights of All Migrant Workers and Members of Their Families, Algeria, U.N. Doc. CMW/C/DZA/CO/1 (May 19, 2010).

HRC, Study of the Office of the United Nations High Commissioner for Human Rights on challenges and best practices in the implementation of the International framework for the protection of the rights of the child in the context of migration, U.N. Doc. A/HRC/15/29 (Jul. 5, 2010).

CERD, Concluding observations of the Committee on the elimination of racial discrimination, Reports submitted by States Parties under article 9 of the Convention Seventeenth and eighteenth periodic reports of States parties due in 2006, Morocco, U.N. Doc. CERD/C/MAR/CO/17–18 (Aug. 27, 2010).

OHCHR, Statement on Protecting the Human Rights of Irregular Migrants (Sep. 30, 2010).

GA, National report submitted in accordance with paragraph 5 of the annex to Human Rights Council resolution 16/21, Morocco, U.N. Doc. A/HRC/WG.6/13/MAR/1 (Mar. 8, 2012).

GA, Summary prepared by the Office of the High Commissioner for Human Rights in accordance with paragraph 5 of the annex to the Human Rights Council resolution 16/21, U.N. Doc. A/HRC/WG.6/13/MAR/3 (Mar. 9, 2012).

GA, Compilation prepared by the Office of the High Commissioner for Human Rights in accordance with paragraph 5 of the annex to Human Rights Council resolution 16/21, Morocco, U.N. Doc. A/HRC/WG.6/13/MAR/2 (Mar. 12, 2012).

SRHRM, Report of the Special Rapporteur on the human rights of migrants,

François Crépeau, U.N. Doc. A/HCR/20/24 (Apr. 2, 2012).
GA, Report of the Working Group on the Universal Periodic Review, Morocco, U.N. Doc. A/HRC/21/3 (Jul. 6, 2012).
GA, Protection of Migrants, U.N. Doc. A/RES/20/3 (Jul. 16, 2012).
CMW, Rapport initial de l'Etat partie devant être soumis en 2004, Maroc, U.N. Document CMW/C/MAR/1 (Nov. 1, 2012).

ILO documents

ILC, 32nd Session, Geneva (1949).
ILO, Migrant Workers, General survey on the reports on the Migration for Employment Convention (Revised) (No. 97), and Recommendation (Revised) (No. 86), Geneva (1949).
Resolution concerning ILO Action for Promoting the Equality of Migrant Workers in All Social and Labour Matters, ILC, 56th Session, Geneva (1971).
ILO, Protecting the most vulnerable of today's workers, Tripartite Meeting of Experts on Future ILO Activities in the Field of Migration, Geneva (1997).
ILC, 60th Session, Record of proceedings, Geneva (1975).
ILC, Migrant workers, Report III (1B), ILO, 87th Session, Geneva (1999).
ILO, Migrant workers, ILC, 87th Session, Geneva (1999).
ILO, Committee on Freedom of Association, Report n. 326–Spain, Case No. 2121 (Mar. 23, 2001).
Report of the General Director, Reducing the Decent Work Deficit: a Global Challenge, Geneva (2001).
ILO, Transformation and migration in Central and Eastern Europe: Final project report, Geneva (2002).
ILO migration survey 2003: Country summaries, Geneva (2004).
ILO, A fair globalization: Creating opportunities for all, World Commission on the Social Dimension of Globalization, Geneva (2004).
ILC, 92nd Session, Provisional Records 22, Report of the Migrant Workers Committee, Geneva (2004).
ILO, Towards a fair deal for migrant workers in the global economy, Report VI, International Labour Conference, 92nd Session, Geneva (2004).
ILO Governing Body, 289th Session, Meetings of experts: Purpose, function and lessons learned GB.289/STM/2, Geneva (March, 2004).
ILC, 92nd Session, Towards a fair deal for migrant workers in the global economy, Geneva (2004).

ILO Multilateral Framework on Labour Migration: Non-binding principles and guidelines for a rights-based approach to labour migration, Geneva (2006).
ILO, Labour Inspection: ILO Survey for the 96th Session of the International Labour Conference, Geneva (2006).
ILO Governing Body resolution, 295th Session, Geneva (March 2006).
ILO, Labour Inspection: ILO Survey for the 96th Session , ILO, Geneva (2007).
ILO, Protecting the rights of migrant workers: a shared responsibility, International Migration Programme, ILO, Geneva (2009).
CEACR, Individual Communication on migrant workers, Italy, 2009.
CEACR, Individual Communication on migrant workers, Cameroon, 2009.
ILO, Governing Body, Six item on the agenda, 353rd (Apr. 20, 2009).
ILO, International Labour Migration:A rights-based approach, ILO, Geneva (2010).
ILO, Labour Inspection in Europe: undeclared work, migration and trafficking, Geneva (2010).

Additional documents

OHCHR, The Rights of Migrant Workers, Fact Sheet No. 24, 1994.
FIDH, Espagne–Maroc: situation des immigrants et demandeurs d'asile, non a la répression comme politique migratoire, 2003.
CIMADE, La situation alarmante des migrants Sub-sahariens en transit au Maroc et les conséquences des politiques de l'Union Européenne, 2004.
Paul Schoukens & Danny Pieters, Exploratory report on the access to social protection for illegal labour migrants, European Committee for Social Cohesion (CDCC), CDCS, 2004.
ECSC, Opinion of the European Economic and Social Committee on the International Convention on Migrants, Resolution A5-0445.2003, SOC/173-CESE 960/2004 ES/JOD/ET/-EN/o-ES-ET/nm, (Jun. 30, 2004).
MSF, Violence et immigration. Rapport sur l'immigration d'origine Sub-Saharienne en situation irrégulière au Maroc, MSF, September 2005.
Global Commission on International Migration (GCIM), Migration in an interconnected world: new direction for action, 2005.
European Commission, Technical Mission to Morocco, Visit to Ceuta and Melilla on Illegal Migration, 7th October to 11th October 2005.
UNICEF, The rights' start to life: A statistical analysis of birth registration, (2005).
Migreurop, Le livre noir de Ceuta et Melilla, June 2006.

OHCHR, Expulsion of Aliens in International Human Rights Law, OHCHR Discussion paper, Geneva, September 2006.

Amnesty International, Spain and Morocco: failure to protect the rights of migrants–Ceuta and Melilla–One year on, Amnesty International Publications, 2006.

House of Lords, Illegal migrants: proposal for a common EU returns policy, Report with Evidence, 32nd Report of Session 2005-06, 2006.

Amnesty International, South Korea: crackdowm against migrants' trade union, 3 December, 2007.

CCDH, Etablissement des faits relatifs aux événements de l'immigrations illégale. Événements de Ceuta et Melilla durant l'automne 2005, CCDH, March 2007.

Médecins du Monde, European Survey on Undocumented Migrants' Access to Health Care, Paris: MDM: European Observatory on Access to Health Care, 2007.

UNHCR, Refugee Protection and Mixed Migration: A 10–Point Plan of Action, January 2007.

UNHCR, The detention of refugees and asylum seekers by reason of their unauthorized entry or presence, July 2007.

GADEM, La chasse aux migrants aux frontières sud de l'Europe, conséquences des politiques migratoires européennes, July 2007.

Amnesty International, The state of the world's human rights, Amnesty International Report 2008, Amnesty International Publications, 2008.

MSF, Violence et immigration, deux ans plus tard, Rapport sur l'immigration d'origine subsaharienne en situation irrégulière au Maroc et dans les zones frontalières, 2008.

OHCHR, The International Convention on Migrant Workers and its Committee, Fact sheet No. 24, 2008.

GMG, International Migration and Human Rights, Global Migration Group, 2008.

Web posting, Illegal Aliens Can Forms Unions, High Court in Soeul Korea has Rules, Feb. 2 2007, *available at* <http://www.digitaljournal.com/article/105113> (last visited Jun. 20, 2012).

ICMC, Improving responses to boat people and other migrants injured or traumatized crossing borders, Geneva, April 2008.

World Health Organization, Health of migrants, WHA A 61/12, 24 January 2008.

OCHA, Congolese espelled from Angola, DR Congo Situation Report, No. 1, 21 July 2008.

FIDH, Statement submitted to the Universal Periodic Review, 2008.

GADEM, Le cadre juridique relatif à la condition des étrangers, GADEM, January 2009.

GADEM, Rapport relatif a l'application par le Maroc de la Convention international sur la protection des droits de tous les travailleurs migrants et les

membres de leur famille, GADEM, February 2009.
The International Steering Committee, Guide on ratification, International Convention on the protection of the rights of all migrants workers and members of their families, The International Steering Committee for the campaign for ratification on the Migrants Rights Convention, Geneva, April 2009.
United States Department of State, Trafficking in Persons Report 2009–Uzbekistan, 16 June 2009.
GADEM, Note informative sur le procès de cinq réfugiés, July 2009.
IOM, Traite transnationale des personnes. Etat de lieux et analyse des réponses au Maroc, Rabat, 2009.
IOM, Migration and the right to health: A Review of International Law, compiled and edited by Paola Pace, No. 19, Geneva, 2009.
MSF, International Report, Morocco 2008, MSF, August 2009.
Hicham Rachidi, Accords de réadmission ou chantage à l'expulsion, Rencontre internationale sur les accords de réadmission, 27 November 2009.
Council of Europe Commissioner for Human Rights, Criminalization of Migration in Europe: Human Rights Implications, CommDH/Issue Paper commissioned and published by Thomas Hammarberg, Council of Europe, 2009.
Amnesty International, Report 2010–Morocco/Western Sahara, 28 May 2010, Amnesty International, 2010.
Human Rights Watch, From the Tiger to the Crocodile–Abuse of migrant workers in Thailand, February 2010.
Refugee Studies Centre, Forced Migration Review No. 34, Issue 34, February 2010.
MSF, Violence sexuelle et migration–La réalité cache des femmes sub-sahariennes arrêtes au Maroc sur la route de l'Europe, MSF, March 2010.
Migration and the Maghreb, Viewpoints, The Middle East Institute, Washington DC, May 2010.
GMG, Background Paper, Rooting migration policies in human rights: ensuring the rights of all migrants and improving human development outcomes, May 2010.
UNHCR, Morocco Fact Sheet, July 2010.
GADEM, Note à l'intention du Comité de lutte contre les discriminations raciales, August 2010.
GADEM, The Human Rights of Sub-Saharan Migrants in Morocco, 2010.
International Council on Human Rights Policy (ICHRP), Irregular Migration, Migrant Smuggling and Human Rights: Towards Coherence, Geneva, 2010.
Migreurop, Aux bords de l'Europe, l'externalisation des contrôles migratoires, Rapport 2010-2011, October 2011.

Association Marocaine des Droits Humains, Rapport Parallèle sur la deuxième examen périodique universel (EPU), Maroc, November 2011.
CCDH, Rapport du Conseil national des droits de l'Homme du Royaume du Maroc, au titre du 2ème cycle d'examen du Royaume du Maroc dans le cadre du l'EPU, 2011.
UNHCR, Submission by the UNHCR for the OHCHR Compilation Report, Universal Periodic Review, Morocco, 2011.
International Commission of Jurists, Submission to the Universal Periodic Review of Morocco, November 2011.
Driss Benzekri Foundation for Human Rights and Democracy, Universal Periodic Review, Morocco July 2012, Joint report, 2011.
GADEM, Foreigners in Morocco: a legal overview, MAROC COSMOPOLITE, No. 1, 2012, 20–21.
AMERM, Colloque organisé sur le thème « Les évolutions de la recherche sur les migrations internationales: Théories, concepts, méthodes et défis contemporains », 29–30 Octobre 2010, forthcoming 2012.

Jurisprudence

At international level

International Court of Justice

Advisory Opinion of 28 May 1951, Concerning Reservations to the Convention on the Prevention and Punishment of the Crime of Genocide, I.C.J. Reports 1951.
South-West Africa Cases (Ethiopia v. South Africa; Liberia v. South Africa) of 18 July 1966, I.C.J. Reports 1966.
Barcelona Traction Light and Power Company (Belgium v. Spain), case of 5 February 1970, I.C.J. Reports 1970.

Human Rights Committee

A v. Australia, Comm. No. 560/1993 (Apr. 30, 1997), U.N. Doc. CCPR/C/59/D/560/1993.
Aage v. Norway, Comm. No. 631/1995 (Jul. 21, 1994), U.N. Doc. CCPR/C/67/D/631/1995.

Adam v. Czech Republic, Comm. No. 586/1994 (Jul. 23, 1996), U.N. Doc. CCPR/C757/D/586/1994.

Ahani v. Canada, Comm. No. 1051/2002 (Jun. 15, 2004), U.N. Doc. CCPR/C/80/D/1051/2002.

Albert Womah Mukong v. Cameroon, Comm. No. 458/1991 (Apr. 3, 1997), U.N. Doc. CCPR/C/51/D/458/1991.

Baban and others v. Australia, Comm. No. 1014/2001 (Aug. 2, 2003), U.N. Doc. CCPR/C/78/D/1014/2001.

Bakhtiyari v. Australia, Comm. No. 1069/2002 (Oct. 29, 2003), U.N. Doc. CCPR/C/79/D/1069/2002.

Barbarin Mojoca v. Dominican Republic, Comm. No. 449/1991 (Jul. 15, 1994), U.N. Doc. CPR/C/51/D/449/1991.

Barrosa Isidora v. Panama, Comm. No. 478/1991 (Jul. 19, 1995), U.N. Doc. CCPR/C/48/D/478/1991.

Ben Said v. Norway, Comm. No. 767/1997 (Mar. 29, 2000), U.N. Doc. CCPR/C/68/D/767/1997.

Albert Berry v. Giamaica, Comm. No. 330/1998 (Apr. 7, 1996), U.N. Doc. CCPR/C/50/D/330/1998.

Byahuranga v. Denmark, Comm. No. 1222/2003 (Nov. 1, 2004), U.N. Doc. CCPR/C/60/D/1222/2003.

Brasilio Lauren Aatachira v. Peru, Comm. No. 540/1993 (Mar. 25, 1996), U.N. Doc. CCPR/C/56/D/540/1993.

C. v. Australia, Comm. No. 990/1999 (Oct. 28, 2002), U.N. Doc. CCPR/C/76/D/990/1999.

Canepa v. Canada, Comm. No. 558/1993 (Jun. 20, 1997), U.N. Doc. CCPR/C/59/D/558/1993.

Ismet Cephali v. Sweden, Comm. No. 322/1994 (Jul. 18, 1994), U.N. Doc. CPR/C/56/D/322/1994.

Charles Chitat v. Canada, Comm. No. 469/1991 (Nov. 5, 1991), U.N. Doc. CPR/C/49/D/469/1991.

El Ghar v. Libya, Comm. No. 1107/2002 (Nov. 2, 2004), U.N. Doc. CPR/C/82/D/1107/2002.

Fuenzalida v. Equador, Comm. No. 480/1991 (Jul. 12, 1996), U.N. Doc. CCPR/C/57/D/480/1991.

Peter Grant v. Giamaica, Comm. No. 597/1994 (Mar. 22, 1996), U.N. Doc. CCPR/ C/57/D/597/1994.

Gueye and others v. France, Comm. No. 196/1985 (Apr. 3, 1989), U.N. Doc. CCPR/ C/D/35/D/196/1985.

Hammel v. Madagascar, Comm. No. 42/1986 (Apr. 3, 1987), U.N. Doc. CCPR/A/42/40.

Keith Ox v. Canada, Comm. No. 539/1993 (Oct. 31, 1992), U.N. Doc. CCPR/C/52/D/539/1993.
Kindler v. Canada, Comm. No. 470/1991 (Jul. 30, 1993), U.N. Doc. CCPR/C/48/D/470/1991.
Hugo van Alphen v. The Netherlands, Comm. No. 305/1988 (Aug. 15, 1990), U.N. Doc. CCPR/C/39/D/305/1988.
Madafferi v. Australia, Comm. No. 1011/2001 (Jul. 28, 2004), U.N. Doc. CCPR/C/59/D/1011/2001.
Nydia Erika de Arellona v. Colombia, Comm. No. 563/1993 (Oct. 27, 1995), U.N. Doc. CCPR/C/55/D/563/1993.
Lauri Petonen v. Finland, Comm. No. 492/1992 (Jul. 21, 1994), U.N. Doc. CCPR/C/51/D/492/1992.
Simunek v. Czech Republic, Comm. No. 516/1992 (Jul. 19, 1995), U.N. Doc. CCPR/C/54/D/516/1992.

Working Group Arbitrary Detention

Opinion 37/2007, United States (Feb. 4, 2009), U.N. Doc. A/HRC/ 10/21/Add.1.
Opinion 45/2006, UK and Ireland (Jan. 16, 2008), U.N. Doc. A/HRC/ 7/4/Add.1.
Opinion 18/2004, United States (Nov. 19, 2004), U.N. Doc. E/CN.4/2005/6/Add.1.
Opinion 34/1999. United States (Nov. 9, 2000), U.N. Doc. E/CN.4/2001/14/Add.1.

Committee Against Torture

Aemei v. Switzerland, Comm. No. 34/1995 (May 29, 1997), U.N. Doc. CAT/C/18/D/34/1995.
Agiza v. Sweden, Comm. No. 233/2003 (May 20, 2005), U.N. Doc. CAT/C/34/D/233/2003.
Arana v. France, Comm. No. 63/1997 (Jun. 5, 2000), U.N. Doc. CAT/C/23/D/63/1997.
Brada v. France, Comm. No. 195/2002 (May 17, 2005), U.N. Doc. CAT/C/D/195/2002.
Dadar v. Canada, Comm. No. 258/2004 (Nov. 23, 2005), U.N. Doc. CAT/C/D/258/2004.
El Rgeig v. Switzerland, Comm. No. 280/2005 (Nov. 15, 2006), U.N. Doc. CAT/C/D/280/2005.
Elmi v. Australia, Comm. No. 120/1998 (May 25, 1999), U.N. Doc. CAT/C/22/D/120/1998.
G.R.B. v. Sweden, Comm. No. 83/97 (May 15, 1998), U.N. Doc. CAT/C/20/D/83/1997.

K.N. v. Switzerland, Comm. No. 94/1997 (May 20, 1998), U.N. Doc. CAT/C/20/D/94/1997.

Kisoki v. Sweden, Comm. No. 41/1996 (May 13, 1996), U.N. Doc. CAT/C/16/D/41/1996.

Korban v. Sweden, Comm. No. 88/1997 (1998), U.N. Doc. CAT/C/21/D/88/1997.

M.A.K. v. Germany, Comm. No. 214/2000 (May 12, 2004), U.N. Doc. CAT/C/D/214/2000.

M.M.P.S. v. Australia, Comm. No. 138/1999 (Apr. 30, 2002), U.N. Doc. CAT/C/28/D/138/1999.

M.S. v. Switzerland, Comm. No. 156/2000 (Nov. 13, 2001), U.N. Doc. CAT/CC/267/D/156/2000.

Mutombo v. Switzerland, Comm. No. 13/1993 (Apr. 7, 1994), U.N. Doc. CAT/C/12/D/13/1993.

N. P. v. Australia, Comm. No. 106/1998 (Jun. 3, 1999), U.N. Doc. CAT/C/22/D/106/1998.

Tebourski v. France, Comm. No. 300/2006 (May 1, 2007), U.N. Doc. CAT/C/D/300/2006.

V.L. v. Switzerland, Comm. No. 262/2005 (Nov. 20, 2006), U.N. Doc. CAT/C/D/262/2005.

Z.T. v. Norway, Comm. No. 127/1999 (Nov. 14, 2005), U.N. Doc. CAT/C/D/238/2003.

X, Y e Z v. Sweden, Comm. No. 61/1996 (May 6, 1998), U.N. Doc. CAT/C/20/D/61/1996.

Committee against Discrimination

Quereshi v. Denmark, Comm. No. 33/2003 (Mar. 9, 2005), U.N. Doc. CERD/C/66/D/33/2003.

At regional level

Inter-American Court on Human Rights

All cases are available at <http://www.corteidh.or.cr/>

I/A Court H.R., Matter of Haitians and Dominicans of Haitian-origin in the Dominican Republic regarding Dominican Republic, 18 August 2002.

I/A Court H.R., Case of Bámaca-Velásquez v. Guatemala. Reparations and Costs, February 2002. Series C No. 91.

I/A Court H.R., Juridical Condition and Rights of the Undocumented Migrants. Advisory Opinion OC–18 of 17 September 2003, Series A No. 18.
I/A Court H.R., Case of the Moiwana Community v. Suriname, Preliminary Objections, Merits, Reparations and Costs, case of 15 June 2005, Series C No. 124.
I/A Court H.R., The Yean and Bosico Children v. Dominican Republic, 8 September 2005, Ser. C No. 130 (2005).

European Court on Human Rights

All cases are available at <http://www.echr.coe.int/echr>

Adbulaziz, Cabales, and Balkandali v. UK, 28 May 1985, A/94.
Ali v. Switzerland, 5 August 1998, Application No. 24881/94.
Al-Nashif v. Bulgaria, 20 June 1992, Application No. 50963/99
Amuur v. France, 25 June 1996, Application 1996-III.
Andric v. Sweden, 23 February 1999, Application No. 45917/99
Assenov v. Bulgaria, 28 October 1998, Application No. 24760/94.
Bader v. Sweden, 8 November 2005, Application No. 13284/04.
Bozano v. France, 18 December 1986, A/111.
Chahal v. UK, 15 November 1996, Application No. 1996-V.
Conka v. Belgium, 5 February 2002, Application No. 51564/99.
Cruz Varas v. Sweden, 20 March 1991, A/201.
D. v. UK, 2 May 1997, Application No. 30240/96.
Dougoz v. Greece, 6 March 2001, Application No. 2001-II.
Drodz and Janousek v. Spain and France, 26 June 1992, A/240.
Hilal v. UK, 8 February 2000, Application No. 45276/99.
H.L.R. v. France, 29 April 1997, Application No. 24573/94.
Hurtado v. Switzerland, 28 January 1994, Application No. 17549/90.
Jecius v. Lithuania, 31 July 2000, Application No. 34578/97.
Kadem v. Malta, 9 January 2003, Application No. 55263/00.
Litwa v. Poland, 4 April 2000, Application No. 26629/95.
M.A.R. v. UK, 16 January 1997, Application No. 28038/95.
Mamaktulov and Abdurasulovic v. Turkey, 6 February 2003, Application No. 46827/99 and 46951/99.
Mansur v. Turkey, 8 June 1995, Application No. 16026/90.
Mubilanzila Mayeka and Kaniti Mitunga v. Belgium, 12 October 2006, Application No. 13178/03.
Ocalan v. Turkey, 12 May 2005, Application No. 46221/99.
Quinn v. France, 22 March1995, Application No. 18680/91.
Rantsev v. Chyprus and Russia, 7 January 210, Application No. 25695/04.

Ribitich v. Austria, 4 December 1995, Application No. 18896/91.
Saadi v. UK, 11 July 2006, Application No. 1329/03.
Sabeur Ben Ali v. Malta, 29 June 2000, Application No. 35892/97.
Selmouni v. France, 28 July 1999, Application No. 25803/94.
Shamsa and others v. Poland, 27 November 2003, Application No. 45355/99 and 45357/99.
Siliadin v. France, 26 July 2005, Application No. 73316/01.
Singh v. Czech Republic, 25 January 2005, Application No. 60538/00.
Slivenko v. Latvia, 9 October 2003, Application No. 48321/99.
Soering v. UK, 7 July 1989, A/161.
Strain v. Romania, 21 July 1995, Application No. 57001/0
T.I. v. UK, 7 July 1989, A/161.
Van der Mussele v. Belgium, 23 November 1983, A/70.
Vasileva v. Denmark, 25 September 2003, Application No. 52792/99.
Vilvarajah and others v. UK, 30 October 1991, A/215.

European Court of Justice

Vatsouras, 4 June 2000, C-22/08.
Said Shamilovish Kadzoev, 30 November 2009, C-357/09 PPU.

At national level

Case Meylan, Court of Appeal, Rabat, 15 May 1969.
Case Cazals, Corte di Appeal, Rabat, 16 December 1969.
Ahmed Fathi v. Administratif Tribunal, No. 395, 29 November 1990.
Abdelaziz el Mahani v. The Prime Minister and others, C.S.A. No. 51, 14 February 1991, REMALD No. 6, January–March 1994, 69–70.
Abdlhakim Irchad v. President of the Council of the Town of Roches, C.S.A. case No. 108, 4 April 1991, REMALD, No. 2–3 January–June 1993, 99–101.
Mohamed Azzam v. President of the Council of Ain Safae, C.S.A. case No. 391, REMALD No. 1, October–December 1992, 64–66.
Mohammed Nasri v. Ministry of Justice, T.A. Rabat 27 June 1994, REMALD No. 7–8, April–September, 153–154.
Società Immobiliare Sidi Yahya v. President of the Council of Oujda Sidi Ziyane, T.A., Casablanca, 13 July 1994, REMALD No. 9, October–December 1994, 70–75.
Mohamed Takouti and other v. Morocco, T.A. Casablanca, O.R. No. 24, 26 July 1994, REMALD No. 0, October–December 1994, 78–79.
Brahim Amrai v. President of the Council of Marrakesh Menara, T.A. Marrakesh, 10 January 1995, REMALD No. 12, July–September 1995, 134–136.

WAFA Banca v. Administration of Customs T.A. Casablanca, O. R. No. 119, 10 October 1996, REMALD No. 20–21, July–December 1997, 139–140.
Said Harmaz v. Ministry of Tourism, T.A. Rabat, 9 December 1996, REMALD No. 19, April–June 1997, 189–190.
Mostafa Mellouki and others v. General Treasurer, T.A. Casablanca, 9 April 1997, REMALD No. 35, November–December 2000, 71–72.
Georgine Chendoub v. General Director of National Security, T.A. Rabat, 28 May1998, REMALD No. 25, October–December 1998, 217–218.
Abdellah El Alami v. Ministry of Interior, REMALD No. 29, October–December 1999, 75–78.
Agente Giudiziario v. Zahra Moutarif, C.S.A. case No 787, 30 July 1998, REMALD No. 34, September–October 2000, 170–171.
Mohammed Sadouk v. Ministry of Interior, T.A. Rabat 19 March1999, REMALD No. 29, October–December 1999, 96–98.
Agente giudiziario v. Ahmed Chaouki, C.S.A. case No. 608, 20 May 1999, REMALD No. 41, November–December 2001, 121–122.
El Aziza Kafifi v. Ministry of Education T.A. Meknes, 23 March 2000, REMALD No. 34 September–October 2000, 192–194.
Abdellah Khalil v. Ministry of Interior, T.A. Oujda, 11 October 2000, REMALD No. 40, September–October 2001, 177–178.
Abdelkader Lakhchin v. Delegate of Education, T.A. Oujda, 13 October 2000, REMALD No. 41, November–December 2001, 150–152.
Jawad Baouch v. *Provisore del Liceo* Imam El Ghazali, T.A. Meknes, 21 December 2000, REMALD No. 40, September–October 201, 201–211.
Ahmed Habibi v. Town of Tamzouzt, T.A. Marrakesh, 31 October 2001, REMALD No. 44–45, May–August, 180–181.
Barawla v. Administratif Tribunal, case No. 382, 3 March 2005.
Deuni Rose Marie v. Administratif Tribunal, case No. 1349/06, 24 January 2007
James Vincent v. Khemisset, Court of Appeal, case No. 564/07, 19 April 2007.

Table of treaties, other international instruments, and legislation

International Instruments

Charter of the United Nations, 1945.
Universal Declaration of Human Rights, 1948.
Convention Relating to the Status of Refugees, 1951.
Convention Against Discrimination in Education (UNESCO Convention against all forms of Discrimination in Education), 1962.
International Convention on the Elimination of All Forms of Racial Discrimination, 1965.
International Covenant on Economic, Social and Cultural Rights, 1966.
International Covenant on Civil and Political Rights, 1966.
Additional protocol to the convention relating to the status of refugees, 1967.
The Convention on the Elimination of All Forms of Discrimination Against Women, 1979.
Convention against Torture and Other Cruel, Inhuman or Degrading Treatment or Punishment, 1984.
Convention on the Rights of the Child, 1989.
International Convention on the Protection of the Rights of All Migrant Workers and Members of Their Families, 1990.
Agreement between Spain and Morocco on the movement of persons, goods in transit and readmission of aliens who entered illegally, B.O. April 25 and May 30, 1992.
United Nations Convention against Transnational Organized Crime, 2000.
Protocol against the Smuggling of Migrants by Land, Sea and Air, 2000.
Protocol to Prevent, Suppress and Punish Trafficking in Persons, especially Women and Children, 2000.
Durban Declaration and Programme of Action, 2001.
Cooperation agreement between Morocco and the High Commissioner for Human Rights of Refugees, 2007.
Association of South East Asian Nations Declaration on the Protection and Promotion of the Rights of Migrant Workers, 2007.

ILO Instruments

All instruments are available at <www.ilo.org/lex>

Constitution of the International Labour Organization, 1919.
Unemployment Convention No. 2, 1919.
Equality of Treatment (Accident Compensation) Convention No. 19, 1925.
Inspection of Emigrants Convention, 1926.
Maintenance of Migrants' Pension Rights Convention No. 45, 1935.
Migration for Employment Convention No. 66, 1939.
Declaration of Philadelphia, 1944.
Social Policy (Non-Metropolitan Territories) Convention No. 82, 1947.
Freedom of Association and Protection of the Right to Organise Convention No. 87, 1948.
Migration for Employment Convention (Revised) No. 97, 1949.
Social Security (Minimum Standards) Convention No. 110, 1952.
Discrimination (Employment and Occupation) Convention No. 111, 1958.
Social Policy (Basic Aims and Standards) Convention No. 117, 1962.
Equality of Treatment (Social Security) Convention No. 118, 1962.
Migrant Workers (Supplementary Provisions) Convention No. 143, 1975.
Migrant Workers Recommendation No. 151, 1975.
Maintenance of Social Security Rights Convention No. 152, 1982.
Equality of Treatment (Accident Compensation) Convention No. 19, 1992.
ILO Declaration on Fundamental Principles and Rights at Work, 1998.
Maternity Protection Convention (C 183), 2002.

European Instruments

Council Recommendation of 30 November 1994 concerning the adoption of a standard travel document for the expulsion of third-country nationals, OJ C 274, 19 September 1996.
Council Recommendation of 30 November 1994 concerning a Specimen Bilateral Readmission Agreement Between a Member State and a Third Country, 30 November 1994.
Council Recommendation of 24 July 1995 on the guiding principles to be followed in drawing up protocols on the implementation of readmission agreements,

OJ C 005, 10 January 1996.
Parliamentary Assembly, Council of Europe, Human rights of irregular migrants, Resolution No. 1509, 2006.
Directive 2008/115/EC of the European Parliament and of the Council of 16 December 2008 on common standards and procedures in Member States for returning illegally staying third-country nationals, OJ L 348/98, 24 December 2008.
European and Social Committee, Opinion on Respect for fundamental rights in European immigration policies and legislation, SOC/335-CESE 1710/2009, 4 November 2009.
Parliamentary Assembly, Committee on Migration, Refugees and Population, Report, Readmission agreements: a mechanism of returning irregular migrants, Doc. 12168, 16 March 2010.
Parliamentary Assembly, Readmission agreements: a mechanism for returning irregular migrants, Resolution 1741 (2010), adopted on 22 June 2010 (22nd Sitting).
European Commission, Communication from the Commission to the European Parliament and the Council-Evaluation of EU Readmission Agreements, COM(2011) 76 final, 23 February 2011.

National Instruments

Dahir No. 1-57-271, 29 *Moharrem* 1377, Aug. 26, 1957, on the implementation of the Geneva Convention of 28 July 1951 (B.O. No. 2341, Sep. 6, 1957, 1161).
Decree No. 2-57-1256, 2 *Safar* 1377, Aug. 29, 1957, on the modalities to apply the Geneva Convention of 28 July 1951 (B.O. No. 2341, Sep. 6, 1957, 1161–1162).
Agreement between Spain and Morocco on the mobility, transit and readmission of irregular migrants (B.O. Apr. 25 and May 30, 1992).
Constitution of the Kingdom of Morocco, 1996.
Law No. 37-99 on civil status (B.O. No. 5054, Nov. 7, 1999).
Dahir No. 1-96-79, Mar. 10, 2000, concerning the Euro Mediterranean agreement, signed in Bruxelles, Feb. 26, 1996 (B.O. No. 4936, Sep. 20, 2001).
Law No. 02-03 on entry and stay of foreigners in Morocco, migration and irregular immigration, 2003.
Code of Nationality 2004, Law No 62-06 (B.O. No. 5513, Apr. 2, 2007), to modify the *Dahir* No. 1-58-250, Sep. 6, 1958 on the Moroccan nationality code.
Decree 2-09-607, Apr. 1, 2010 (B.O. No. 5836-21 I 1431, May 6, 2010).

Index

Kolibri 360 GmbH
Ferdinand-Jühlke-Straße 7
99095 Erfurt, Deutschland
produktsicherheit@kolibri360.de